Microsoft® Office Specialist 2016 Series

# Microsoft®
# Excel 2016
## Core Certification Guide

Exam 77-727

June 2018

© CCI Learning Solutions Inc.

# CCI Learning™

## Microsoft® Excel 2016 Core Certification Guide

This courseware is one in a series prepared by CCI Learning Solutions Inc. for use by students and instructors in courses on computer software applications. CCI designed these materials to assist students and instructors in making the learning process both effective and enjoyable.

Funded by the Government of Canada | Canada

Courseware Team: Kenny Lee, Kelly Hegedus, Kim Williams, Sue Wong, Irina Heer, Ken Kozakis

Copyright © 2016 CCI Learning Solutions Inc.

ISBN: 978-1-55332-473-7

All rights reserved.

Printed in Canada.

CCI Courseware#: 3263-2

Any brand name or product mentioned in this publication is a trademark or registered trademark of their respective companies and are used for identification purposes only.

## Working with the Data Files

The exercises in this courseware are designed to utilize a specific set of data files, which are available for download. Follow these instructions to download the data files for this courseware.

1  Launch your browser and navigate to the CCI Web site location http://www.ccilearning.com/data.

2  Enter: 3263 in the Courseware # box and click **Find Data**.

3  Click **Run** in the File Download – Security Warning window. (Alternatively, you can choose to **Save** the file to a location on your computer.)

4  In the Internet Explorer – Security Warning window click **Run** again.

5  In the **WinZip Self-Extractor** dialog box, use the **Browse** button to specify the Windows Desktop as the location to unzip the file and then click **Unzip**.

The *3263 Student Files* folder containing the required student work files has now been downloaded to your desktop. It is recommended that you rename the folder using your own name before starting the exercises in this courseware. You can reinstall and use the work files as many times as you like.

# What is the Microsoft Office Specialist Certification?

Microsoft Office Specialist (MOS) certification is the leading IT certification in the world. More than 1 million MOS exams are taken every year in over 140 countries.

The Microsoft Office Specialist Program enables you to demonstrate the knowledge, skills, and abilities to productively use Microsoft Office. MOS enables you to tap into the full features and functionality of the Microsoft Office system, resulting in heightened levels of individual performance, confidence, and differentiation.

# Microsoft
## Office Specialist

The Microsoft Office Specialist (MOS) certification exams validate skills within the applicable Microsoft Office programs. The 2016 exams are more powerful for assessing student skills and preparing students for real-world application. Skill assessments include performance-based formats, revised instructions, multiple projects, and questions integrated with objective domains.

The available Microsoft Office Specialist Program 2016 exams include*:

- Microsoft Office Specialist: Word 2016
- Microsoft Office Specialist: Excel 2016
- Microsoft Office Specialist: PowerPoint 2016
- Microsoft Office Specialist: Outlook 2016
- Microsoft Office Specialist: Access 2016

**Prepare for your Microsoft Office Specialist exam with Jasperactive!**

Learn more about Jasperactive at www.jasperactive.com

**Jasper**active™

**Microsoft** [W] [X] [P] [O] [A]
Office Specialist

Founded on CCI Learning's world-leading courseware, Jasperactive is the world's first kinesthetic Microsoft Office learning and validation system mapped to the Microsoft Office Specialist Global Standard.

**For more information:**

To learn more about Microsoft Office Specialist exams, visit https://www.microsoft.com/en-us/learning/mos-certification.aspx

To learn about other Microsoft approved courseware from CCI Learning Solutions, visit mos.ccilearning.com

To learn more about Jasperactive, visit www.jasperactive.com

* The availability of Microsoft Office Specialist certification exams varies by Microsoft program, program version and language. Visit www.microsoft.com/learning for exam availability.

Microsoft, Access, Excel, the Office Logo, Outlook, PowerPoint, SharePoint, and Windows Vista are either registered trademarks or trademarks of Microsoft Corporation in the United States and/or other countries. The Microsoft Office Specialist logo is used under license from Microsoft Corporation.

# Table of Contents

## Lesson 1: Introducing Excel

## Lesson 2:  Constructing Cell Data

# Lesson 3: Using Formulas

# Lesson 4: Formatting the Worksheet

# Lesson 5: Viewing and Printing Workbooks

# Lesson 6: Working with Charts and Graphics

# Lesson 7: Organizing Data

# Lesson 8: Using Data Tools

# Appendices

# Course Description

This *Microsoft® Excel 2016 Core Certification Guide* teaches the student how to create and edit professional-looking worksheets using a variety of core and intermediate features. Comprehensive step-by-step instruction combined with the 'why' behind a skill allows students to enhance their level of understanding and proficiency as they work through the exercises. Students who complete this course will have reviewed all the exam objectives and be on their way to preparing for Microsoft Office Specialist Excel 2016 Core Exam #77-727. Successful completion of the certification exam provides a competitive advantage by validating the knowledge and skill sets for individuals who may be seeking employment or further job opportunities in their careers.

## Course Series

This guide is one of seven courses in CCI's Microsoft Office Specialist series. The courses available in the series include:

- Word 2016 Core
- Excel 2016 Core
- PowerPoint 2016
- Outlook 2016
- Access 2016
- Word 2016 Expert
- Excel 2016 Expert

## Course Prerequisites

This course is designed for students who are familiar with personal computers, using a keyboard and using a mouse. The course assumes that students have completed the *Microsoft Windows* course or have equivalent Microsoft Windows knowledge and experience.

- ☐ start and run Windows
- ☐ use the taskbar
- ☐ use the Start button
- ☐ use the Help feature
- ☐ use Minimize, Restore Down/Maximize, or Close
- ☐ use the left and right mouse buttons
- ☐ understand file management techniques
- ☐ navigate between files, folders, or drives

## System Requirements

This courseware was developed using specific software and hardware configurations. To complete this courseware, you should have the following for each student:

- A desktop or laptop system running Microsoft® Windows 10 and Microsoft® Office 2016
- Mouse or comparable pointing device
- 101-key enhanced keyboard
- A headset with a microphone for each student for recording a presentation

**Note:** Internet access is required to perform some of the hands-on exercises.

In the materials contained in this courseware, we assume that you have met these criteria, and that you have successfully installed both Windows and Office on your computer.

If you subscribe to Office 365, features may be added or updated.

## Classroom Setup

The features and exercises shown in this courseware were developed using the standard installation of the Microsoft Office 2016 Desktop applications on a system with Windows 10. If your computers have another version of Windows installed, you will need to adjust accordingly to accommodate for the differences in dialog boxes when saving or opening files.

It is likely your teacher set up the classroom computers based on the system requirements to run the software for this course. Most software configurations on your computer are identical to those on your teacher's computer. However, your teacher may use additional software to demonstrate network interaction or related technologies.

Teacher Resources are available and are produced specifically to help and assist an instructor in preparing to deliver the course using the CCI materials. Contact your coordinator or administrator, or call your CCI Account Manager for information on how to access these resources.

# Course Design

This course book was developed for teacher-led training and will assist you during class. Together with comprehensive instructional text and objectives checklists, this course book provides easy-to-follow hands-on lab exercises and a glossary of course-specific terms.

This course book is organized in the following manner:

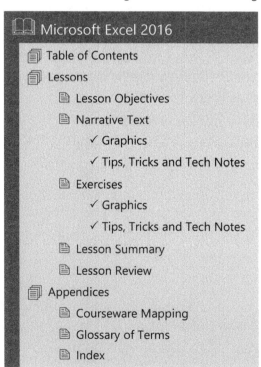

When you return to your home or office, you will find this course book to be a valuable resource for reviewing exercises and applying the skills you have learned. Each lesson concludes with questions that review the material. Lesson review questions are provided as a study resource only and in no way guarantee a passing score on a certification exam. Appendices in the back of this course book provide additional information.

# Course Objectives

This course book teaches the skills you will need to successfully complete the Microsoft Office Specialist Excel 2016 Core exam. These skill sets are introduced using multiple types of business and personal documents that are commonly used in practical life.

After completing this course, you will be able to:

- create and manage worksheets and workbooks
- manage data cells and ranges
- create tables
- perform operations with formulas and functions
- create charts and objects

# Conventions and Graphics

The following conventions are used in CCI learning materials.

**File and Folder Names** – Names of folders and files are indicated in *italic* font style.

**Database Fields** – Names of database fields are indicated in *purple italic* font style.

**Exercise Text** – Content to be entered by the student during an exercise appears in `Consolas` font.

**Procedures** – Procedures and commands you are instructed to activate are indicated in **bold** font style.

**Objective 1.1.1, 1.1.2** – This indicates the numbered objective from the Microsoft Office Specialist exam being covered in this topic. Refer to the Appendix for a complete listing of exam objectives.

**Technical Notes** point out exceptions or special circumstances that you may find when working with a particular procedure, or may indicate there is another method to complete the task.

# Learn Exercise

Learn Exercise headings signal the start of step-by-step, hands-on exercises or other activities.

Microsoft®

# Excel 2016

## Core Certification Guide

# Lesson 1: Introducing Excel

## Lesson Objectives

In this lesson you will be introduced to the Excel program, learn how it works, and understand how to move in the program, create a workbook, enter data into a worksheet, and work with files. Upon completion of this lesson, you should be able to:

☐ understand what an electronic spreadsheet is

☐ understand what Excel is and what it can do

☐ identify elements on the Excel screen

☐ understand some basic terminology

☐ use the Quick Access Toolbar

☐ move around in Excel

☐ use keyboard shortcuts

☐ enter text, numbers, dates, and times

☐ move around a worksheet

☐ use the Backstage view to save, create new, open, and close a workbook

☐ switch between workbooks

☐ save in a previous version Excel format, and check for compatibility issues

☐ manage files and folders

☐ select cells

# What is Excel?

Excel is an electronic spreadsheet program developed by Microsoft, originally for the Windows environment, but is now available for the Apple Mac or any computer with a web browser. A powerful tool for analyzing and presenting information, Excel actually consists of three programs in one:

**Spreadsheet** – Entering and analyzing numeric data in applications such as financial forecasting and statistical problems. Excel performs math calculations so quickly that they appear to be simultaneous. Excel uses the term worksheet in place of spreadsheet.

**Graphics** – Creating charts to represent numeric data.

**Database** – Compiling and sorting lists of data.

Some of Excel's advantages are:

- It is relatively easy to learn. All Microsoft Office Suite programs, such as Word, Excel, and PowerPoint, operate similarly. Many of the skills you learn in one program carry over to others.

- It enables data to be exchanged easily between the different Office programs. For example, you can create a chart in Excel and insert it into a document you are writing using Word.

- Excel can produce output of print-shop quality using features such as the spelling checker and other tools that enhance your work and provide it with a professional look.

- Excel has a large selection of mathematical, financial, statistical, and database functions. It includes 14 basic chart types and each of the commonly-used chart types have four or more subtypes. There are also some tools for forecasting or analysis, and a function helper.

- Worksheets can be grouped together in a single file rather than separate files. In Excel, these files are called workbooks. Inside a workbook, there are several ways to manage the multiple worksheets such as renaming worksheet tabs.

- Excel uses AutoFill to fill selected cells with data that follows from the information in the first of the selected cells. For example, if you select four cells, and the first cell contains Qtr 1, AutoFill will fill in the next three cells with Qtr 2, Qtr 3, and Qtr 4.

- By default, edits occur directly in the cell. This includes formatting portions of text and making font changes. Alternatively, you can perform edits in the Formula bar.

Although Excel is a very large program, it is enjoyable to learn and use. Most people find it takes them less time to become competent and productive with Excel than they initially anticipated. For the purpose of this courseware, we will assume that you are using Excel on a Windows computer.

## Starting Excel

In Windows 10, there are several ways to start the Excel program:

- if it is present in the Start window, click or tap the Windows **Start** button, then select the **Excel 2016** tile from the Start window.

- click the Windows **Start** button, then select **All apps**, and then **Excel 2016**.

- in the taskbar, click or tap the **Excel 2016 Quick Launch** icon.

# Looking at the Screen

When Excel starts, a new workbook opens and the screen displays as follows:

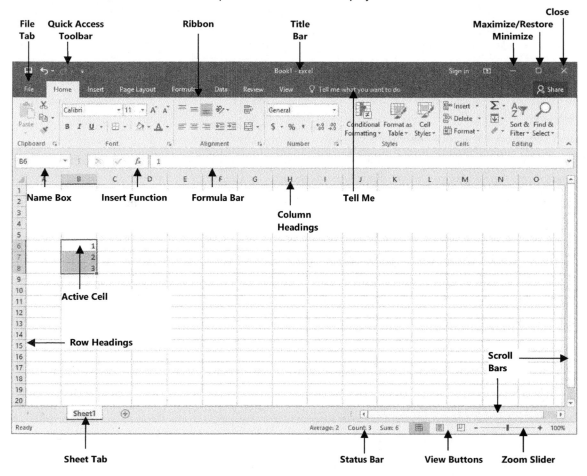

**File Tab** – Click this tab to open the Backstage view from which you can select commands to manage files, such as create, save, open, print, export or change Excel options. A panel at the left displays commands that may include tabs with a set of sub-commands to manage the file.

**Quick Access Toolbar** – Located above the Ribbon, this provides quick access to frequently used commands. You can customize the toolbar to contain commands you use regularly.

**Title Bar** – Located at the top of the screen, the title bar indicates the contents of the window (for example, *Book1, Department Budget*). It may also show the text *[Compatibility Mode]* if the workbook you are using has been saved to be compatible with a previous version of Excel. If more than one window is open on the screen, the one with a title bar that has a darker color or intensity is the active window.

**Minimize, Maximize, Restore Down, Close** – Located in the upper right-hand corner of the window, these buttons enable you to minimize (▬) the application window to a button on the taskbar, maximize (□) the program to full screen, restore (▫) the window to its original size, or close (✕) the application window.

**Ribbon** – A collection of tabs (for example, File, Home, Insert, Page Layout) provides quick access to commands you need to complete a task. Each Ribbon tab relates to a type of activity such as inserting objects in a worksheet, or modifying the format of data in a worksheet. In the example above, the Home tab is currently selected, and all of the icons and options for that Ribbon tab are displayed.

**Ribbon Group** – Each Ribbon tab contains groups of related commands to edit, format, or enhance items in your documents. Some groups have a Dialog box launcher button at the bottom right, which displays a dialog box or window with more commands and options.

**Ribbon Display Options** – Controls whether to hide or display the Ribbon with the tabs or with both tabs and command buttons.

**Name Box** – Located on the left below the Ribbon, this displays the cell address of the active cell. For example, if the Name Box displays A21, this indicates that A21 (the cell at the intersection of column A and row 21) is the active cell. In the example on the previous page, three cells are selected. Cell B6 is the upper left-most cell of that cell range and therefore its cell address is displayed in the Name Box to designate it as the active cell.

**Insert Function** – This tool opens a dialog box to help you choose and insert a built-in function.

**Formula Bar** – Located to the right of the Name Box, the Formula bar displays the contents of the active cell. Under certain circumstances, the Formula bar can be used to make entries into the worksheet.

**Tell Me** – This allows you to enter a description of what you are looking for. Unlike the simpler help feature in older versions of Excel, the Tell Me feature will display a customized menu of the commands that you are looking for. You can also choose the Smart Lookup option which will use the Microsoft Bing search pane to find related topics from the Internet in a task pane. The traditional help feature is also offered in the menu.

**Column Headings** – Sequential letters at the top of each column enable you to track columns.

**Row Headings** – Sequential numbers on the left side of each row enable you to track rows.

**Status Bar** – Displays the current cell mode, auto calculations, the View buttons, and the Zoom slider. You can customize the Status bar to display keyboard locks and other features.

**View Buttons** – These buttons change the on-screen views for the worksheet. The views are Normal, Print Layout, and Page Break Preview.

**Zoom Slider** – The buttons at either side of the slider allow you to increase or decrease the zoom by 10%, or you can drag the slider button to choose a particular zoom percentage. Excel displays the current zoom percentage in the Zoom level button, at the right of the View buttons. You can also click this button to set a custom or specific zoom percentage.

The previous screen shot displays various commonly used areas of the Excel screen. Because you can customize the screen's appearance, not all parts always appear. For instance, some people prefer to have the workbook displayed as a window on the screen, while others prefer to maximize the workbook. It is also possible to change the overall color scheme for the Excel window, as well as individual components within each worksheet.

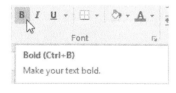

ScreenTips help identify buttons or elements on the tabs of the Ribbon and the screen. To view a ScreenTip, position the mouse cursor on the item. A tip then displays the name of the button along with a description of the purpose of this item. For some items, a keyboard shortcut may also display as an alternative for activating this feature.

Many Ribbon Groups also have a dialog box launcher button. By hovering the mouse cursor over it, the Screen Tip will display a summary of its purpose, as demonstrated in this example:

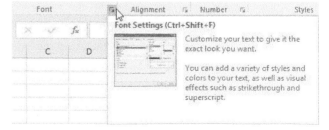

A number of the elements shown in this section can be set to show or hide, as you prefer. In most cases, you can change your display options by clicking the **File** tab, clicking **Options,** and then clicking the **General** or **Advanced** categories.

# Understanding Basic Terminology

A worksheet is similar to an extremely large sheet of paper divided into rows and columns. In Excel, the rows are numbered from 1 to 1,048,576. Each of the 16,384 columns is named with a letter combination starting with A to Z, then AA to ZZ, then AAA to AZZ, up to column XFD.

**Workbook** – A single Excel file containing one or more worksheets (for example, Sheet1, Sheet2, Sheet3) is called a workbook. You can have more than one workbook open at any time but you can only work in one of them at any one time. The workbook that is currently open and on top of all other workbooks or other Windows programs is called the *active workbook*.

**Worksheet** – A worksheet is a two-dimensional arrangement of cells in rows and columns. When you use a workbook with multiple worksheets, you can only use one worksheet at any one time. The worksheet that is currently displayed is called the *active worksheet*.

**Cell** – Located at the intersection of every row and column, a cell holds a single value, label, or formula. It may also contain comments, formatting, and other related data. The cell where you are entering data or the current location of the cursor is called the *active cell*.

**Cell Address** – Excel has more than 17 billion (x $10^9$) cells available per worksheet (1,048,576 rows x 16,384 columns). Each cell has its own distinct address (its point of column-by-row intersection) such as B6 (column B at row 6).

**Sizing** – When the Excel window is not maximized, you can change its overall size and aspect ratio. By positioning the mouse over any of the four edges of the window, the mouse pointer will change to a double-headed arrow ($\leftrightarrow$ or $\updownarrow$). You can then click and drag the edge to change the width or height of the window. If you position the mouse over any of the four corners of the window, you will see a diagonal double-headed arrow (e.g. $\searrow$), which will allow you to drag both adjacent edges at the same time.

# Mouse Symbols

This section introduces some of the common mouse symbols and their purposes:

⬦ Select a cell or range of cells in the worksheet.

⬥ Move or copy selected cells by dragging and dropping.

◹ Select items, command buttons, and menu options.

↔↕↖ Size objects.

I Edit text within the Formula bar or a cell.

+ Indicates the use of the AutoFill feature to copy the contents of cells.

+ Provides a guide for the top left and bottom right corners when creating objects.

↔↕ Change the column width or row height.

↕↔ Move the split bar between the window panes.

→↓ Select an entire row or entire column.

It is possible to use Excel with a touchscreen, however, you will find it is generally easier to use a mouse and keyboard.

## Using the Quick Access Toolbar

The Quick Access Toolbar (also known as QAT) is located at the left of the title bar above the Ribbon and contains buttons for frequently used commands. By default, this toolbar contains the Save, Undo, Redo, and Customize Quick Access Toolbar buttons.

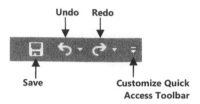

## Using the Ribbon

The Ribbon can help you quickly find commands you require to complete a task. Commands are grouped in tabs with each tab relating to a type of activity such as inserting items, changing the view, and formatting text in the document. You can customize the Ribbon to display commands you use frequently in a particular order, or to add or remove commands for a Ribbon tab.

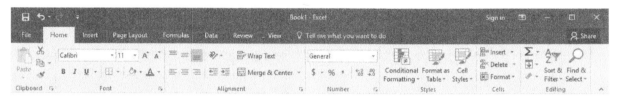

To reduce screen clutter, contextual tabs appear only when they are applicable (for example, Chart Tools, Design, Add Chart Element).

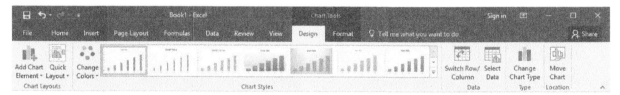

The active button is the one that appears in a different color or has an outline around it. Many of these deactivate when you click the same button or click another choice. For example, the Bold command can be applied to selected text by clicking that button. To turn off the boldface, click the same button again. If you want text to be larger, click the down arrow for the Size button and choose the required size. When you need to change the font size again, click the down arrow for Size and then select the new size.

When the Ribbon displays different choices (as shown in the Chart Styles list in the screen above), one item has a border around it to indicate it is active. To see how the text would appear with another style, point the mouse on one of the other items. Excel previews the effect that will take place if it is selected.

Each tab on the Ribbon contains groups with similar commands. For example, the Home tab has a group called Font that contains buttons for formatting text characters, and the Insert tab contains a group with different types of graphics or illustrations that can be inserted into a worksheet.

If a group shows a feature with a vertical scroll bar, it also has a button below the bottom scroll button, a triangle with a bar above it, which you can click to display the full list or gallery for that option.

This is the More button and, when clicked, it displays a gallery with more options, as seen below. As you point the mouse cursor at an option, Excel displays a Live Preview for how the selected item will appear if you apply this feature. You can turn off this feature in Excel Options.

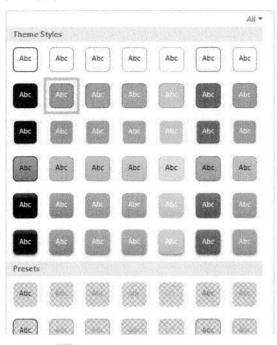

Click the 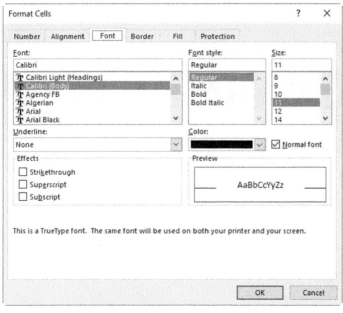 dialog box launcher button at the lower right of a group to show the corresponding dialog box with more options for this feature. In some cases, a task pane may appear at the left or right side of the screen instead of a dialog box. The dialog box launcher button displays the name of the dialog box or task pane window that will appear when clicked.

**Dialog Box**

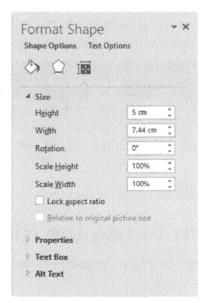

**Task Pane**

Within the dialog box, you can select items from the lists, use the arrow for a list box to display more choices for that list, or click a command to turn the feature on or off. It may display a preview of the changes.

A dialog box displays the various options that you can select to perform a change to a worksheet or cells within a worksheet. Once you click OK to perform the change, the dialog box closes. A task pane is similar to a dialog box because it is used to make changes to parts of the worksheet, except that it remains open until you close it. An example of a task pane is the Office Clipboard which collects and displays the items selected when the Cut or Copy command is used.

If you want to show more lines on the screen or you do not want to display the Ribbon, you can minimize it. To minimize the Ribbon, use one of the following methods:

- point at the 🖼 button at the upper right of the screen, then click **Show Tabs**, or
- right-click anywhere on the Ribbon and then click **Collapse the Ribbon**, or
- double-click on any Ribbon tab, or
- press CTRL+F1.

## Using the Keyboard

You can also access commands in Excel using the keyboard. Some users consider the keyboard to be a faster method for accessing commands. There is also the benefit of consistency between Windows programs, in that many keyboard shortcuts are the same in all Windows programs such as pressing CTRL+C to copy, CTRL+S to save, or CTRL+P to print.

To access the Ribbon using the keyboard, press ALT or F10 to display the keyboard buttons for the commands in the Ribbon.

When you press the key for the appropriate feature, Excel displays the next set of keys you can use to select a command or feature. For example, pressing P displays the Page Layout tab.

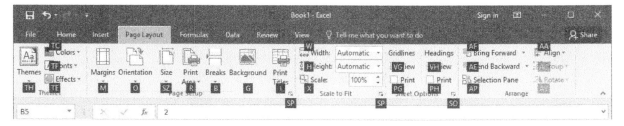

If the Ribbon command displays more options, then you can select from those available key options as well.

# Learn to use the Ribbon

This exercise demonstrates how to use various features on the Ribbon.

1   Start Microsoft Excel.

The Excel Startup screen is displayed. From here, you can choose to open an existing workbook or create a new one using a workbook template.

2   Click **Blank workbook** to create a new blank workbook.

3   Click the **File** tab to display the Backstage view.

4   Click the ⊙ (**Back**) button to return to the workbook.

5   Use the mouse pointer to point to the View tab.

    Notice how the View tab changes color even though you have not clicked it.

6   Click the **View** tab to activate it.

7   Point to Page Layout in the Workbook Views group and notice how the background color of the button changes.

8   Click the **Page Layout** button in the Workgroup Views group to see how the worksheet changes.

9   On the View tab, in the Workbook Views group, click **Normal** to switch back to the default view.

10  Move the cursor to the Zoom slider at the bottom right of the screen. Click and drag the **slider** to the right until you see the zoom percentage change to approximately 200%.

11  At the far right of the Ribbon, click the ⌃ (**Collapse the Ribbon**) button.

    Notice how you now can see a few more rows on the screen. To display a Ribbon tab again temporarily, simply click on any of the tabs.

12  Click the **Home** tab, then click the **Formulas** tab.

13  Click a blank area of the Excel title bar to hide the Ribbon again.

14  Click and drag the slider the other way so the percentage changes to **50%**, then drag the slider to return the zoom to **100%**.

15  Click the ⊞ (**Ribbon Display Options**) button, then click **Show Tabs and Commands** to re-display the entire Ribbon.

**16** Now move the cursor to the top of the screen and click some of the tabs to see how the commands are categorized and grouped on the tabs.

**17** Press ALT to display the keyboard shortcuts on the tab.

**18** Press P to display the Page Layout tab.

**19** Then press M to display the Margins options.

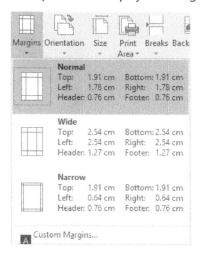

**20** Press ESC to cancel this option.

Notice that the keys are still displayed on the tab, so you can continue to use the keyboard to choose another command.

**21** Press ESC twice more until the keyboard shortcut no longer appear.

**22** Click in the **Tell Me** entry box, and type: create a chart.

**23** Click on the first entry (**Insert Column or Bar Chart**) in the menu that displays below the Tell Me entry box, then position the mouse over each of the chart icons that appear in the sub-menu that appears on the right.

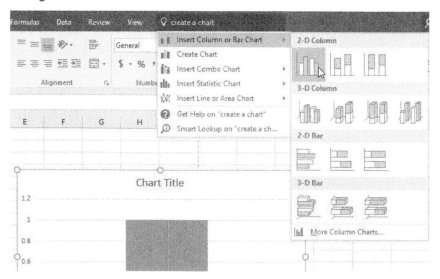

As you position the mouse over each chart icon, a live preview of the selected chart type is displayed on the worksheet.

**24** Move the cursor back to the menu displayed below the Tell Me entry box, and click on the **Get Help on "create a chart"** option.

A window is displayed showing various help information about chart-related topics.

**25** Scroll down the Help window to view the different topics displayed.

**26** Close the Help window.

## Identifying Screen Symbols

Occasionally, you may see different types of symbols appear after performing a task or activating a command. These symbols are visual cues provided within Excel to help you identify a particular status or recognize that other options may be available.

Some of these symbols include:

Circular References: E13 – The **Circular References** indicator appears in the status bar if Excel finds this problem in the current worksheet. A circular reference occurs when a formula in one cell references another cell that references back to the first cell, either directly or indirectly through other cells. Excel will display the double-headed blue arrow between these offending cells. You will learn more about cell references later in this courseware.

**Auto Fill options** – This appears when you use the AutoFill feature to copy data or formulas into adjacent cells. Excel provides you with options for this item. When you point to this button, it appears with a drop-down arrow. Click the arrow to display more options for this item.

**Paste Options** – Excel identifies that you have pasted an item and provides other options for the paste action. When you point to this button, it appears with a drop-down arrow. Click the arrow to display more options for this item.

# Entering Data in a Worksheet

If you design and build it in a logical manner, an Excel worksheet is a very powerful tool. The basic building block of every worksheet is entering data into the cells.

## Types of Data

You can make three main types of entries when you insert data into worksheet cells:

**Numeric** – Numeric data form the core of all worksheets. This type of data consists of number, date, or time values that you enter directly into a worksheet cell. By default, numeric values align to the right in a cell.

**Text** – Text data consist of alphabetic and numeric characters and most printable symbols. Text data are usually labels or titles used to describe and explain the data in adjoining cells. Text is seldom included in calculations, but Excel does include several functions that apply to text data. If you enter a text value that is wider than the cell, it will flow into the adjacent cells as long as those cells are empty. By default, text data align to the left in a cell.

**Formulas** – Formulas, which you enter in individual cells, are composed of values, cell references, arithmetic operators, and special functions for calculating and displaying result. These results may then become part of other formulas located in other cells. The ability to use formulas is what differentiates spreadsheets from word processing software like Microsoft Word.

## Entering Text

To enter data, move your pointer to the desired cell, click in it, and type the entry. If you make a typing error while still entering information in a cell, press the BACKSPACE key to erase your mistake. When you have finished entering data in a cell, press the ENTER key to move the cell pointer automatically to the next cell down. Alternatively, use your mouse to click another cell (or press any arrow key), which performs the same result of storing the data in that cell and moving the cell pointer to the new location.

The best way to begin any worksheet is to enter column and row titles that identify the purpose of the numeric data. When you enter titles for the worksheet, you are creating an outline of the relationships you will later represent mathematically.

When typing information, notice that Excel displays the text in two places:

- You can enter or edit data directly in the active cell where the pointer appears, or you can enter or edit it in the Formula bar. The latter method is especially useful for very long data entries. In either case, the data is displayed in both places.

- Text entries can be up to 32,767 characters, although a maximum of 255 characters are displayed. If a text entry is longer than the width of the cell, it will extend past the column border on the right after you have pressed ENTER, as long as there is nothing entered in those adjoining cells. Any value entered into the cell on the immediate right will truncate the display of the text at the border. For long entries, the entire text value will be stored in the cell, but only the portion that fits in the available space is visible. By default, Excel aligns text data on the left side of the cell. You can easily change the appearance and alignment of a text entry.

## Learn to enter text data

This exercise demonstrates how to enter text data into a worksheet cell, which will serve as a label or title for other cells containing numeric data.

1   In the blank workbook, click in cell **A2**.

2   Type: Price Quote and press ENTER.

    Notice the current active cell is now A3. When you press ENTER, Excel completes the entry of data in the current cell, then moves the cell pointer to the next cell down.

3   Press ENTER twice to move down two rows.

4   In cell **A5**, type: Airfare and press ENTER.

5   In cell **A6**, type: Hotel and press ENTER.

6   In cell **A7**, type: Car Rental and press ENTER.

7   In cell **A8**, type: Taxes and press ENTER.

**Note:** If you entered the wrong value into a cell, simply select the cell and type the entire correct entry again to replace the incorrect value.

Now try a feature called AutoComplete, in which Excel determines whether you are repeating the same text as in a previous cell and completes it for you. If it is the text you want, you simply press ENTER to accept it.

8   In cell **A9**, type: A.

Notice that Excel automatically offers you a text label, based on your previous entry. You can now press the ENTER key to accept it or continue typing the value that you want.

**9** Ignore the suggested label and continue typing the rest of the text: `irport Fees` and press ENTER.

Notice that the text extends further than the default column width for this text entry. If you enter data in the next column, the part of this new label that overflows into the next column will appear to be cut off.

**10** In cell **A12**, type: `Airline:` and press ENTER.

Notice this time that the AutoComplete feature did not turn on. This is because of the blank cells (**A10** and **A11**) that are preventing Excel from "looking up" a previous similar value in this column.

**11** Enter the following in the remaining cells:

| Cell | Text |
|------|------|
| A13 | Hotel: |
| B12 | Great West Airline |
| B13 | Hotel Zathura |

## Entering Numbers

Numbers, such as those representing dollar and percentage values, are constant – that is, they do not change. They are typically used as part of calculations, with results appearing in other parts of the workbook.

By default, Excel aligns numeric values to the right side of a cell. They are displayed with no commas unless you enter them at the same time. Extraneous zeroes at the far left or right are not displayed, even if entered at the same time. You can format the values to your preference at a later time.

If you enter a value that contains a mixture of alphabetic and numeric digits (for example, T-1000), Excel treats the entire entry as text and aligns it to the left of the cell.

## Learn to enter numeric data

This exercise demonstrates how to enter numeric data into a worksheet cell.

**1** In cell **B5** of the workbook, type: `450` and press ENTER.

**2** In cell **B6**, type: `1,050` and press ENTER.

**3** In cell **B7**, type: `225` and press ENTER.

**4** In cell **B8**, type: `46.50` and press ENTER.

**5** In cell **B9**, type: `9.9` and press ENTER.

**6** Click in cell **A9**.

Notice in cell A9 that the part of the text entry that had overflowed into cell B9 is now hidden because a value was entered into cell B9. However, the Formula bar shows that the data in cell A9 is unchanged.

**7** Click in cell **D8**, and type: `3.1%` and press ENTER.

Excel interprets the entered values as numeric and aligns them on the right of their cells. However, if you enter any non-recognizable characters, or insert any commas or decimal points in the wrong position, Excel will treat the entire contents of that cell as a label, and align it on the left side of the cell.

8   In cell **D9**, type: 2,2% (including the comma) and press ENTER.

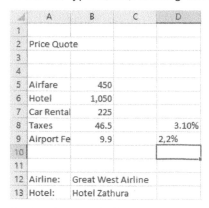

Notice that Excel aligned the data on the left side of the cell. Because you entered a comma instead of a period, Excel assumes that the cell entry is a text value.

9   Move back to cell **D9** and type: 2.2% to replace the incorrect contents of that cell.

# Entering Dates and Times

Excel is also capable of handling date and time values. When entering dates, note the following:

- If you enter a full date value including the month, day, and year value, the date value will display as dd-mmm-yy by default.

- The date value does not have to be the full day, month, and year. It can be just the day and month (format is dd-mmm), or the month and year only (format is mmm-yy).

- If you enter only the name of a month, Excel will treat it as a text value. If you enter only a day or year value, Excel will treat it as a numeric value. In these cases, Excel will not recognize that you intended to enter a part of a date value.

- When entering the date, Excel attempts to interpret what you have entered. For example, the following are acceptable date values:

      September 15, 2016 (you must include the comma followed by a space)
      Sep 15, 16
      15-Sep-16
      09/15/16 (month, day, year sequence — see next bullet)
      9-15-16
      Sep 2016
      Sep 15

- If you enter the date using only numeric values (for example, 09/15/16 as shown above), the sequence of the values must match the date sequence specified in the Windows Control Panel, Region settings. For the United States, the normal date sequence is month/day/year. For Canada and the United Kingdom, the sequence is day/month/year. If Excel is not able to interpret the date value, it will appear as a text label (left aligned in the cell).

When entering time values, note the following:

- The time must consist of hours and minutes, as a minimum, in the format of hh:mm. You can also add seconds and the AM/PM indicator. The alternative to the latter is to use the 24-hour clock format.

The following are acceptable time values:

> 1:15 PM (be sure to add a space before the AM/PM indicator)
> 13:15
> 13:15:01
> 1:15:01 PM
> 1:15

# Learn to work with dates

This exercise demonstrates the use of dates.

1   In cell **A3**, type: As of: and press TAB.

2   In cell **B3** type: 30 Jun and press ENTER.

Notice that Excel puts the date in the default format and aligns it to the right.

3   In cell **D3** type: Expires: and press TAB.

4   In cell **E3** type: Jul 15, 2016 and press ENTER.

| | A | B | C | D | E |
|---|---|---|---|---|---|
| 1 | | | | | |
| 2 | Price Quote | | | | |
| 3 | As of: | 30-Jun | | Expires: | 15-Jul-16 |
| 4 | | | | | |
| 5 | Airfare | 450 | | | |
| 6 | Hotel | 1,050 | | | |
| 7 | Car Rental | 225 | | | |
| 8 | Taxes | 46.5 | | 3.10% | |
| 9 | Airport Fe | 9.9 | | 2.20% | |
| 10 | | | | | |
| 11 | | | | | |
| 12 | Airline: | Great West Airline | | | |
| 13 | Hotel: | Hotel Zathura | | | |

5   Select cell **E3**.

The date value for this cell also appears in the Formula bar. The date value sequence corresponds to the setting in the Windows Control Panel.

6   Select cell **B3**.

Because you have not included a year in this date value, Excel assumes it is the current year and adds it for you. If you want a different year, you have to enter it as part of the date.

## Moving Around the Worksheet

You can move around the cells of a worksheet very quickly by either using the keyboard or scrolling with the mouse. Use one of the following methods to move around in the worksheet:

**Scroll Bars** – Click the arrow buttons at either end of the scroll bars to move one row or column at a time. Click on the scroll box (the size will vary depending on the zoom percentage) and drag to display another location in the worksheet.

**LEFT, RIGHT, UP, DOWN ARROW** – Press one of these directional keys to move one cell at a time.

**HOME** – Press this key to move to column A in the current row.

**CTRL+HOME** – Press this key combination to move to cell A1, regardless of where you are in the worksheet.

**CTRL+END** – Press this key combination to move to the last cell in the data table.

**CTRL+G / F5** – Display the Go To dialog box so you can move quickly to a cell reference, range name, or bookmark, or use the Special button to find specific types of information (for example, Comments, Blanks).

# Working with Workbooks

As you begin using workbooks, you need to consider how to organize your files for quick and easy access. This includes considerations such as how you name the file, where you save it, whether it needs to be saved as a specific file type, and whether you want to add or change the file properties to make it easier to find at a later date. The Save commands are located in the Backstage view via the File tab.

## Saving Workbooks

To be able to recall your work later, you must save your workbook before exiting Excel or turning off your computer. The saved file also provides an excellent fall-back option if you try something in your worksheet that does not work as you expected, and you are unable or unwilling to undertake all the necessary steps to correct the problem.

When naming a workbook, keep the following in mind:

- Workbook names must follow the same basic rules as naming files in Windows: a maximum of 255 characters (including the drive and folder path), and none of these characters: / \ : * ? " < >|

- File names should be descriptive so that you can identify the contents quickly.

- Excel automatically assigns a .xlsx extension or file type at the end of the file name, so you need not do this. You only have to type in the name for the workbook.

- Files can be saved with two different types of save commands:

  - Use Save As to save a new document or to save an existing document with a new name or new location.

  - Use Save to save changes to the active workbook but retain the existing name and keep the file in the existing location.

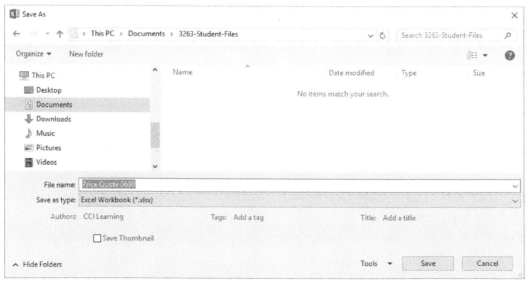

---

- When the file name appears in the Save As dialog box as highlighted text, begin typing the new file name to insert the new file name for this workbook. Use the arrow direction keys to move anywhere in the existing file name to add or delete text to the file name.

- To save a workbook as a different file type, such as an earlier version of Excel, use Save as type in the Save As dialog box to find the file format you need.

- By default, Windows sets up the Documents library to store files. Excel draws on this, but you are not restricted to this folder. You can:

  - Create your own folders to help organize files by clicking **New folder** on the command bar in the Save As dialog box.

  - Save in any location that you can access (hard drive, thumb drive, flash disk, network drive).

If you are unsure whether you have saved a file previously, look at the workbook name in the title bar to see if it is the default name of *Book1* (or *Bookx* where the *x* is a number). Alternatively, use Save As to give the workbook a different name, thereby ensuring you do not accidentally overwrite the workbook currently stored on the hard drive with the one on your screen.

Even if the file already exists in one location, you can save the same file to another location. Be careful with having files with the same name in different locations, as it may be difficult to determine which is the most current or valid version to use.

To view the file type (the extension part of the file name), you need to turn on this option using File Explorer. Click **View**, and on the Show/hide group, click **File name extensions** to activate it. Showing the file types can be helpful when determining which file you want to use. For example, two files may have the same name, but the file extensions show that one is in .xlsx format (Excel 2007 and later) while the other is in .xls format (Excel 2003 and earlier).

To save changes made to the current workbook using the same file name, use one of the following methods:

- click **File** and then **Save**, or
- on the Quick Access Toolbar, click **Save**, or
- press CTRL+S.

You can use Views in the Save As dialog box to help display the folders and files in the way you prefer (for example, list or thumbnails).

# Learn to save workbooks

In this exercise, you will save the new workbook you have just created.

**1** In the Quick Access Toolbar, click **Save**.

The Backstage view is displayed, and the Save As command is selected. Even though you clicked Save, Excel will automatically skip to Save As for any new workbook that was never previously saved. The Save command will save the current workbook to disk using the same workbook name and storage location. The Save As command is needed to ask you to assign the workbook name and storage location.

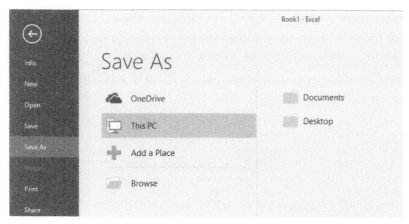

2   Click **This PC**, then click **Documents**.

The Save As dialog box is now displayed with the *Documents* folder contents displayed. Alternatively, click the **Browse** button if the desired folder is not displayed under the Recent Folders or Current Folder headings.

3   Navigate to the student data files folder location. Refer to page ii of the Preface for instructions on how to access the student data files.

4   Click in the **File name** field, and type: Price Quote 0630.

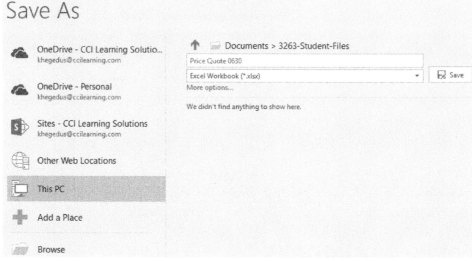

5   Click **Save**.

Notice that the title bar now contains the new file name as visual confirmation that the file is now saved.

**Note:** You can also press ENTER after entering the file name to save the file.

## Creating a New Workbook

**Objective 1.1.1**

While you are using a workbook, you can also create a new workbook at any time. You can have more than one workbook open and on the screen at any time. Each workbook is created in its own window, and each window can only have one workbook. Also, each workbook window can be placed anywhere on the Desktop, independent of any other workbook window that is open at the same time.

Each time you create a new blank workbook in a current session, Excel numbers it sequentially, starting at 1 as *Book#*, with # representing the number of new workbooks you have created up to that moment. The document numbering will begin at 1 again when you start a new session of Excel.

To create a new blank workbook, use one of the following methods:

- to create a new blank document, click **File**, click **New**, click **Blank workbook**, or
- press CTRL+N.

Instead of starting with a blank workbook, you can create a workbook using a template. A template is simply a pre-designed workbook that may already contain data, formulas, and other objects, which saves you time and effort. Examples of common templates are sales invoices, balance sheets, and loan amortization schedules. Whenever you use the New option to create a new workbook, you will be presented with many pre-made templates (in addition to the blank workbook) that you can begin using immediately. You can also search for additional templates online from the Microsoft Office.com website using the search text box at the top of the window. In reality, all of these templates are downloaded from the Microsoft Office website. The New window simply displays some examples that may be of interest to you.

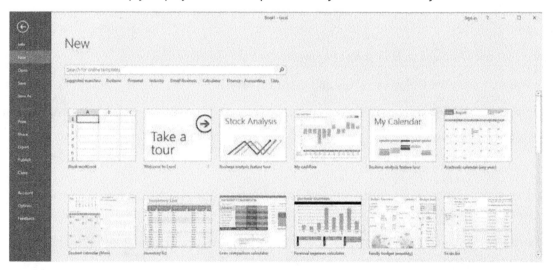

In the Excel 2016 Expert courseware, you will learn how to create and save your own customized template.

To create a new workbook from a template, click **File**, click **New**, click a template, and then click **Create**.

# Learn to create new workbooks

In this exercise, you will create a new workbook using different methods.

**Note**: This exercise (and several that follow) refers to specific templates. If you cannot find a specified template, you may select a different template. You may need to adjust the steps to reflect the template you chose.

1   Press CTRL+N.

You should now have a new blank workbook titled as *Book2* on the screen, appearing in front of any other workbooks currently open.

2   If the Excel window is maximized to the full screen, click the 🗗 (**Restore Down**) button to change it to a window.

Two workbooks are now visible on your screen.

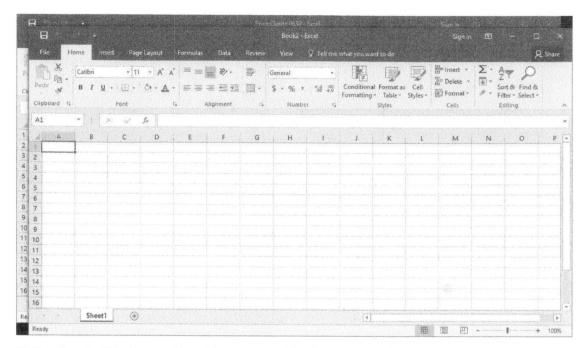

Notice that the Windows taskbar shows two workbooks are currently open.

**3**   Click **File** to display the Office Backstage and then click **New**.

In addition to the Blank workbook option, several other workbook templates are also readily available.

**4**   Scroll down the screen, click **To do list**, and then click **Create** in the next pop-up window.

Excel now displays a to do list.

This is an example of how templates can save you time and effort when creating a workbook. Many of the elements you see in this document will be covered in more depth later in this courseware.

You can also select from your own templates, from Microsoft's website, or other Internet websites. To use templates from Microsoft's website, use the search feature.

**5**   Click **File** once more and then click **New**.

**6**   Type: budgets in the search text box, and press ENTER.

All available templates in the website that are related to your search key are now displayed. A quick glance at the vertical scroll bar indicates that there are many budget-related templates available. You can use the Category panel on the right to act as a filter to find the templates that are best suited to what you are looking for.

**7**   In the Category panel on the right, click **Budgets**, **Business**, **Industry**, and **Travel**.

**8**   Click **Business trip budget**, and then click **Create** in the next pop-up window.

# Switching Between Workbooks

When you have multiple workbooks open on the screen, you can switch between workbooks quickly and easily using one of the following methods:

- on the View tab, in the Window group, click **Switch Windows,** or

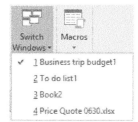

- hover the mouse cursor over the **Excel** button on the taskbar to display a preview of each open workbook, or

**Tip:** In this example, there is only one Excel icon in the Windows Taskbar even though you have four workbooks currently open. You can reconfigure the Taskbar so that one Excel icon will appear for each open workbook by right-clicking on the Taskbar, selecting **Properties**, and in the Taskbar tab, change the **Taskbar buttons** option to **Combine when taskbar is full.**

- press CTRL+TAB to jump to the next open workbook, or
- if the workbooks are restored down as windows on the Desktop screen, click the title bar for the appropriate workbook to pull it to the front.

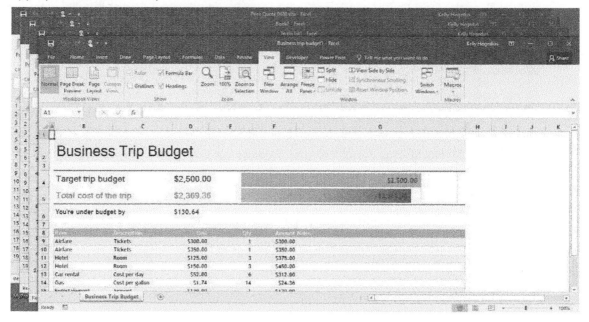

# ▎Learn to switch between workbooks

This exercise demonstrates how to switch between multiple workbooks that are open at the same time.

1  Click the **View** tab.

2  In the Window group at the right, click **Switch Windows**.

3  Click **To do list1**.

   This workbook should now be displayed on top of the other workbooks.

4  Point at the **Excel** button on the taskbar at the bottom of the screen.

5  Click **Price Quote 0630**.

   This workbook should now be displayed on top of the other workbooks.

## Opening a Workbook

If you want to work with a previously created and saved workbook, you must first open it. You can open as many workbooks as needed. The only limitation is the amount of memory available on your system to handle multiple workbooks.

If you do not recall the name or location of the Excel workbook, use the File Explorer to try to find the workbook on the computer or on the network. Alternatively, Excel displays a list of the most recently opened workbooks, which you can use if you know that the workbook was recently used on the computer you are using.

Use one of the following methods to open a workbook:

- if Excel is starting up, click the desired workbook in the Recent(ly used workbooks) section of the Excel startup screen or click **Open Other Workbooks**, or

- right-click on the Excel Quick Launch icon in the taskbar and select the recently used workbook from the Recent list, or

- with a workbook currently open, click **File**, click **Open**, and then click the file from the list of **Recent Workbooks**, or

  As you open workbooks, Excel displays the files in the same order as you opened them, with the most recent at the top of the list. As you reach the maximum number of files that show in this list, the oldest drops from the list. You can click the pin icon at the right of the file name to make this file always available in the list until it is unpinned. By default, you can see a list of up to 50 recent workbooks at a time. This number can be customized.

- click **File**, click **Open**, then click **This PC** and use this Open screen as a simplified File Explorer to navigate around your PC, then click on the workbook to open, or

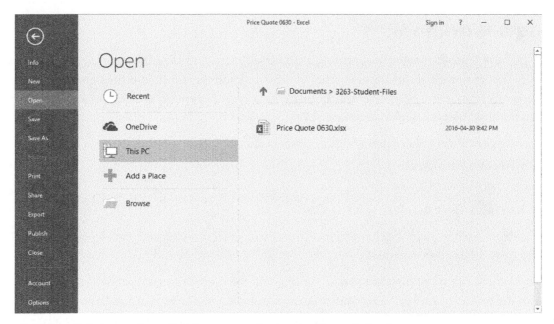

- click **File**, click **Open**, then click **Browse** to display the Open dialog box.

The Open screen in the Backstage displays several options to look for your workbooks: your most recently used folders, a link to your OneDrive service, a link to all files and folders on your local computer, and a **Browse** button for you to use the Open dialog box to find your workbooks. You can also press CTRL+O to display this same Backstage view.

The Open dialog box looks and works like the File Explorer: the navigation pane on the left side allows you to quickly jump to different storage areas connected to your computer, whether they are on your local physical drives, storage drives available on the network, or remote storage on the Internet. If you prefer using it, you can press CTRL+F12 to go directly to the Open dialog box without displaying the Backstage view.

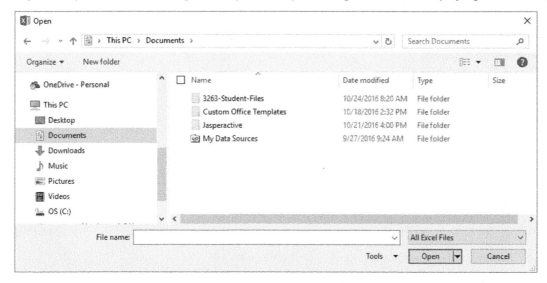

In the main display pane, you can navigate using the mouse or keyboard to display the files or folders and then use one of the following methods to open a document:

- double-click the file name, or
- click on the file name to select it, and then click **Open** or press ENTER.

# Closing a Workbook

Once you have finished creating or updating a workbook, close it to clear the screen and free up computer memory. This ensures that any unsaved data for that workbook is saved onto the hard drive, and protects the workbook from unintended changes. Closing your workbook is much like closing a book and putting it back on the shelf before opening another book.

You can use one of the following methods to close a workbook:

- click **File** and then **Close**, or
- press CTRL+W or CTRL+F4 , or
- click the ⊠ **Close** button.

**Note:** Because each workbook is running in its own Excel application window, closing one workbook will not affect any other open workbooks.

If you add or change something in a new or existing document, which has not yet been saved, Excel prompts you with the option of saving the workbook before closing it. If the workbook has been open for more than 10 minutes (this time interval can be changed), an additional note is added to the message box to indicate that it will still be available even if you accidentally discard the workbook without saving it.

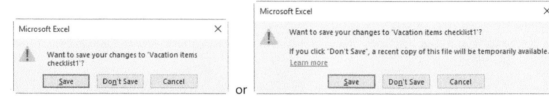

You can choose to close the workbook without saving the changes.

# Learn to close workbooks

In this exercise, you will use several different techniques to save and then close multiple workbooks.

1   Click **File** and then **Open**.

2   Click **This PC**, then click **Browse**.

3   Navigate to the student files folder.

4   Click the **Popular Tours** file, and click **Open**.

Assume that you are now satisfied with viewing the contents of this workbook, and you no longer need to continue viewing it.

5   Click **File**, and then click **Close**.

The *Popular Tours* file is no longer on the screen. Now close another workbook using the close button.

6   On the View tab, in the Windows group, click **Switch Windows**.

7   Click **To do list1**.

8   Click the ⊠ **Close** button in the upper right corner.

9   If a pop-up message box is displayed with this question: "Do you want to save the changes you made to To do list1?", click **Don't Save**.

Close another workbook, but use the close button in the taskbar preview this time.

**10** Point to the Excel button in the taskbar, then point to the *Business trip budget1* workbook, and click the ▨ **Close** button for that workbook. Click **Don't Save** in the pop-up message box if it appears.

**11** Point to the Excel button in the taskbar, then click on the **Book2** workbook to make it active, and press CTRL+W. Click **Don't Save** in the pop-up message box if it appears.

**12** Click the ▨ **Close** button in the upper right corner of the remaining *Price Quote 0630* workbook. Click **Don't Save** in the pop-up message box if it appears.

All workbooks should now be closed and Excel has closed.

## Working with the Compatibility Mode

**Objective 1.5.8**

Excel 2007 and later versions (including Excel 2016) all use the same file format for saved workbooks, which have the extension .xlsx at the end of the file name. If you have a user who is using Excel 97, 2000, 2002, or 2003, then you must save your workbook as a new and different file using the older format to enable them to open it. These workbooks use the file extension of .xls. To save a workbook in this format, click **File**, click **Save As** and then click the arrow for Save as type and select **Excel 97-2003 Workbook**.

Excel 2016 is able to open any of these workbooks – even though they were created by older Excel versions – make changes to their contents, and save the workbook back to the older format. Excel will inform you that the workbook is using an older format by displaying the words "Compatibility Mode" next to the workbook name in the title bar.

However, Excel 2016 has many features and capabilities that did not exist or worked differently in these earlier versions. Excel provides a few tools to help you check the workbook and ensure that it is compatible with earlier Excel versions. These tools are available in Backstage via the File tab and the Info category.

To check if there may be problems with converting your workbook to a different file format than .xlsx, click **File**, click **Info**, click **Check for Issues**, and then **Check Compatibility**.

Any potential problems between the versions appear in the list. You then need to decide whether to continue saving the file in this file format or return to the document to make appropriate changes.

# Learn to check compatibility

In this exercise, you will check a workbook for compatibility before saving it in the .xls format.

**1** Start Excel and open a new, blank workbook.

**2** Click **File**, **Open**, then click **Browse**. Navigate to the student files folder, then double-click the **Retirement Planner** workbook to open it. The workbook includes formulas that will calculate the required earnings and savings each year to achieve your retirement goals.

**3** Click **File**.

**4** Click **Check for Issues**.

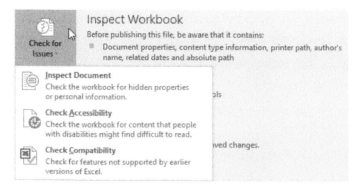

**5** Click **Check Compatibility**.

A quick look at the relative size of the elevator button to the length of the vertical scroll bar indicates how many compatibility issues you have when trying to save the workbook to the older format. In addition, this window shows the number of occurrences of each problem.

**6** Read through the list of findings, then click **OK**.

For the purpose of this exercise, you will proceed with saving this workbook in the older format, even though there are unresolved compatibility issues.

**7** Click **File** and then click **Save As**.

**8** Click **Browse**, then navigate to the student files folder.

**9** In the Save As dialog box, click the arrow for the Save as type list, and then click **Excel 97-2003 Workbook (*.xls)**.

The Save As dialog box displays all other existing workbooks of the same type. There are no others in this folder.

**10** Change the **File name** to My Retirement Planner and click **Save**.

The Compatibility Checker dialog box is displayed again as a warning.

**11** Click **Continue**.

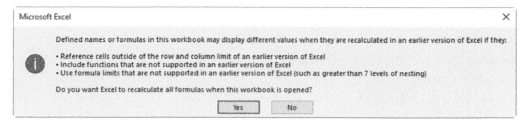

This message box describes some of the problems you may have when using the older version of Excel. The Compatibility Checker dialog box gave you the details of the differences. Because this is a standard warning for any workbook containing formulas, these problems may not apply to this workbook.

**12** Click **Yes**.

**13** Close the workbook.

**14** Click **File**, **Open**, **Browse**, navigate to the student files folder, and select the **My Retirement Planner** workbook and click **Open**.

The workbook name in the title bar now shows the label [Compatibility Mode] next to it. This indicates that this workbook uses the file format for an earlier version of Excel.

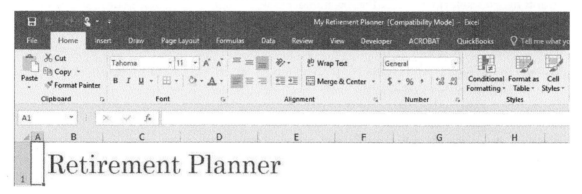

**15** Close the workbook again and don't save any changes.

# Selecting Cells

The ability to select a range of cells is a fundamental skill in Excel. Prior to issuing a command or undertaking a procedure, you must indicate what part of the worksheet you wish to affect with the command. Range selection is the means to indicate this area.

A range selection can be as small as a single cell, or as large as the entire spreadsheet. Excel keeps the cell(s) highlighted until you change or remove the selection. Clicking a cell or using an arrow key will remove the selection.

In a worksheet, you can select:

- a single cell, that is, the active cell
- a single range, for example, a rectangular section of a worksheet containing two or more cells
- multiple ranges of cells

Excel displays the selected range by reversing the color of the cells. Within the selected range, one cell appears in a normal color. This is the active cell of the range.

You can use the mouse to select different ranges as follows:

**A single cell** – Click the cell.

**Extend the selection** – Click the cell, hold the left mouse button down, drag to the end of the desired range, and then release the mouse button.

**An entire row** – Click the row heading.

**An entire column** – Click the column heading.

**The entire worksheet** – Click the **Select All** button in the top left corner of the worksheet (the triangle to the left of the column headings and above the row headings).

**Make a selection** – Click the beginning cell in the range, then point to the ending cell in the range and hold SHIFT down while clicking on the ending cell in the range.

**Extend/shrink a selection** – Hold SHIFT and click inside the previously selected range to shrink the selection, or click outside the range to extend the selection.

Other selection techniques include:

**Non-adjacent columns**, **rows**, or **cells** – Click the cell, column, or row. Move the pointer to the next cell, column, or row, hold CTRL down, then click and drag.

**Extend the row selection** – Click the row number, hold the left mouse button down, and drag.

**Extend the column selection** – Click the column letter, hold the left mouse button down, and drag.

In some cases, you may want to use the keyboard to select cells by using SHIFT with the arrow keys. Generally, you have better control when selecting large cell ranges with the keyboard, especially when having to scroll to other parts of the worksheet at the same time. Note that you cannot select non-adjacent rows, columns or cells using the keyboard only.

# Learn to select cell ranges

This exercise demonstrates how to select ranges of cells using the mouse in a blank worksheet so you can quickly identify the ranges.

1   Create a new blank workbook if necessary.

2   Select a single cell by clicking cell **A9**.

3   Select a range of cells by holding the left mouse button down in cell **A9**, drag the mouse to cell **C5**, and then release the mouse button.

4   Select an entire column by clicking on the column **E** header at the top of the worksheet.

5   Select an entire row by clicking on the row **14** header on the left side of the worksheet.

6   Select the entire worksheet by clicking **Select All** in the top left corner of the worksheet (the gray triangle to the left of the column **A** header and above the row **1** header).

Now select more than one non-contiguous range of cells.

7   Select the range of cells **B4** to **B7**.

8   Hold CTRL and select cells **D11** to **E18**.

9   Continue holding CTRL and select cells **F2** to **D3**. Release CTRL.

Now use the keyboard to select a range of cells.

**10** Select cell **A9**.

**11** While holding down SHIFT, press the appropriate arrow keys to extend the range to cell **C5**. Release SHIFT.

Now try selecting another range of cells using an alternate method with the keyboard.

**12** Select cell **E10**.

**13** While holding down SHIFT, click in cell **G15**.

**14** Close and discard the workbook.

# Lesson Summary

Now that you have completed this lesson, you should be able to:

☑ understand what an electronic spreadsheet is

☑ understand what Excel is and what it can do

☑ identify elements on the Excel screen

☑ understand some basic terminology

☑ use the Quick Access Toolbar

☑ move around in Excel

☑ use keyboard shortcuts

☑ enter text, numbers, dates and times

☑ move around a worksheet

☑ use the Backstage view to save, create new, open, and close a workbook

☑ switch between workbooks

☑ save in a previous version Excel format, and check for compatibility issues

☑ manage files and folders

☑ select cells

# Review Questions

1.  You should use an electronic spreadsheet if you want to:

    a.  Create a presentation for viewing at a kiosk.

    b.  Perform a large number of mathematical calculations and display charts and graphs.

    c.  Track extremely complex data relationships.

    d.  Create and print a full-color brochure for investment brokers.

2.  What is the difference between a workbook and a worksheet?

    a.  A worksheet is a document created in Access, while a workbook is created in Excel.

    b.  A worksheet can contain numbers, text and formulas, whereas a workbook can contain only numbers.

    c.  A worksheet is a document divided into columns and rows, whereas a workbook is a single Excel file containing one or more worksheets.

    d.  A worksheet contains data for viewing onscreen only, whereas a workbook can be printed.

3.  If you want to access the Ribbon using the keyboard, you should:

    a.  Press the ALT or F10 key.

    b.  Turn on Excel's built-in accessibility features.

    c.  Press CTRL+ALT+DEL.

    d.  Press the WINDOWS key.

4. The Auto-hide Ribbon, Show Tabs, and Show Tabs and Commands options are available when you click which button?

   a. Formula bar

   b. Ribbon display options

   c. Quick access toolbar

   d. Dialog button

5. Text, numeric and formula are examples of:

   a. Types of data.

   b. Types of cell formats.

   c. Types of worksheets.

   d. Types of cell addresses.

6. Which of the following entries will NOT be recognized as a date by Excel?

   a. 9/15            c. 9//15

   b. 9/15-16         d. 9-15

7. Amanda has just updated her Budget 2016 workbook with new values for 2017. She wants to save her revised file as Budget 2017. Which command should she use?

   a. Save            c. Update

   b. Save as         d. Rename

8. You should create a new workbook using a template when:

   a. You want to enter information using your own layout.

   b. You want to use a design and layout previously created, either to enter data or to use as a base for your own reports.

   c. You want to create a workbook that is automatically password-protected.

   d. You want to start out with one blank worksheet.

9. You need to share your Excel 2016 workbook with a colleague who uses Excel 2003. What should you do?

   a. Use the Check Compatibility tool to inspect the workbook for any compatibility issues with Excel 2003, then save your workbook in Excel 97-2003 format.

   b. Encourage your colleague to upgrade to Excel 2016 so he can work with your data.

   c. You don't need to do anything – Excel 2003 can open an Excel 2016 workbook with no difficulties.

   d. Allow your colleague to use your computer when working on the file.

10. How do you select different areas of a worksheet at the same time?

   a. Use the ALT key as you click to select other cells.

   b. Use the WINDOWS key as you click to select other cells.

   c. Use the F1 key as you click to select other cells.

   d. Use the CTRL key as you click to select other cells.

Microsoft®

# Excel 2016

## Core Certification Guide

# Lesson 2:
# Constructing Cell Data

## Lesson Objectives

In this lesson, you will learn how to make changes to data in the worksheet, change the structure of the worksheet, and add and remove worksheets in the workbook. Upon completion of the lesson, you should be able to:

- ☐ edit cells and undo changes
- ☐ cut, copy, and paste data
- ☐ use Paste Special
- ☐ change column widths
- ☐ change row heights
- ☐ use AutoFit with columns or rows
- ☐ hide and unhide rows and columns
- ☐ insert and delete rows and columns

- ☐ insert and delete cells
- ☐ use AutoFill and Flash Fill to copy and fill cells
- ☐ rename worksheets
- ☐ insert and delete worksheets
- ☐ move and copy worksheets
- ☐ hide and unhide worksheets
- ☐ add color to the worksheet tabs

# Editing Cells and Undoing Changes

Once you have entered your data into a worksheet, you may want to rearrange the data or change it to suit your needs and preferences. If your "spreadsheet" is a very large piece of paper, you will waste a lot of time erasing and rewriting your data each time your requirements changed. With an electronic spreadsheet, you can easily make quick changes to the display and arrangement of the data on the worksheet.

There are two ways to modify a cell containing data:

- Enter the new value into the cell and press ENTER to replace the original contents with the new contents. This method is popular because it does not require the use of any special keys or modes.

- Activate Excel's editing mode by pressing the F2 key, then use the LEFT ARROW, RIGHT ARROW, BACKSPACE, DELETE, HOME and END keys to move inside the cell and make the changes. Note that anything you type is added to existing content. You can also type over the cell contents by pressing INSERT while you are in the editing mode. You may still have to delete any remaining characters from the previous text.

**Note:** You can also activate the editing mode by double-clicking on the data in a cell, or by clicking in the Formula bar.

If you are entering data into an empty cell (a cell that does not have a value currently), you can only make corrections by pressing BACKSPACE prior to pressing ENTER. Excel only allows you to use the cursor movement keys when you are in edit mode (F2).

Excel has an Undo function that enables you to undo commands that you have executed in your worksheet. You can undo a maximum of 100 most recently used commands. This history of commands is listed in reverse order (the most recent action is listed at the top, followed by the next most recent) and can be accessed by clicking the arrow next to the Undo button. The list remains available to you even if you save the workbook, but will be lost once you close it.

To undo an action, use one of the following methods:

- on the Quick Access Toolbar, click **Undo** to reverse the last action. Alternatively, click the arrow next to **Undo** to display the history of the most recently used commands; or

- press CTRL+Z to reverse the last action. Each time you press this key sequence, you will undo a previous action.

Some actions cannot be undone—specifically any Backstage actions such as saving, opening or printing a workbook.

In addition to undoing commands, Excel enables you to redo commands. If you reverse a command, then immediately want to undo your undo, you can redo the command to put it back in your worksheet. The Redo function is only available if one or more commands were undone.

To redo an action, use one of the following methods:

- on the Quick Access Toolbar, click **Redo** to reverse the last undo. Alternatively, click the down arrow next to Redo to display the list of all actions that can be reversed, or

- press CTRL+Y to reverse the last action. Each time you press this key sequence, you will redo a previous action.

# Learn to edit cell content

This exercise demonstrates how to edit the contents of cells containing text, numbers and dates.

1   If necessary, start Excel and open the *World Travel Destinations* workbook and save it to the student data files folder as: `World Travel Destinations - Student`.

First, you will notice that Egypt and France have each other's capital city. You will switch them around by replacing the cells with the correct values.

2   Select cell **B8**, type `Cairo` and press ENTER.

3   Select cell **B9** and enter: `Paris`.

Now try using the editing mode to modify the contents of a cell.

4   Select cell **A2** and press F2.

5   Press BACKSPACE twice.

6   Type: `na` and press ENTER.

The contents of the cell should now be Argentina.

Next, make some corrections to numbers.

7   Select cell **C4** and enter: `30,510`.

8   Select cell **C3**, press F2 and press HOME. Type: `768` and press ENTER so the final value shows as 7,686,850.

You can also modify date values. Note that the month and day sequence on your computer will depend on your computer's region setting.

9   Select cell **B22**, press F2 and press HOME or LEFT ARROW to position the cursor to the left of the month value of 5. Press DELETE and type: `6` to change the month to June, then press ENTER.

Finally, make the corrections to the rest of the worksheet.

10  Use F2, LEFT ARROW, RIGHT ARROW, DELETE, BACKSPACE and other keyboard keys as necessary to correct the indicated cells as follows:

| Cell | Should Be |
|------|-----------|
| A5   | `Brazil` |
| A10  | `Germany` |
| A14  | `Italy` |
| A20  | `United States of America` |
| B14  | `Rome` |
| B19  | `London` |
| C13  | `3,287,590` |
| C11  | `1,092` |

| | A | B | C |
|----|------------------------|---------------|-------------|
| 1  | Country | Destination | Size (sq km) |
| 2  | Argentina | Buenos Aires | 2,766,890 |
| 3  | Australia | Melbourne | 7,686,850 |
| 4  | Belgium | Brussels | 30,510 |
| 5  | Brazil | Rio de Janeiro | 8,511,965 |
| 6  | China | Shanghai | 9,596,960 |
| 7  | Cuba | Havana | 110,860 |
| 8  | Egypt | Cairo | 1,001,450 |
| 9  | France | Paris | 547,030 |
| 10 | Germany | Berlin | 357,021 |
| 11 | Hong Kong | Hong Kong | 1,092 |
| 12 | Iceland | Reyjkavik | 103,000 |
| 13 | India | Mumbai | 3,287,590 |
| 14 | Italy | Rome | 301,230 |
| 15 | Netherlands | Amsterdam | 41,526 |
| 16 | South Africa | Cape Town | 1,219,912 |
| 17 | Spain | Barcelona | 504,782 |
| 18 | Thailand | Bangkok | 514,000 |
| 19 | United Kingdom | London | 244,820 |
| 20 | United States of America | New York | 9,629,091 |
| 21 | | | |
| 22 | List updated on: | 02-Jun-16 | |

**11** Save the workbook but don't close it.

Suppose you change your mind at this point and need to reverse the last change made.

**12** On the Quick Access Toolbar, click **Undo**.

The value in cell C11 has changed back to *101,092*.

If you then decide that the change was actually correct, you can redo or repeat the last change made.

**13** On the Quick Access Toolbar, click **Redo**.

The value in cell C11 has changed back to *1,092*.

**14** Save and close the workbook.

# Copying and Moving Data
## Cutting, Copying and Pasting Data

### Objective 2.1.2

Excel enables you to copy or move cell contents and their formats to simplify editing tasks and streamline worksheet construction. There are very significant differences between copying the contents of a cell and moving the contents to another worksheet cell.

You can move the contents of a cell or range of cells to a different part of the worksheet, a different part of the workbook, or even a different workbook. This removes the values from the original location and places them in the new location.

Alternatively, you can copy the contents of a cell and range of cells to a different location. By copying, you do not affect the original cells. The originating data remain in their current cells.

**Cut** – Marks the contents of a cell or a range of cells for removal, and places a copy on the Clipboard.

**Copy** – Marks the contents of a cell or a range of cells for copying and places a copy on the Clipboard.

**Paste** – Puts the contents of the marked cell or range of cells into the new cell location. If the previous action was Cut, then the contents of the marked cell(s) are removed. If the previous action was Copy, the marked cells remain unchanged. If the new cell location already contains data or formatting, the pasted data will overwrite the existing data and formatting.

**Paste Special** – Modify the effects of the paste option (for example, you can paste the contents or format only). In comparison, the Paste command is non-selective and pastes all features of the originating cells.

When you select either the Cut or Copy command, a marquee (a rectangle outlined with a moving, dotted line) appears around the selected cell range. This marquee identifies the cell range that you can paste to another part of the worksheet or to another worksheet. At the same time, the contents of this cell range is also copied into an internal Clipboard, which is used as a temporary storage area to enable the subsequent Paste command. You can remove the marquee (cancelling the copying or moving action) by pressing ESC. You can also cancel the copying or moving action by typing new data into a cell. When you enter new data, Excel interprets that you want to continue the editing process on your spreadsheet, and so the marquee disappears.

- You can copy or move any kind of data—text, numbers, dates, formulas, drawing objects and charts – that you have embedded in a worksheet.

- You can copy a range of cells more than once. On the Home tab, in the Clipboard group, click **Copy** and click **Paste** as many times as necessary in several cells.
- You can also cut or copy more than one cell range and retain up to 24 cell ranges on the Clipboard at one time. You can then paste any or all of these cell ranges from the Clipboard in any sequence you want.

To copy an item, select it and then use one of the following methods:
- on the Home tab, in the Clipboard group, click **Copy**, or
- press CTRL+C, or
- right-click the item, and then click **Copy**.

To cut or move an item, select it and then use one of the following methods:
- on the Home tab, in the Clipboard group, click **Cut**, or
- press CTRL+X, or
- right-click the item, and then click **Cut**.

To paste an item, move to the cell where you want to paste it, and then use one of the following methods:
- on the Home tab, in the Clipboard group, click **Paste**, or
- press CTRL+V, or
- right-click the destination cell, and then click **Paste**.

More data can be added at any time simply by entering the data into the blank rows below, or into blank columns to the right of the existing data. In many cases, you should not leave any blank rows or columns in your data if all of the data is related to each other. In some cases, you can use blank rows and columns to improve the readability of your data.

# Learn to copy and paste data

This exercise demonstrates how to copy and move the contents of cells from one part of a worksheet to another. It also demonstrates the use of text labels as row and column titles.

1   Open the *Office Expenses* workbook and save it to the student data files folder as: Office Expenses - Student.

Suppose that another expense item needs to be added to the spreadsheet. To do this, you can simply enter the data into the blank cells immediately below the existing data.

2   Enter the following new data:

| Cell | Should Be |
| --- | --- |
| A12 | Utilities |
| B12 | 325 |

More data can also be added across columns.

3   Enter the following new data:

| Cell | Should Be |
| --- | --- |
| C4 | February |
| D4 | March |

Suppose some expenses stay the same every month. These values can be copied to other cells.

4   Click cell **B5** and drag the mouse down to select cell **B8**.

**5** On the Home tab, in the Clipboard group, click **Copy**.

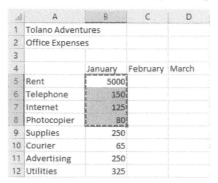

Notice that the marquee appears around cells B5 down to B8 to indicate that you have copied their contents onto the Clipboard.

**6** Select cell **C5** and, in the Clipboard group, click **Paste**.

Notice how Excel has copied the data from all marked cells into the correct place, even though you only chose one cell. Excel will automatically replace the contents of the existing cell(s) with the copied entries.

You can also press ENTER to paste the entries into this location. However, this technique will only allow you to paste the entry once, and then will automatically turn off the marquee.

**7** Select cell **D5** and press ENTER.

**Hint:** Alternatively, you can continue using the Paste button to paste these values into as many destination cells as you want, as long as the marquee appears around the cells being copied.

**8** Select cells **B9** to **B12** and click **Copy**.

**9** Select cells **C9** to **D12** and click **Paste**.

**10** Select cell **E9** and click **Paste**.

**11** Select cell **F9** and click **Paste**.

**12** Select cell **G9** and click **Paste**.

**13** Click **Undo** in the Quick Access Toolbar, then click it three more times.

Next, see how the Office Clipboard works.

**14** Enter the following new data:

| Cell | Should Be | Cell | Should Be |
|------|-----------|------|-----------|
| C9   | 95        | D9   | 175       |
| C10  | 150       | D10  | 160       |
| C11  | 325       | D11  | 300       |
| C12  | 350       | D12  | 300       |

**15** Save and close the workbook.

# Using Paste Special

### Objective 2.1.3

The standard Paste command will paste the cells you have selected with Cut or Copy into the target cell(s), including data, formulas, formatting, and any comments. In some cases, you may not want to paste all of this together at the same time.

The Paste Special menu gives you the full range of all options available for pasting the selected cell contents to a target cell range. This menu enables you to selectively choose to paste only the data values, formulas, formatting, comments, or a combination of these.

To activate the Paste Special command, on the Home tab, in the Clipboard group, click the arrow for Paste, then click **Paste Special**.

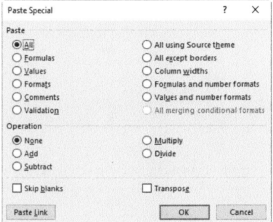

**Paste** – Specifies what components of the data in the Clipboard are pasted to the target cells. For example, if Formulas is specified, then only the formulas are selected and other components such as cell formatting will not be pasted. If Values is selected, then only the data (if a cell contains a formula, then the formula result is used) is pasted and other components such as cell formatting will not.

**Operation** – Specifies how any data in the target cells will be treated. For example, if Multiply is selected, then any existing data will be multiplied by the data pasted into the target cells.

**Skip blanks** – If selected, this will avoid overwriting any existing data in the target cells if there is no data from the clipboard to be put into that cell.

**Transpose** – If selected, this will rotate the data. Therefore, the data in the clipboard listed down a column will now be listed across a row in the target cells. Similarly, data listed across cells in a row will be listed down cells in a column.

# Learn to use Paste Special

This exercise demonstrates how to use the Paste Special feature using a specialized workbook that highlights its capabilities.

**1** Open the *Paste Special* workbook and save it to the student data files folder as: Paste Special - Student.

Columns A and C contain data values in the cells. Column B contains formulas that reference cells in column A. Formulas will be discussed in more detail in a later lesson in this courseware.

First, try pasting just values from columns A and B to a set of target cells.

**2** Select cells **A2:B6**, and on the Home tab, in the Clipboard group, click **Copy**.

**3** Select cell **G3**. On the Home tab, in the Clipboard group, click the arrow for **Paste**.

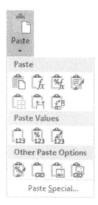

**4**  Click **Paste Special** at the bottom of the drop-down menu.

**5**  In the Paste Special dialog box, click **Values** and click **OK**.

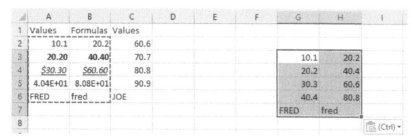

**Hint:** Alternatively, you can also select the left-most icon in the Paste Values section of the drop-down menu. This is a faster method of accessing the feature instead of using the Paste Special dialog box.

Now compare the contents of each of these two sets of cells—all of the data in the selected source cells were pasted into the target cells.

**6**  Select cell **B2**, look at the Formula bar, then select cell **H3** and look at the Formula bar again.

**7**  Repeat step 6 for each corresponding set of cells below **B2** and **H3**.

Because you had selected Values, the formulas in column B were evaluated, and the calculated results were pasted into the target cells.

Note also that none of the cell formatting was pasted into the target cells.

**8**  Select cells **B2:B6**, and on the Home tab, in the Clipboard group, click **Copy**.

**9**  Select cell **H3**. On the Home tab, in the Clipboard group, click the arrow for **Paste**, and point to the left-most icon in the Other Paste Options section of the drop-down menu.

Notice that the cells in **H3:H7** are displayed using the formats that are about to be pasted, even though you have not actually clicked the paste icon yet. This is a demonstration of the Live Preview capability of Excel – you can preview the effects of a formatting change as it will appear on the worksheet. If you then move your mouse cursor away without clicking, the formatting reverts back. The Live Preview capability is available for most of the formatting options on the Ribbon. It is not available from any of the formatting dialog boxes.

**10**  Click the left-most icon in the Other Paste Options section of the drop-down menu to make the change permanent.

Now see what happens when you paste just the formulas to the target cells.

**11** With cells **B2:B6** still selected, select cell **D2**.

**12** On the Home tab, in the Clipboard group, click the arrow for **Paste** to display the Paste menu.

**13** Point to different icons (but do not click on any of them) in the **Paste** drop-down menu to see how the worksheet is affected.

**14** Click the **Formulas** icon (top row, second from the left in the Paste section) in the drop-down menu.

| | A | B | C | D | E | F | G | H | I |
|---|---|---|---|---|---|---|---|---|---|
| 1 | Values | Formulas | Values | | | | | | |
| 2 | 10.1 | 20.2 | 60.6 | 121.2 | | | | | |
| 3 | 20.20 | 40.40 | 70.7 | 141.4 | | | 10.1 | 20.2 | |
| 4 | $30.30 | $60.60 | 80.8 | 161.6 | | | 20.2 | 40.40 | |
| 5 | 4.04E+01 | 8.08E+01 | 90.9 | 181.8 | | | 30.3 | $60.60 | |
| 6 | FRED | fred | JOE | joe | | | 40.4 | 8.08E+01 | |
| 7 | | | | | (Ctrl) ▾ | | FRED | fred | |
| 8 | | | | | | | | | |

The formulas in column B are now copied into column D, referencing the values in column C. This is an example of relative addressing, which is explained in more detail in a later lesson in this courseware. Notice that this option did not copy the formatting from column B.

**Hint:** Alternatively, you can also select the Formulas option from the Paste Special dialog box.

Now try the Transpose option.

**15** Select cells **A2:B6**, and on the Home tab, in the Clipboard group, click **Copy**.

**16** Select cell **B9**. On the Home tab, in the Clipboard group, click the arrow for **Paste**, and click the last icon (second row, far right) in the Paste section of the drop-down menu.

**Hint:** Alternatively, you can also select Transpose from the Paste Special dialog box.

| | A | B | C | D | E | F | G | H | I |
|---|---|---|---|---|---|---|---|---|---|
| 1 | Values | Formulas | Values | | | | | | |
| 2 | 10.1 | 20.2 | 60.6 | 121.2 | | | | | |
| 3 | 20.20 | 40.40 | 70.7 | 141.4 | | | 10.1 | 20.2 | |
| 4 | $30.30 | $60.60 | 80.8 | 161.6 | | | 20.2 | 40.40 | |
| 5 | 4.04E+01 | 8.08E+01 | 90.9 | 181.8 | | | 30.3 | $60.60 | |
| 6 | FRED | fred | JOE | joe | | | 40.4 | 8.08E+01 | |
| 7 | | | | | | | FRED | fred | |
| 8 | | | | | | | | | |
| 9 | | 10.1 | 20.20 | $30.30 | 4.04E+01 | FRED | | | |
| 10 | | 20.2 | 40.40 | $60.60 | 8.08E+01 | fred | | | |
| 11 | | | | | | (Ctrl) ▾ | | | |

**17** Save and close the workbook.

# Copying and Moving Cells Using the Mouse

**Objective 2.1.2**

Instead of cutting and pasting cell contents, you can simply move the cell(s) directly to the new location using the drag-and-drop method. This method requires the use of the mouse. As with the cut and paste method, the target cell(s) will lose all existing data and formatting.

You can also use the drag-and-drop method to copy a cell or range of the cells by pressing CTRL at the same time. Using the drag-and-drop method does not involve either the Windows or Office Clipboards.

# Learn to copy and move data with the mouse

This exercise demonstrates how to copy and move the contents of cells from one part of a worksheet to another.

1   Open the *Office Expenses - Student* workbook.

2   Select cell **A12**.

3   Position the cursor over any of the four edges of cell **A12**.

    The cursor should change to a white pointer with a four-headed arrow at its tip (✥).

4   Click and hold down the left mouse button and drag the cell down to cell **C13**. Release the left mouse button.

    Notice that, as you drag the data around the worksheet, the cell address of the selected cell is updated and displayed next to the selected cell.

Next, move the contents of this cell to another cell that contains data.

5   Repeat steps 3 and 4 to drag cell **C13** to **A6**.

    A message box appears. If you accidentally selected the wrong cell, you can cancel this operation. Otherwise, you can proceed with the move.

6   In the message box, click **OK**.

Next, try moving a group of cells to another location.

7   Select cells **C4** to **D12**.

8   Click and drag these cells down so that the upper left corner of the range of cells is in **D9**. Release the left mouse button.

Now use the drag-and-drop method for copying cells.

9   With the cell range **D9** to **E17** still selected, move the cursor to one of the four edges.

10  Press and hold down CTRL, then click and hold down the left mouse button.

11  Drag the selected range to cells **B7** to **C15**.

    Notice the + symbol next to the arrow while you are holding down CTRL. You can actually press or release CTRL at any time while you are dragging the mouse. This enables you to change your mind between moving and copying, and back again.

12  Release the mouse button and CTRL.

| | A | B | C | D | E |
|---|---|---|---|---|---|
| 1 | Tolano Adventures | | | | |
| 2 | Office Expenses | | | | |
| 3 | | | | | |
| 4 | | January | | | |
| 5 | Rent | 5000 | | | |
| 6 | Utilities | 150 | | | |
| 7 | Internet | February | March | | |
| 8 | Photocopier | 5000 | 5000 | | |
| 9 | Supplies | 150 | 150 | February | March |
| 10 | Courier | 125 | 125 | 5000 | 5000 |
| 11 | Advertising | 80 | 80 | 150 | 150 |
| 12 | | 95 | 175 | 125 | 125 |
| 13 | | 150 | 160 | 80 | 80 |
| 14 | | 325 | 300 | 95 | 175 |
| 15 | | 350 | 300 | 150 | 160 |
| 16 | | | | 325 | 300 |
| 17 | | | | 350 | 300 |

**13** Close the workbook without saving the changes.

# Inserting and Deleting Rows and Columns
## Inserting Rows and Columns

**Objective 1.3.5**

Excel can insert new rows and columns, even between rows or columns containing data. This feature enables you to add information to a previously created spreadsheet, or to separate parts of your spreadsheet with blank rows or columns.

Worksheet columns start at A and end at column XFD (16,384 columns). For every new column inserted between A and XFD, one column is pushed off the far right side of the worksheet and deleted. Similarly, new rows inserted between rows 1 and 1,048,576 will result in the same number of rows being pushed off the bottom of the worksheet and deleted.

New rows or columns are added at the current cell position. That is, rows are always inserted directly above and columns are inserted to the left of the cell that you select before issuing the insert command. If you want to insert a row below the current active cell, simply move down one row to the next row and then use the Insert command. Similarly, to insert a column to the right of the active cell, shift to the right by one column before using the Insert command.

You can insert one or more rows or columns at the same time by selecting that number of rows or columns before using the Insert command. The rows or columns do not have to be next to each other.

To insert a row or column, use one of the following methods:

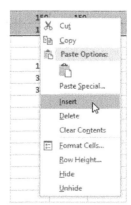

- on the Home tab, in the Cells group, click the arrow for Insert, and click **Insert Sheet Rows** or **Insert Sheet Columns**, or

- select the row heading or column heading where the new row or column is to be inserted, and then press CTRL+ + (Plus) on the numeric keypad or the keyboard, or

- select the row heading or column heading where the new row or column is to be inserted, and then on the Home tab, in the Cells group, click **Insert**, or

- right-click a row or column heading and click **Insert**, or

- right-click a cell in the row or column where the new row or column is to be inserted, click **Insert**, select **Entire row** or **Entire column** and click **OK**.

Be careful when using these commands, as they affect the entire worksheet and therefore may affect areas of the worksheet that are not visible on the screen.

# Deleting Rows and Columns

Just as Excel enables you to insert new rows and column, you can also delete unnecessary rows and columns.

Before deleting entire rows or columns, take some time to verify that these rows or columns do not contain any valuable data elsewhere in the worksheet that is not visible on the screen.

To delete a row or column, use one of the following methods:

- on the Home tab, in the Cells group, click the arrow for Delete, and then click **Delete Sheet Rows** or **Delete Sheet Columns**, or

- select the row heading or column heading for the row or column to be deleted, and then press CTRL+− (Minus) on the numeric keypad or on the keyboard, or

- select the row heading or column heading for the row or column to be deleted, and then on the Home tab, in the Cells group, click **Delete**, or

- right-click a cell in the row or column to be deleted, click **Delete** and then click **Entire row** or **Entire column**, or

- right-click a row or column heading and click **Delete**.

You can delete more than one row or column at a time. The selected rows or columns do not have to be next to each other.

# Inserting and Deleting Cells

### Objective 2.1.5

You may also choose to insert or delete one or several cells. When you insert new cells, Excel shifts the existing cells to the right or down to make space for the new cell(s). When you delete existing cells, Excel shifts the remaining cells over from the right or below to take the place of the deleted cell(s). When you delete cells, any formulas that reference the cell(s) will display an error (the topic of formulas is discussed in more detail later in this courseware).

Alternatively, you may delete the contents of one or more cells by simply pressing DELETE. Unlike deleting the cell itself, using DELETE will leave the structure of the worksheet intact, and formulas that reference the cell will assume the cell value is zero.

# Learn to add and delete rows, columns and cells

This exercise demonstrates how to add and delete rows, columns and cells in a workbook.

**1** Open the *Office Expenses - Student* workbook.

**2** Select any cell in row **5**.

**3** On the Home tab, in the Cells group, click the arrow for Insert and click **Insert Sheet Rows**.

Note that if you had clicked the Insert button instead of the arrow below it, all the data below the active cell in the same column would have shifted down by one row, and the data in the surrounding columns would not have moved. When you click Insert, Excel interprets that you mean to insert cells only and not entire rows.

Now insert two rows in the middle of the data.

**4** Click the gray row headers for rows **7** and **8**.

Notice the ➡ row heading symbol that appears to show you that the entire row will be selected.

**5** On the Home tab, in the Cells group, click **Insert**.

Because you selected entire rows (two of them in this case), Excel inserts rows rather than cells.

The combination of steps 4 and 5 is a popular method of adding a new row to a worksheet. Another method, at step 5, is to right-click anywhere in the selected area, then click Insert. This method is popular because the shortcut menu only shows the most relevant commands for the selected cell(s) at the time of the right-click.

Now insert one column on the left side of the data.

**6** Click the heading for column **B**.

Notice the column heading symbol that appears ⬇ shows you that the entire column will be selected.

**7** On the Home tab, in the Cells group, click **Insert**.

**Hint:** Alternatively, on the Home tab, in the Cells group, click the arrow for Insert and click Insert Sheet Columns.

**8** Enter the following values:

| Cell | Value |
|------|-------|
| A7 | Janitorial |
| A8 | Vehicle |
| C7 | 100 |
| C8 | 475 |

**9** Type or copy the values in cells **C7** to **C8** across to cell **D7** to **E8**.

Now delete a row of data.

**10** Click the row selector button for row **8** to select the entire row.

**11** Right-click anywhere in row **8**, then click **Delete**.

Notice that when an entire row is selected, Excel will remove the entire row without waiting for further commands. You can do the same thing for an entire column.

12  Select any cell in column **B**.

13  On the Home tab, in the Cells group, click the arrow for Delete and click **Delete Sheet Columns**.

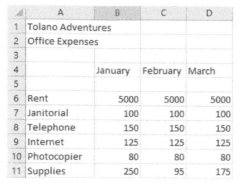

Now delete the contents of one cell.

14  Select cell **C8**.

15  Press DELETE.

Note that this key removes the contents of the cell, but not the cell formatting (this will be demonstrated in a different lesson in this courseware). The structure of the worksheet is also unaffected. Now try to delete the entire cell.

16  On the Quick Access Toolbar, click **Undo** to reverse the deletion.

17  On the Home tab, in the Cells group, click **Delete**.

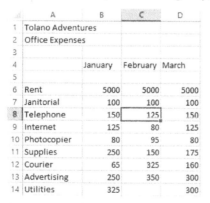

Because you have selected only one cell, Excel removes only that cell and all data in the column below shifts up. If you want to see all delete cell options, open the Delete cells dialog box.

18  Click **Undo** to reverse the deletion.

19  With cell **C8** still selected, on the Home tab, in the Cells group, click the arrow for Delete and click **Delete Cells**.

20  With the Shift cells up option selected, click **OK**.

Let's see what happens when you delete a range of cells.

21  Click **Undo** to reverse the deletion.

22  Select cells **C7** to **C8**, and on the Home tab, in the Cells group, click **Delete**.

In this situation, Excel assumed you wanted to shift the cells to the left, instead of up.

**23** Click **Undo** to reverse the deletion.

**24** Save and close the workbook.

# Adjusting the Columns and Rows

As you work with data in Excel, you may want to improve the readability of your worksheets by adjusting the column width and row height so that you can see more or fewer characters in that column or row.

## Changing the Column Widths

**Objective 1.3.7**

The standard column width in a new worksheet may not be enough to accommodate some of the entries you make in the cells. If the adjacent cells to the right are empty, Excel will display your entire text label by overflowing into those cells. If those adjoining cells have entries, the text labels will appear truncated at the cell boundary.

You can select between zero and 255 for the width of your column. When you change a column width, the stored contents of the cells do not change. Only the number of the characters displayed changes.

Numbers represent a special problem when there is insufficient space to display the whole number. Excel cannot simply truncate numbers as it does with text labels. If it did, the number would be misleading. For example, you would not want 1,000,000 to be displayed as 1,000 if there is not enough space to display the whole number. Excel uses several different rules to determine how to display a numeric value in a cell:

- If you enter a numeric value that is slightly larger than the current column width, Excel will automatically widen the column width to show the number with the current cell format.

- If you enter a numeric value that is much larger than the current column width, Excel automatically changes the cell format to scientific notation.

- If you reduce the width of a column that already contains numeric data, Excel may be unable to display the number. In this case, a series of pound signs (######) will be displayed in the affected cell(s). Excel will redisplay the number when you increase the column width to accommodate the number in its current format.

A quick way of checking the width of the column is to click the vertical bar between the column headers. Excel displays the width in a screen tip located above and to the right of the mouse pointer.

To change the width for a column manually, use one of the following methods:

- on the Home tab, in the Cells group, click **Format** and click **Column Width**, or

- place the mouse cursor on the vertical line on the right of the column heading for the column to be adjusted. When the cursor changes to the ↔ symbol, click and drag to the appropriate width, or

- right-click the column heading for the column to be adjusted, and then click **Column Width**.

# Adjusting the Row Height

**Objective 1.3.7**

Similar to column widths, the height of a row can be changed. This capability is not used as frequently as adjusting the width of columns, but there will be occasions when you need to override the default row height setting used by Excel when you re-format the data in cells.

To adjust the height for a row, use one of the following methods:

- on the Home tab, in the Cells group, click **Format** and click **Row Height**, or

- place the mouse cursor at the bottom of the row heading to be adjusted. The cursor will change to a ⤯ symbol and you can then drag to the desired new height, or

- right-click the row heading for the row to be adjusted, and then click **Row Height**.

# Using AutoFit

AutoFit is a time-saving feature of Excel that will automatically adjust column width for you.

To fit the contents to the column's width automatically, use one of the following methods:

- on the Home tab, in the Cells group, click **Format** and click **AutoFit Column Width**, or

- use the mouse to double-click the vertical line on the right of the heading for the column you want to adjust. The cursor will change to a ⟷ (double-headed arrow).

These two methods can produce different results. When you use the AutoFit feature from the Ribbon, Excel will change (either widen or reduce) the column width to fully display the contents of the selected cell(s). When you use the mouse method, Excel will automatically adjust the width so that it is just wide enough for the widest value in the entire column.

You can also select multiple columns and use either of these two methods. The result will be same as if you apply AutoFit to each of the columns.

Similarly, you can set row height to fit the height of the cell contents using one of the following methods:

- on the Home tab, in the Cells group, click **Format** and click **AutoFit Row Height**, or

- use the mouse to double-click at the bottom of the row heading to be adjusted.

# Learn to modify column widths

This exercise demonstrates how to modify column widths, and how cell contents are displayed.

1   Open the *Price Quote 0730* workbook and save it to the student data files folder as: Price Quote 0730 - Student.

2   Select any cell in column **A**.

3   On the Home tab, in the Cells group, click **Format** and click **Column Width**.

4   In the Column Width box, type: 14 and press ENTER.

**5**   Repeat steps 2 to 4 for column **C** with a width of 6.

Now try using the AutoFit option for column B. You will choose cell B13 because it is wider than the current column width, but will not make the entire column too wide for many of the cells.

**6**   Select cell **B13**.

**7**   On the Home tab, in the Cells group, click **Format** and click **AutoFit Column Width**.

You can also use the mouse to AutoFit a column. It is a faster method than using the menu because it chooses the widest cell in the selected column.

**8**   Move the mouse pointer to the right edge of the column **A** header. The mouse pointer will change to a double-headed pointer.

**9**   Double-click that position.

Column A is now too wide to be visually appealing. Use the mouse to adjust the width.

**10**   Move the mouse pointer to point to the right edge of the column **A** header. The mouse pointer will change to a double-headed pointer.

**11**   Click and drag to the left to reduce the width.

Notice that a screen tip appears as you drag the column width, giving you the current column width as a visual reference.

**12**   Release the mouse button when the column width is just right for displaying the full contents of cell **A9** (Airport Fees).

| | A | B | C | D | E | |
|---|---|---|---|---|---|---|
| 1 | Tolano Adventures | | | | | |
| 2 | Price Quote | | | | | |
| 3 | As of: | 03-Jul | | Expires: | 18-Jul-16 | |
| 4 | | | | | | |
| 5 | Airfare | 450 | | | | |
| 6 | Hotel | 1,050 | | | | |
| 7 | Car Rental | 225 | | | | |
| 8 | Taxes | 46.5 | | 3.10% | | |
| 9 | Airport Fees | 9.9 | | 2.20% | | |
| 10 | | | | | | |
| 11 | | | | | | |
| 12 | Airline: | Great West Airline | | | | |
| 13 | Hotel: | Hotel Zathura | | | | |

Use the mouse to adjust the height of some of the rows.

**13**   Move the mouse pointer to the bottom edge of the row **1** header.

The mouse pointer will change to a double-headed pointer.

**14**   Click and drag the row **1** header down until it is twice the current height—about **30.00 (40 pixels)**.

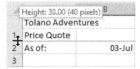

**15**   Click and drag the row **4** header up to a height of about **9.00 (12 pixels)**.

**16**   Save and close the worksheet.

---

## Hiding/Unhiding Rows & Columns

**Objective 1.4.2**

On occasion, you may need to hide one or more rows or columns in your worksheet. You may want to do this for different reasons. For example:

- You may be printing a worksheet with more columns or rows than the page width allows. If you print all of the data, you will have to either break it up across multiple pages or reduce the scale – and, therefore, reduce the readability – of the data.

- The columns or rows may contain formulas used for intermediate calculations only. In some cases, you may be developing complex calculations that you cannot perform in one formula, or you may want to view how Excel is calculating the data across multiple cells containing simpler formulas.

- You may want to prevent other users from viewing these hidden rows or columns, or the formulas used in these hidden cells. Note that you will have to prevent users from unhiding the data by activating the workbook protection feature.

You can easily identify hidden rows or columns by the gaps in the row or column headers. Also, the row and column header divisions for hidden rows and columns will appear as double lines. They remain hidden until you unhide them again. Excel will continue to correctly calculate any formulas in hidden cells, or formulas in visible cells that reference hidden cells.

Hidden rows and columns will not appear, even if you print the worksheet, until you unhide them again.

To hide a row or column, select the row or column headings first, and then use one of the following methods:
- on the Home tab, in the Cells group, click **Format**, click **Hide & Unhide**, and then **Hide Columns** or **Hide Rows**, or
- right-click the selected rows or columns and then click **Hide**, or
- drag the right edge of the column to the left or the bottom edge of the row upwards until it is hidden.

To unhide a row or column, select the appropriate headings on both sides of the hidden row(s) or column(s), and then use one of the following methods:
- on the Home tab, in the Cells group, click **Format**, click **Hide & Unhide**, and then **Unhide Columns** or **Unhide Rows**, or
- right-click the double line header division that indicates hidden rows or columns and then click **Unhide**, or
- drag the right edge of the hidden column to the right or the bottom edge of the hidden row downwards until the desired width or height is attained.

# Learn to use hide and unhide

This exercise demonstrates how to hide and unhide rows and columns.

1   Open the *Political Contributions* workbook.

   Notice that there appears to be a gap between columns B and D, and between rows 15 and 17.

2   Select columns **B** to **D**.

**Hint:** Alternatively, you can select any range of cells that include both columns B and D to indicate that you are selecting the hidden column between these two columns.

3   On the Home tab, in the Cells group, click **Format**, click **Hide & Unhide** and then click **Unhide Columns**.

A column header now appears with an intriguing description.

4   Right-click the double line header division between rows **15** and **17** (as shown here) and then click **Unhide**.

The worksheet should now look similar to the following:

| | A | B | C |
|---|---|---|---|
| 1 | Political Contributions Declaration | | |
| 2 | For John Goodheart | | |
| 3 | | | |
| 4 | Contributor | Amount | Add'l Amt |
| 5 | J. Abrams | 450 | |
| 6 | P. Bodwick | 100 | |
| 7 | B. Cherry | 300 | |
| 8 | K. Gurmit | 500 | |
| 9 | M. Jenns | 250 | |
| 10 | T. Koehns | 100 | |
| 11 | A. Moham | 95 | |
| 12 | G. Muir | 250 | |
| 13 | M. Nohrs | 175 | |
| 14 | F. Peans | 375 | |
| 15 | G. Singh | 150 | |
| 16 | S. Smith | 500 | 350,000 |
| 17 | T. Wong | 325 | |
| 18 | Total | 3,570 | |

Now hide the row and column again to cover your tracks.

5   Select column **C**.

6   On the Home tab, in the Cells group, click **Format**, click **Hide & Unhide** and then click **Hide Columns**.

Use the mouse to hide a row.

7   Move the mouse pointer to the bottom edge of the row **16** header.

The mouse pointer will change to a double-headed pointer.

8   Click and drag the row **16** header upwards until the height is 0.00 (touching the bottom edge of row 15).

9   Close the workbook without saving.

# Using AutoFill and Flash Fill

**Objective 2.1.4**

Entering a lot of data into a worksheet can be a tiring exercise, which could lead to errors being entered. Fortunately, Excel has two features that may help reduce some of the workload, simply by using patterns in the data that has already been entered into the worksheet.

The AutoFill feature is very useful when you have entered numbers or dates into the first one or two cells of your data series, and you are now facing entering the rest of data into the remaining cells using the same sequential pattern. Instead of continuing to manually enter the rest of the data, AutoFill will insert the data for you. You simply select the cells you want to use as your data pattern and then drag the AutoFill handle (the small black square at the bottom right corner of the cell pointer) across the target cells. When you release the mouse, the cells will be filled with the new data. For example, if your source cells contain the values 1 and 2, then the AutoFill feature will continue with the next logical values of 3, 4, followed by the remaining numbers for the rest of the target cells.

The AutoFill feature will do its best to continue the pattern that it sees in the source cells to fill the target cells, such as adding 1 or some other number to calculate the next value.

Text data generally (except for special cases such as names of months or days of the week) are not used in sequential patterns. For this type of data, AutoFill will only copy the same values into the target cells. For example, if the source cells contain the values John and Joe, then the AutoFill feature will copy John and Joe to the remaining cells.

AutoFill is not only used to fill or copy cells with numeric, date, and text data, it is actually most often used to copy formulas into adjacent cells. This will be demonstrated in the next lesson of this courseware.

The Flash Fill feature is another labor-saving feature that will extract, combine, and/or re-sequence cell contents from one or more cells to create new values.

In order to use this feature, you must use the column to the immediate right of the column(s) that you want Flash Fill to obtain its data from. The target cells must also be empty with no data.

# Learn to use AutoFill

This exercise demonstrates how the AutoFill and Flash Fill features work.

1  Open the *Customer List AutoFill* workbook and save it to the student data files folder as: Customer List AutoFill - Student.

Your first task is to combine all of the first, middle, and last names in columns A to C together as one name in column D. Start by entering the first name.

2  Select cell **D2** and enter: Jayel Sasha Wylie.

But when you start entering the second name, Excel will recognize the pattern from the first row and apply it to the remaining rows.

3  Select cell **D3**, type: B but do not press any more keys.

The Flash Fill feature then completes the rest of the customer's name in not only this cell, but also every cell below, saving you a lot of work. At this point, the flash fill data is only tentative: it is displayed in a light gray color to show what they will look like, and you have to confirm your acceptance.

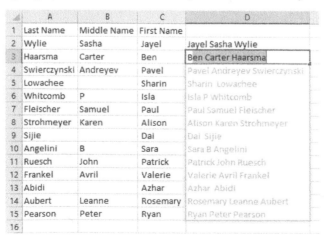

**4**  Press ENTER to let the Flash Fill feature complete the data entry for you. If the flash fill data did not display for you or the names do not appear correctly, press the ESCAPE key twice to abandon the Flash Fill, then go back to step 2 above to check the name was entered into cell D2 correctly. Once you have done that, continue with the next step because the Flash Fill feature will not launch automatically at this point.

You can also manually invoke the Flash Fill feature.

**5**  Select cells **D3** to **D15**, and press the DELETE key to delete all of these entries.

**6**  Select cells **D2** to **D15**, then on the Data tab, in the Data Tools group, click **Flash Fill**.

You can also use the Flash Fill feature to pick out a specific word from a text string such as a name. For example, extract out just the first name from column D.

**7**  Select cell **E2**, and enter: Jayel.

**8**  Select cell **E3**, type: B and press ENTER to accept the Flash Fill data.

Now pick out the middle name from column D, if there is any.

**9**  Select cell **F2**, and enter: Sasha.

**10**  Select cell **F3**, type: C and press ENTER to accept the Flash Fill data.

And finally extract the family name from column D.

**11**  Select cell **G2**, and enter: Wylie.

**12**  Select cell **G3**, type: H and press ENTER to accept the Flash Fill data.

You can also change the pattern of the middle name to just the first letter.

**13**  Select cells **F2** to **F15**, and press the DELETE key.

**14**  Select cell **F2**, and enter: S. (uppercase letter "S" followed by the period at the end).

**15**  Select cell **F3**, type: C and press ENTER to accept the Flash Fill data.

This same technique can be applied in reverse to combine the contents of multiple cells together.

**16**  Select cells **D2** to **D15**, and press the DELETE key.

**17**  Select cell **D2**, and enter: J. S. Wylie.

**18**  Select cell **D3**, type: B and press ENTER to accept the Flash Fill data.

| | A | B | C | D | E | F | G | H | I |
|---|---|---|---|---|---|---|---|---|---|
| 1 | Last Name | Middle Name | First Name | | | | | | Phone |
| 2 | Wylie | Sasha | Jayel | J. S. Wylie | Jayel | S. | Wylie | | 2064858314 |
| 3 | Haarsma | Carter | Ben | B. C. Haarsma | Ben | C. | Haarsma | | 2533574805 |
| 4 | Swierczynski | Andreyev | Pavel | P. A. Swierczynski | Pavel | A. | Swierczynski | | 2067881452 |
| 5 | Lowachee | | Sharin | S. Lowachee | Sharin | | Lowachee | | 3605647884 |
| 6 | Whitcomb | P | Isla | I. P. Whitcomb | Isla | P. | Whitcomb | | 2064257753 |
| 7 | Fleischer | Samuel | Paul | P. S. Fleischer | Paul | S. | Fleischer | | 2533770435 |
| 8 | Strohmeyer | Karen | Alison | A. K. Strohmeyer | Alison | K. | Strohmeyer | | 2069367601 |
| 9 | Sijie | | Dai | D. Sijie | Dai | | Sijie | | 2539623056 |
| 10 | Angelini | R | Sara | S. R. Angelini | Sara | R | Angelini | | 2537463077 |

Numeric values can also be re-patterned as text strings, such as phone numbers.

**19**  Select cell **J2** and enter: (206) 485-8314.

**20** Select cell **J3**, type: ( and press ENTER to accept the Flash Fill data.

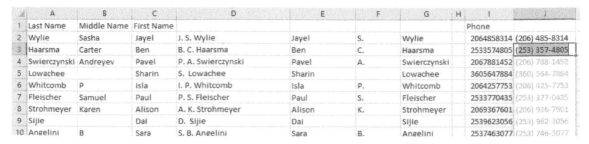

Now let's look at how the AutoFill feature works. As a first example, you will create a sequential series of numbers. You can start with any number, so for this exercise you will use 21. To establish the pattern, you will also need to enter the next sequential number next to it, which will be 22.

**21** Scroll the worksheet to the right so that columns L to Q are fully visible on your screen.

**22** Select cell **L2** and enter: 21 then select cell **L3** and enter: 22.

**23** Select cells **L2** to **L3** again and position the mouse pointer on the AutoFill handle at the bottom right corner of cell **L3**.

The mouse cursor will change to a + icon. You can now create the rest of the series.

**24** Select and drag the mouse down to cell **L9**. As you drag the AutoFill handle down, you will see the current AutoFill value as a screen tip.

You can also set the series to increment by any value other than 1, such as 5.

**25** Select cell **L3** and enter: 26.

**26** Select cells **L2** to **L3** again and drag the AutoFill handle down to cell **L9**.

AutoFill is normally used on numbers and dates, which are naturally used in series with incrementing values. Words are not usually grouped in series, except for month names and days of the week.

**27** Enter the following new data:

| Cell | Should Be |
| --- | --- |
| M2 | July |
| N2 | Sep |
| O2 | Tuesday |

You can also use AutoFill to create a series using multiple rows or columns at the same time.

**28** Select the cell range **M2** to **O2**, and drag the AutoFill handle down to cell **O9**.

You can see here that the series "loops back" to the first value in a series when it reaches the last value. In this case, it entered January after December, and Monday after Sunday.

When AutoFill does not recognize a word that belongs in a series, then it will simply copy the cell contents into the target cells. For example, the words "one" and "two" are not recognized as being the same as the numbers 1 and 2.

**29** Select cell **P2** and enter: One then select cell **P3** and enter: Two.

**30** Select the cell range **P2** to **P3**, and drag the AutoFill handle down to cell **P9**.

You can also use AutoFill to copy a formula to adjacent cells. This formula will calculate a new value by multiplying the value from the cell above it by two. You will learn more about formulas in the next lesson of this courseware.

**31** Select cell **Q2** and enter: 3.

**32** Select cell **Q3** and enter: =Q2*2, then select cell **Q3** again, and drag the AutoFill handle down to cell **Q9**.

| | L | M | N | O | P | Q |
|---|---|---|---|---|---|---|
| 1 | | | | | | |
| 2 | 21 | July | Sep | Tuesday | One | 3 |
| 3 | 26 | August | Oct | Wednesday | Two | 6 |
| 4 | 31 | September | Nov | Thursday | One | 12 |
| 5 | 36 | October | Dec | Friday | Two | 24 |
| 6 | 41 | November | Jan | Saturday | One | 48 |
| 7 | 46 | December | Feb | Sunday | Two | 96 |
| 8 | 51 | January | Mar | Monday | One | 192 |
| 9 | 56 | February | Apr | Tuesday | Two | 384 |

**33** Save and close the workbook.

# Managing Worksheets

By default, new workbooks are created with one worksheet, which is sufficient for most purposes. However, every Excel workbook is capable of having multiple worksheets. Each of these worksheets can be treated as being independent of one another although typically, they are related to one another. For example, one worksheet may contain the list of expenses for a company, another worksheet may contain the revenues for each product sold, and a third worksheet may have the summary of both the revenues and expenses. Formulas can be used to refer to any cell, in any worksheet, to bring data together into one worksheet and to perform calculations.

You can rename worksheets, as well as add, delete, copy, or move them around in a workbook. You shift the display from one worksheet to another by using worksheet tabs. By default, the first worksheet is named *Sheet1*, and every new worksheet added is given the next number. For example, *Sheet2*, *Sheet3*, and higher numbers.

To navigate between the worksheets, use the tab scrolling buttons at the bottom left of each workbook's window. If your workbook has many worksheets (for example, more than six) or the worksheet names are very long, your screen may not display all of the worksheet tabs at the same time and some may become hidden behind the horizontal scroll bar. Use these buttons to shift the hidden worksheet tabs to the left or right. Alternatively, you can view more worksheet tabs by shrinking the horizontal scroll bar.

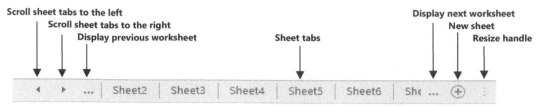

## Renaming Worksheets

**Objective 1.3.2**

Excel's use of *Sheet1, Sheet2, Sheet3,* and similar names is useful to identify the different sheets when you first access your workbook. However, it is not very descriptive after you have entered information on several worksheets. Assigning more descriptive names to the tabs will make navigating your worksheets much easier, particularly when you have used several sheets to enter the information.

As you rename your worksheets, Excel will adjust the size of the tabs based on the number of characters in the name. Even though Excel permits up to 31 characters per tab, it is best to keep the tab names short. If you have several worksheets with long sheet tab names, you will not be able to see very many of the worksheet tabs on the screen at one time.  This will make navigating between them more difficult.

To rename a worksheet tab, use one of the following methods:

- double-click the sheet tab to put it in editing mode for renaming, or
- right-click the sheet tab and click **Rename**, or
- click the sheet tab, then on the Home tab, in the Cells group, click **Format**, click **Rename Sheet**.

# Learn to rename worksheet tabs

This exercise involves changing sheet tab names in a workbook.

1   Open the *Department Budget* workbook and save it to the student data files folder as: Department Budget - Student.

2   Double-click the **Sheet1** tab.

    The tab label for this sheet is now highlighted.

3   Type: Quarter 1 to rename the tab and press ENTER.

Now rename the other 2 tabs.

4   Right-click the **Sheet2** tab, and click **Rename**.

5   Enter: Quarter 2 to rename this tab.

6   Click the **Sheet3** tab.

7   On the Home tab, in the Cells group, click **Format**, click **Rename Sheet**.

8   Enter: Quarter 3 to rename this tab.

Switch back to display the first worksheet tab.

**9** Click the *Quarter 1* sheet tab.

**10** Leave the workbook open for the next exercise.

# Inserting or Deleting Worksheets

## Objective 1.1.3

When you create a new workbook, Excel includes one worksheet by default. You can add more worksheets to a workbook at any time. There is no limit to the number of worksheets that you can add to a workbook, except the total amount of computer memory available. On a practical level, you should avoid using a single workbook to store all of your information. The workbook would become unwieldy to manage, take too long to load and save, and consume too many computer resources when it is open. Instead, put unrelated information – such as the list of employees for the company – in a different workbook from the one containing a list of sales office addresses.

If there are more worksheet tabs than the status bar can display at one time, you can use the tab scrolling buttons to display the other worksheet tabs.

When you no longer need worksheets, you can remove them from the workbook. You should save your workbook before deleting a worksheet because, once deleted, you cannot retrieve a worksheet with the Undo command. You should also check every worksheet for error messages after deleting it. There may be formulas in the other worksheets that depend on values in the deleted worksheet.

To insert a new blank worksheet into a workbook, use one of the following methods:

- on the Home tab, in the Cells group, click the arrow for Insert, and click **Insert Sheet**, or
- click the **New sheet** button, or
- right-click the sheet tab where the worksheet is to be inserted and click **Insert**. In the Insert dialog box, click the **Worksheet** template and then click **OK**.

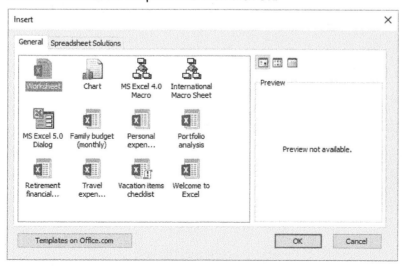

If you use the New sheet button method, Excel will add the new worksheet to the right of the active worksheet. If you use either of the other two methods, Excel will add the new worksheet to the left of the active worksheet.

To delete a worksheet, use one of the following methods:

- on the Home tab, in the Cells group, click the arrow for Delete, and then click **Delete Sheet**, or
- right-click the sheet tab to be deleted and click **Delete**.

## Moving or Copying Worksheets

**Objective 1.1.4, 1.3.3**

You may occasionally want to change the sequence in which the worksheets appear in a workbook. This feature is useful in organizing multi-worksheet workbooks. For example, placing related worksheets close together enables you to switch between them without the additional step of using the tab scrolling buttons.

It is also easy to make an exact copy of an existing worksheet. This is a useful feature for creating different scenarios when performing a what-if analysis. After copying the worksheet, some data values can be changed. You can then flip between the worksheets to compare results of these differences.

To move or copy a worksheet within a workbook, use one of the following methods:

- right-click the sheet tab to be moved or copied and click **Move or Copy**, or
- to quickly move a worksheet, click the sheet tab for the sheet to be moved and then drag the sheet tab to the new location, or
- to quickly copy a worksheet, click the sheet tab for the sheet to be copied, press; CTRL and then drag the sheet tab to the new location.

You can also move or copy a worksheet from one workbook to another workbook by dragging the worksheet tab. To do this, place the two workbooks next to each other on the Windows Desktop, then click and drag the worksheet tab from one workbook to the other.

# Learn to insert, delete, move and copy worksheets

This exercise involves adding a new worksheet to a workbook, and moving and deleting worksheets.

1   In the *Department Budget – Student* workbook, click the **Quarter 1** worksheet tab, if necessary, to display this worksheet.

2   Click the **New sheet** button to add a new worksheet.

Note that the new worksheet is added to the right of the worksheet currently being displayed.

3   Right-click on the new worksheet tab and click **Rename**.

4   Enter: Company to rename the tab.

5   On the Home tab, in the Cells group, click the arrow under **Insert** and click **Insert Sheet**.

Notice that this procedure adds the new worksheet to the left of the active worksheet instead of the right. The worksheet should now look similar to the following:

With the addition of this second worksheet, the number of tabs may now exceed the space available to display them all, resulting in some worksheet tabs being hidden from view.

6    Position the cursor over the **Resize handle** located at the left side of the horizontal scroll bar so that the mouse cursor changes to ◀▐▶.

7    Click and drag the **Resize handle** to the right or left as necessary to fully display all of the worksheet names.

Now enter data into this new worksheet and try deleting it.

8    Select the *Sheet2* worksheet and type your first name in cell **A1**.

9    On the Home tab, in the Cells group, click the arrow for **Delete** and then click **Delete Sheet**.

If nothing has been entered into the worksheet, Excel deletes it without any further prompting. However, if the worksheet contains data, Excel issues a warning message regarding data contents that might affect other data in the workbook.

10  Click **Delete**.

The worksheet has been deleted from the workbook, and the blank *Company* worksheet is displayed. You will now create the Quarter 4 worksheet by making a copy of the Quarter 1 worksheet.

11  Right-click the *Quarter 1* worksheet tab and click **Move or Copy**.

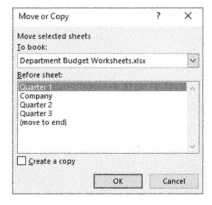

The Move or Copy dialog box now appears in front of the *Quarter 1* worksheet. By default, Excel moves the current active worksheet to a new position.

At the top of the dialog box, the current active workbook is displayed in the To book list box. So the worksheet move or copy will happen within the same workbook. If you have another workbook open at the same time, you can select it in the To book list box so that the selected worksheet can be moved or copied to that workbook. For this exercise, you will stay in the same workbook.

Selecting the Create a copy check box indicates that you want the current active worksheet to be copied. You also want this worksheet at the far right.

**12** Click the **Create a copy** check box to activate it.

**13** Click **(move to end)** in the Before sheet list and click **OK**.

Excel has now created a copy of the current worksheet, including the worksheet name. Because no two worksheets can have the exactly the same name, Excel has appended a number at the end of the new worksheet name.

**14** Double-click the **Quarter 1 (2)** worksheet tab and change it to Quarter 4.

**15** Select cell **C4**. Enter: Oct and select cell **C4** again. Use the mouse to drag the AutoFill handle across to column **E**.

Now move one of the worksheets to a different location.

**16** Click the **Company** tab and drag it to a new position to the left of the *Quarter 1* sheet tab, but do not release the mouse button yet.

Notice the icon and arrow indicating that you are moving a sheet into this location.

**17** At the new location, release the mouse button.

**18** Save the workbook.

# Hiding/Unhiding Worksheets

### Objective 1.4.1

Similar to hiding and unhiding a column or row, you can also hide or unhide an entire worksheet. The main reason for hiding a worksheet is to prevent other users from viewing the data or formulas used there.

You can hide as many worksheets in a workbook as you want, in any sequence. However, you must have at least one unhidden worksheet in a workbook. If you need to hide all worksheets, then you likely need to apply protection to the workbook instead.

When unhiding worksheets, you will be presented with a dialog box displaying all hidden worksheets for this workbook. From this list, you can select the worksheets to unhide.

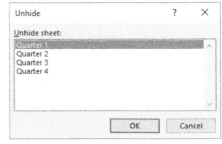

# Learn to hide and unhide worksheets

This exercise demonstrates how to hide and unhide one or more worksheets.

**1** In the *Department Budget – Student* workbook, select the **Quarter 1** worksheet.

**2** On the Home tab, in the Cells group, click **Format**, point to **Hide & Unhide**, and then click **Hide Sheet**.

The Quarter 1 worksheet is now hidden.

**3** Right-click the **Quarter 2** worksheet tab, and click **Hide**.

Next, hide all of the remaining worksheets.

**4** Repeat step 3 with the Quarter 3 and Quarter 4 worksheets.

**5** Attempt to repeat step 3 with the **Company** worksheet.

**6** Click **OK** to close the message box.

Unhide each of the hidden worksheets. Excel does not allow you to unhide more than one worksheet at a time.

**7** On the Home tab, in the Cells group, click **Format**, point to **Hide & Unhide**, and then click **Unhide Sheet**.

**Note:** If a workbook does not have any hidden worksheets, the Unhide Sheet menu item is grayed out.

The Unhide dialog box displays a list of all worksheets currently hidden in this workbook.

**8** Select the **Quarter 1** worksheet and click **OK**.

Use the right-click method to display the Unhide dialog box.

**9** Right-click the **Quarter 1** worksheet tab and click **Unhide**.

**10** Select the **Quarter 4** worksheet and click **OK**.

**11** Repeat steps 9 and 10 for the Quarter 2 and Quarter 3 worksheets.

The workbook is now restored with all sheets showing in their original sequence.

**12** Save the workbook.

## Adding Color to the Worksheet Tabs

**Objective 1.3.1**

You can add color to the worksheet tabs to help identify your worksheets. The selected color will appear as a background in the tab, similar to a divider tab. This can be handy if, for example, you are creating a budget for multiple departments in your company. You can use different colors for each department and then color code the budget in each worksheet tab for the corresponding departments.

The one exception is the active worksheet: the tab color will appear as a gradient shaded background behind the worksheet name. This helps you to easily identify which is the active worksheet.

Similar to background colors for worksheet cells, you can choose from the standard or various theme colors using the color palette. To display it, click the worksheet tab and then use one of the following methods:

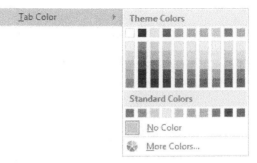

- on the Home tab, in the Cells group, click **Format** and click **Tab Color**, or

- right-click the worksheet tab and click **Tab Color**.

# Learn to add color to worksheet tabs

This exercise demonstrates how adding color to worksheet tabs can help you identify the worksheets.

**1**   With the *Department Budget - Student* workbook open, select the **Quarter 1** worksheet.

**2**   On the Home tab, in the Cells group, click **Format** and point to **Tab Color** to display the color palette.

**Note:** The color palette can also be displayed by right-clicking the worksheet tab.

**3**   Click **Blue** in the Standard Colors section (third from the right) of the color palette.

Notice how the worksheet tab now shows a blue gradient shade, darker at the bottom of the tab and becoming white at the top.

**4**   Click the **Quarter 2** tab.

Notice how Excel now displays the Quarter 1 tab with a full blue background. The Quarter 2 tab does not have a color, so it only shows a colored line at the bottom.

**5**   Repeat steps 1 to 3 for the remaining tabs: Quarter 2, Quarter 3, and Quarter 4 tabs, picking different colors for each tab.

| Tab | Color |
|-----|-------|
| Quarter 2 | purple  (Standard Colors section, far right) |
| Quarter 3 | red  (second from the left) |
| Quarter 4 | green  (sixth from the left) |

**6**   When complete, click the **Company** tab.

Your worksheet tabs should look similar to the following:

**7**   Save and close the workbook.

# Lesson Summary

Now that you have completed this lesson, you should be able to:

☑ edit cells and undo changes

☑ cut, copy, and paste data

☑ use Paste Special

☑ change column widths

☑ change row heights

☑ use AutoFit with columns or rows

☑ hide and unhide rows and columns

☑ insert and delete rows and columns

☑ insert and delete cells

☑ use AutoFill and Flash Fill to copy and fill cells

☑ rename worksheets

☑ insert and delete worksheets

☑ move and copy worksheets

☑ hide and unhide worksheets

☑ add color to the worksheet tabs

# Review Questions

1. Which key/combination activates Edit mode in Excel?

   a. F2

   b. ALT+E

   c. WINDOWS key

   d. CTRL+E

2. Suppose you used the Copy and then the Paste command to copy the contents of cells A1 to cell B1, but you do not want to copy the cell formatting to cell B1. What can you do to fix it?

   a. Use the Paste Special command instead, and select the Formats option.

   b. Use the Paste Special command instead, and select the Values option.

   c. Use the Paste Special command instead, and select the All using Source theme option.

   d. Use the Paste Special command instead, and select the Transpose option.

3. What is the difference between pressing Delete to delete the contents of a cell and using the Delete Cells command?

   a. Deleting the contents of a cell clears all formatting from the cell. If you use the Delete Cells command, the formatting is still applied to the cell.

   b. Deleting the contents of a cell places the deleted contents into the Clipboard. If you use the Delete Cells command, the cell contents are not copied to the Clipboard.

   c. Deleting the contents of a cell leaves the structure of the worksheet intact. If you use the Delete Cells command, you have the option of shifting the cells after the delete action is complete.

   d. Deleting the contents of a cell leaves any formatting still applied. If you use the Delete Cells command, the formatting is also cleared from the cell.

4. Ruby wants all the entries in Column D in her worksheet to display fully. What is the best method for ensuring Column D is wide enough?

   a. Dragging the right border of Column D to the right edge of the Excel window.

   b. Using the AutoFit command.

   c. Using the Resize command.

   d. Entering a very large number in the Column Width dialog box.

5.  Dean needs to print a worksheet for distribution at a meeting. The worksheet currently includes sensitive information that Dean needs to see, but which should not be seen by the meeting attendees. What is the easiest way for Dean to print an appropriate version of the worksheet for his meeting?

    a.  Make a copy of the worksheet, delete the sensitive information from the new worksheet, and then print the new worksheet.

    b.  Use a conditional printing command that skips over the cell ranges containing sensitive information.

    c.  Delete the sensitive information, print the worksheet, then enter the deleted information back into the worksheet.

    d.  Hide the rows or columns that contain the sensitive information before printing the worksheet.

6.  In which figure can you drag the AutoFill handle to create a series with 7 days between dates?

    a.   b.   c.

7.  What is the maximum length of a worksheet tab name?

    a.  8 characters          c.  250 characters

    b.  31 characters         d.  255 characters

8.  How many new worksheets can you add to an Excel workbook?

    a.  Three                 c.  As many as the available memory of your system will permit.

    b.  One hundred           d.  One thousand

9.  When you insert a new worksheet using the New sheet button, the new worksheet tab appears:

    a.  To the left of the current worksheet tab.

    b.  To the far left of all worksheet tabs.

    c.  To the far right of all worksheet tabs.

    d.  In a random position, depending on which worksheet is active.

    e.  To the right of the current worksheet tab.

10. Sam has painstakingly created a worksheet of Sales figures for the Eastern region. His worksheet is beautifully formatted and contains accurate formulas. Now he needs to create a worksheet just like it for the Western region. How should Sam proceed?

    a.  He should open a new workbook, line his two windows up side-by-side, and create a Western worksheet from scratch, using the Eastern worksheet as a guide.

    b.  He should add a new worksheet to the current workbook, view both worksheets side-by-side, and create the Western worksheet from scratch, using the Eastern worksheet as a guide.

    c.  He should create a copy of the Eastern worksheet, rename the copy Western, and then enter the figures as appropriate.

    d.  He should rename the Eastern worksheet to Western, and then enter the figures as appropriate.

Microsoft®

# Excel 2016

Core Certification Guide

# Lesson 3: Using Formulas

## Lesson Objectives

In this lesson, you will learn about formulas—what they are, how they work, how to insert simple formulas and use built-in functions to create some formulas. Upon completion of this lesson, you should be able to:

- [ ] know what formulas are
- [ ] create and edit simple formulas
- [ ] use math operators and understand the precedent order of calculations
- [ ] use formulas for what-if analysis
- [ ] reference other worksheets
- [ ] use common functions
- [ ] use the SUBTOTAL function
- [ ] use the IF function
- [ ] use conditional summary functions
- [ ] use text functions
- [ ] use absolute and relative cell references
- [ ] use mixed absolute and relative cell addresses
- [ ] display and print formulas

# Using Formulas

## Creating and Editing Formulas

In Excel, every worksheet cell is capable of using a formula. A formula is simply a calculation involving any number and combination of values, cell references, and/or built-in functions.

Worksheets typically contain formulas that refer to other worksheet cells. It is to your advantage to use cell references in your formulas whenever possible rather than the actual values. When these values or amounts change, the dependent cells (the cells containing the formulas) are automatically recalculated.

A formula can be up to 8,192 characters long. Enter your formula in the cell where you want the results to appear. Formulas are easy to recognize – all of them begin with the equal sign (=).

Suppose you have a worksheet with some formulas:

The formulas used in this worksheet are as follows:

| Cell | Formula/Value | Description |
| --- | --- | --- |
| A1 | 10 | A constant value – numeric in this case. Every workbook with formulas will usually have at least one constant value. |
| B1 | =A1 | References the current value in cell A1. No changes or calculations are done to the value in cell A1, other than copy it over. If the value in cell A1 is changed, cell B1 will automatically display the new value. |
| C1 | =A1*8 | References the value in cell A1 and multiplies it by eight. |
| D1 | =C1/5 | References the value in cell C1 and divides it by five. Digits to the right of the decimal point will also be displayed if necessary. Note that if the value in cell A1 changes, then the value in cell C1 will change, which will cause the value in this cell to change in a cascading effect. |
| E1 | =SUM(A1:D1) | References a built-in function called SUM to calculate the sum total of all cells in the range from A1 to D1. Note that if the value in cell A1 changes, then the values in cells B1, C1, and D1 will also change at the same time, which will cause the value in this cell to change as well. |

Let's change the value in cell A1. All of the formulas are automatically recalculated and the worksheet will now appear as follows:

Here is a comparison of how these numbers were calculated using the previous and new value in A1:

| Cell | Formula | Old Value | New Value |
| --- | --- | --- | --- |
| A1 | | 10 | 11 |
| B1 | =A1 | 10 | 11 |
| C1 | =A1*8 | 80 (=10 x 8) | 88 (=11 x 8) |
| D1 | =C1/5 | 16 (=80 ÷ 5) | 17.6 (=88 ÷ 5) |
| E1 | =SUM(A1:D1) | 116 (=10 + 10 + 80 + 16) | 127.6 (=11 + 11 + 88 + 17.6) |

This example demonstrates that by using formulas, you can have the computer do all of the work of performing the calculations for you quickly, which is a significant time savings for you. You changed the value in only one cell. Excel knows which sequence to perform all of the calculations, so that all of the results will be correct.

Excel does not display the formula you type into a cell in the worksheet, only the result of the formula. To view the formula, select the cell and you will see the formula and cell references in the Formula bar. You can also change a setting to display all formulas in a worksheet. This topic is covered later in this lesson.

You can also copy formulas to other cells. Excel will make a copy of the formula and the cell formatting while automatically adjusting cell references for the offset distance and direction. This may appear illogical at first, but it is actually a desirable feature in worksheets because the copied formulas are usually supposed to refer to different sets of input values.

Most worksheets have the same formulas used in multiple cells down a column or across a row. Excel will helpfully review these cells for you and displays a ⊤ symbol if it sees a formula that is different than the others in the same column or row. When you click on the ⧉ ▾ smart tag, a pop-up menu is displayed with the error message in the first line, followed by suggestions below on how you could correct it. This feature can be very handy to help you review the worksheet for differences or discrepancies.

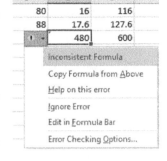

If you had deliberately entered a different formula, then you can simply ignore it or click the Ignore Error option in the menu to turn the flag off.

# Cell References

**Objective 4.1**

A cell reference simply means copying the current value from another cell in the workbook. A formula can have as many cell references as you want. After pressing the '=' key to start the formula, there are two ways to enter a cell reference:

- type the cell reference (or cell address) directly, or
- click on the cells being referenced.

For example, you may set up a cell with a formula to use the value from another cell and perform a calculation on it. Cells C1 and D1 in the example worksheet above demonstrate this. However, cell B1 is a very simple cell reference with no additional calculation.

You can also set up another cell with a formula to perform a calculation with two or more cells, such as =A1+B1, or =A1*B1+C4.

A third alternative is to create a formula that uses a function to operate on a range of cells. This is demonstrated in cell E1 in the example worksheet above. A cell range is any rectangular block of cells, written in this format:

> **<starting cell address>:<ending cell address>**

An example of a cell range is C11:E18. Note the use of the ":" to separate the two cell addresses. These cell addresses mark the two opposite corners of the rectangular group of cells. All cells inside this rectangle are used together in the formula.

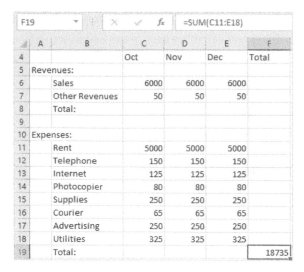

Cell ranges can only be used in functions or arrays, for example =SUM(C11:E18). You can't use a cell range on its own in a formula. The formula =F9+C11:E18 will result in an error in Excel.

The cell range can be one-dimensional with all cells in the same row or column, or two-dimensional with multiple rows and columns.

You can enter the cell range address in any sequence, as long as you use the cell addresses from the two opposite corners. The follow cell range addresses are equivalent for the same range of cells: C11:E18, E11:C18, C18:E11, E18:C11. Excel will accept every one of these range addresses and will change them to C11:E18, marking the top left and bottom right corner cells.

Cell range addresses can also include entire rows or columns. For example, the formula =SUM(B:C) will calculate the sum total of all values in columns B and C in the worksheet. Similarly, the formula =SUM(3:3) will calculate the sum total of all values in row 3 in the worksheet.

## Mathematical Operators

The following shows the symbols used in Excel to represent the standard mathematical operators:

- ^ Exponentiation and roots
- * Multiplication
- / Division
- + Addition
- − Subtraction

You generally use formulas to perform calculations, such as ordinary arithmetic. Excel calculates formulas using the standard precedence rule used in mathematics, as follows:

1. Brackets or parentheses
2. Negation (for example -2)
3. Exponents and roots
4. Multiplication and division
5. Addition and subtraction

Multiplication and division operators have the same level of precedence, so Excel performs them in the sequence they appear starting from the left to right. In the same manner, the addition and subtraction operators are performed as they appear from left to right.

You can alter this standard order of operation by placing components of the formula within parentheses. Excel will then calculate the portion of the formula in parentheses before defaulting to calculations in the order listed above. Thus, you can control the order of calculations in your formulas with careful use of parentheses.

# Learn to use formulas

This exercise demonstrates some of Excel's formula capabilities.

1   Open the *Quarterly Income Statement* workbook and save it to the student files folder as: Quarterly Income Statement - Student. Be sure that the *Quarter 1* worksheet is selected.

2   Select cell **C8** and type: =c6+c7 (but do not press ENTER yet).

Excel now shows which cell(s) you selected as part of the formula. You can use this visual tool to see what is happening on the screen when you set up a formula.

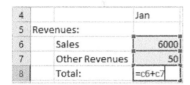

| 4 | | Jan |
|---|---|---|
| 5 | Revenues: | |
| 6 | Sales | 6000 |
| 7 | Other Revenues | 50 |
| 8 | Total: | =c6+c7 |

3   Press ENTER to complete the formula.

4   Select cell **C8** again.

In cell **C8**, Excel displays the number *6050*, which is the sum of the numbers in cells C6 and C7. Note the formula displayed in the Formula Bar.

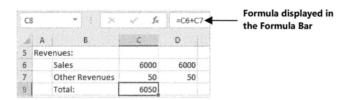

Formula displayed in the Formula Bar

5   In cell **C7**, enter: 125.

Excel has automatically recalculated the displayed value in cell C8 because it contains a formula that refers to the values in cells C6 and C7, and a change in either (or both) cells will cause Excel to update the total in cell C8. This demonstrates the advantage of using formulas in a worksheet and using a cell reference rather than the cell contents.

6   In cell **D6**, enter: 6100.

This time, the displayed value in cell C8 does not change when you change the value in cell D6. Remember that the formula in cell C8 has the cell reference to cell C6, not D6.

Once you enter a formula into the worksheet, you can copy the formula to another location, if the formula operation for the new location is the same. For instance, you can use the same formula to calculate the total revenues for each of the next two months, except that you must use the respective cells for each of those two months. Rather than entering the formula in each of the two cells twice, you can simply copy the formula.

7   Select cell **C8** and, on the Home tab, in the Clipboard group, click **Copy**.

**8**   Select cells **D8** to **E8** and, on the Home tab, in the Clipboard group, click **Paste**.

If you change a value in a referenced cell, all cells that depend on that value will also change.

**9**   Select each of the cells in the range **C8** to **E8**.

Notice that Excel has adjusted the formula in each of these cells. This is called *relative addressing*.

Now enter a similar formula, this time adding across three columns.

**10**  Select cell **F4** and enter: Total.

**11**  Select cell **F6** and enter: =C6+D6+E6.

**12**  Select cell **F6** again and copy this formula down to cells **F7** to **F8**.

If a value is changed in one cell, Excel will recalculate all formulas that directly or indirectly reference this cell automatically.

**13**  In cell **E7**, enter: 80.

**14**  On the Quick Access Toolbar, click **Undo** to see that the displayed values in cells **E7**, **E8**, **F7** and **F8** change back to their previous values.

**15**  On the Quick Access Toolbar, click **Redo** to re-apply the change in cell **E7**.

| | A | B | C | D | E | F |
|---|---|---|---|---|---|---|
| 1 | Tolano Adventures | | | | | |
| 2 | Department Budget | | | | | |
| 3 | | | | | | |
| 4 | | | Jan | Feb | Mar | Total |
| 5 | Revenues: | | | | | |
| 6 | | Sales | 6000 | 6100 | 6000 | 18100 |
| 7 | | Other Revenues | 125 | 50 | 80 | 255 |
| 8 | | Total: | 6125 | 6150 | 6080 | 18355 |
| 9 | | | | | | |
| 10 | Expenses: | | | | | |
| 11 | | Rent | 5000 | 5000 | 5000 | |
| 12 | | Telephone | 150 | 150 | 150 | |
| 13 | | Internet | 125 | 125 | 125 | |
| 14 | | Photocopier | 80 | 80 | 80 | |
| 15 | | Supplies | 250 | 250 | 250 | |
| 16 | | Courier | 65 | 65 | 65 | |
| 17 | | Advertising | 250 | 250 | 250 | |
| 18 | | Utilities | 325 | 325 | 325 | |
| 19 | | Total: | | | | |
| 20 | | | | | | |

Company | **Quarter 1** | Quarter 2 | Quarter 3

Repeat these same formulas in the other quarterly worksheets.

**16**  Select cell **C8** and, on the Home tab, in the Clipboard group, click **Copy.**

**17**  Select the *Quarter 2* worksheet, then select cells **C8** to **E8** and, on the Home tab, in the Clipboard group, click **Paste**.

**18**  Select the *Quarter 1* worksheet, then select cells **F4** to **F8** and, on the Home tab, in the Clipboard group, click **Copy.**

**19**  Select the *Quarter 2* worksheet, then select cell **F4** and, on the Home tab, in the Clipboard group, click **Paste**.

The series of steps from 16 to 19 demonstrates one way of copying formulas from one worksheet to others. The same end result can be achieved faster by knowing that you can paste the same cells as many times as you need to until you do something different.

**20** Select the *Quarter 3* worksheet, then select cell **F4** and, on the Home tab, in the Clipboard group, click **Paste**.

**21** Select the *Quarter 4* worksheet, then select cell **F4** and, on the Home tab, in the Clipboard group, click **Paste**.

Now copy the other set of formulas.

**22** Select the *Quarter 1* worksheet, then cells **C8** to **E8** and, on the Home tab, in the Clipboard group, click **Copy**.

**23** Select the *Quarter 3* worksheet, then select cell **C8** and, on the Home tab, in the Clipboard group, click **Paste**.

**24** Select the *Quarter 4* worksheet, then select cell **C8** and, on the Home tab, in the Clipboard group, click **Paste**.

With more experience in copying and pasting, you will find your own shortcuts to make tasks easier.

**25** Save and close the workbook.

# What-If Analysis

Spreadsheets can easily perform calculations such as simple arithmetic (such as add and multiply) on a large volume of numbers. You don't need an expensive computer to do this type of task. It can be done easily even with a basic calculator because the problem only needs to be solved once and then the task is completed.

Spreadsheets become invaluable when you need to perform what-if analysis, which involves repeating the calculation of a set of formulas many times using different numbers. The trial-and-error method of doing calculations is commonly used when there are multiple competing demands, and users try to find the best compromise between the many choices to make. The name "what-if" describes the thinking process that users face: "what if I change this number, then what will the result look like".

A spreadsheet created to perform what-if analysis often uses simple formulas, although there will usually be a large number of formulas.

Imagine that you are a prospective first-time home buyer. This worksheet in the next exercise will help you determine how large a mortgage you can assume given your current income level and spending priorities. Many financial institutions rely on two calculations when deciding whether to approve a mortgage application: the gross debt service and the total debt service. The gross debt service is the percentage of gross income required to cover the basic costs of a house, including mortgage payments (principal and interest), property taxes, heating, and condo fees. The total of this cannot exceed 32% of the buyer's gross income. The total debt service is the percentage of gross income required to cover the house and all other debts, such as credit card payments and car loans. This percentage cannot exceed 40% of the buyer's gross income.

# Learn to use formulas for what-if analysis

This exercise demonstrates how to use formulas to perform what-if analysis.

1   Open the *Personal Budget* workbook and save it to the student data files folder as: Personal Budget -
    Student.

First, calculate your monthly take home pay by reducing the monthly gross salary by 25%. This calculation
assumes that income taxes and other payroll deductions add up to 25% of your gross pay. You need both
your gross pay and take home pay amounts for these calculations.

2   Select cell **B4**, enter: =b3*0.75.

Now calculate the excess of your take home pay over your expenses, which you accumulate as savings in a
bank account.

3   Select cell **B22**, enter: =b4-b20.

    At first glance, you appear to be ready to apply for a mortgage to buy your very first home! It seems very
    reasonable that your current rent payments will become the new monthly mortgage payment, and you
    can afford a home in that price range.

4   Select cell **A7**, enter: Mortgage payments.

After looking at some homes, you can now estimate your property taxes and monthly condominium fees.

5   Select cell **B8**, enter: 125.

6   Select cell **B9**, enter: 100.

    Your income can no longer cover all of your expenses. You will have to cut back some of your expenses.

7   Select cell **B17**, enter: 100.

8   Select cell **B14**, enter: 100.

    Your cost cutting will have to include getting a smaller mortgage.

9   Select cell **B7**, enter: 1285.

    With your monthly expenses now under control, calculate the mortgage qualification ratios.

10  Select cell **D3**, enter: =A7.

    Notice that you can make a cell reference to a cell containing a text value, as demonstrated here.

11  Select cell **E3**, enter: =B7.

    Alternatively, you can copy the formula from cell D3 to cell E3. Excel will automatically adjust the formula
    to reference the next cell to the right.

12  Enter the following formulas in the specified cells:
    D4  =A8
    D5  =A9
    D6  =A15
    D7  Total housing costs
    D8  Ratio (max 32%)

Steps 10 to 12 demonstrate using formulas to copy values from one cell to another. In this group of cells, selected numbers are taken from the personal budget and used for another calculation in a formula entered in step 15 below. If the numbers in the personal budget are changed, these calculations are updated at the same time.

**13**   Select cells **D4** to **D6** and, on the Home tab, in the Clipboard group, click **Copy**.

**14**   Select cell **E4** and, on the Home tab, in the Clipboard group, click **Paste**.

**15**   Enter the following formulas in the specified cells:

E7          =E3+E4+E5+E6

E8          =E7/B3

You calculate the gross debt service as 39% (0.39), which is higher than the maximum allowable 32%. Now calculate the total debt service ratio.

**16**   Enter the following formulas in the specified cells:

D12         =D7

D14         =A11

D15         =A18

D16         =A19

D17         Total debt costs

D18         Ratio (max 40%)

**17**   Copy the contents of cell **D12** to cell **E12**.

**18**   Select cells **D14** to **D16**, then click the AutoFill handle (**+**) in the bottom right corner of this block and drag it across to column **E**.

**19**   Enter the following formulas in the specified cells:

E17         =E12+E14+E15+E16

E18         =E17/B3

You have calculated the total debt ratio as 55.25% (0.5525)—much higher than the maximum allowable 40%. You have too many debt (and other mandatory) payments to make every month to qualify for this mortgage. You will need to make more adjustments in your lifestyle to qualify for a mortgage, such as reducing or paying off your credit card debt, student loans, and car payments. You should also consider looking for ways to increase your monthly income, such as changing to another job with higher pay.

This is an unexpected surprise: your personal budget indicates that you can afford the mortgage payments, but your financial institution requires two additional calculations to determine your eligibility. These calculations seem unreasonable, but are in fact designed to prevent prospective home buyers from accumulating more debt than they can handle, which may result in serious financial problems in the future and possibly even personal bankruptcy or mortgage foreclosure.

Let's assume that you delay buying your new home for several months and concentrate on paying off debts. You were also able to improve your income by another $100 a month. Lastly, you reluctantly lowered your expectations for a home, settling for a less expensive one.

**20** Enter the following values in the specified cells:

| | |
|---|---|
| B19 | 100 |
| B18 | 0 |
| B7 | 1000 |
| B3 | 4100 |

This income level is still not enough. Your Gross Debt Service Ratio (cell E8) is 31%, which is below the maximum allowable rate of 32%. However, your Total Debt Service Ratio (cell E18) is 40.85%, which is higher than the maximum allowable rate of 40%.

Let's assume that you are able to increase your income by another $100 a month.

**21** Change the contents of cell **B3** again to: 4200.

This demonstrates how you can use cell references very effectively in what-if analyses. The spreadsheet contains many formulas, but they are calculated very quickly so that you can see the results when adjustments are made. With these changes, you will be able to apply for a mortgage and be confident that your application will be successful.

The completed worksheet should look similar to the following:

| | A | B | C | D | E |
|---|---|---|---|---|---|
| 1 | Personal Budget | | | | |
| 2 | | | | Gross Debt Service: | |
| 3 | Monthly Gross Salary | 4200 | | Mortgage payments | 1000 |
| 4 | Monthly Take Home Pay | 3150 | | Property taxes | 125 |
| 5 | | | | Condo monthly fee | 100 |
| 6 | Expenses: | | | Heat & electricty | 50 |
| 7 | Mortgage payments | 1000 | | Total housing costs | 1275 |
| 8 | Property taxes | 125 | | Ratio (max 32%) | 0.303571 |
| 9 | Condo monthly fee | 100 | | | |
| 10 | Food | 250 | | | |
| 11 | Car payments | 300 | | Total Debt Service: | |
| 12 | Car insurance | 150 | | Total housing costs | 1275 |
| 13 | Parking | 130 | | Other debts: | |
| 14 | Clothing | 100 | | Car payments | 300 |
| 15 | Heat & electricty | 50 | | Student loan payments | 0 |
| 16 | Phone | 60 | | Credit card payments | 100 |
| 17 | Entertainment | 100 | | Total debt costs | 1675 |
| 18 | Student loan payments | 0 | | Ratio (max 40%) | 0.39881 |
| 19 | Credit card payments | 100 | | | |
| 20 | Total Expenses | 2465 | | | |
| 21 | | | | | |
| 22 | Savings/Withdrawals | 685 | | | |

**22** Save and close the workbook.

# Referencing Other Worksheets

**Objective 4.1.1**

In addition to referencing other cells within the same worksheet, formulas can reference cells in other worksheets within the same workbook. The general format of this kind of reference is:

'<worksheet name>'!<cell reference>

Excel uses the ! (bang) symbol to indicate that this cell is located in a different worksheet. The single quotes are required if the worksheet name has blank spaces in it.

Furthermore, you can also use cell references for cells located in a different workbook. This topic will be covered in the Expert level courseware.

# Learn to reference cells in other worksheets

This exercise demonstrates how to create formulas that reference cells located in other worksheets.

**1**   Open the *Quarterly Income Statement - Student* workbook.

**2**   Click the *Company* worksheet tab to make it the active worksheet.

**3**   In cell **C4**, enter: Qtr 1.

**4**   In cell **C6**, type: = (but do not press ENTER yet).

**5**   Click the *Quarter 1* worksheet and select cell **F6**.

Notice that a marquee now appears around cell **F6** and the Formula bar shows =*'Quarter 1'!F6* with single quotes around the worksheet name.

**6**   Press ENTER.

**7**   Copy the contents of cell **C6** (in the *Company* worksheet) to cells **C7** to **C8** using your preferred method.

Notice that Excel automatically adjusts only the cell reference part, while keeping the worksheet reference component unchanged.

**8**   Select cell **C4**. Then click the AutoFill handle (✚) in the bottom right corner and drag it across the worksheet to column **F**.

**9**   Repeat steps 4 to 7 for column **D**, but referencing the cells in the *Quarter 2* worksheet.

Alternatively, you can set up the first formulas that reference the various worksheets, and then use the copy command on multiple cells.

**10**   Repeat steps 4 to 6 for column **E**, but referencing the cells in the *Quarter 3* worksheet.

**11**   In cell **F6**, enter: ='Quarter 4'!F6 (be sure to avoid entering any blank spaces inside this formula except between the two single quotes).

Now use the very useful AutoFill feature to copy these formulas to the remaining cells.

**12**   Select cells **E6** to **F6**, and drag the AutoFill handle (✚) in the bottom right corner down to cell **F8**.

| | A | B | C | D | E | F |
|---|---|---|---|---|---|---|
| 1 | Tolano Adventures | | | | | |
| 2 | Quarterly Income Statement | | | | | |
| 3 | | | | | | |
| 4 | | | Qtr 1 | Qtr 2 | Qtr 3 | Qtr 4 |
| 5 | Revenues: | | | | | |
| 6 | | Sales | 18100 | 22500 | 20000 | 18000 |
| 7 | | Other Revenues | 255 | 105 | 105 | 150 |
| 8 | | Total: | 18355 | 22605 | 20105 | 18150 |
| 9 | | | | | | |
| 10 | Expenses: | | | | | |
| 11 | | Rent | | | | |
| 12 | | Telephone | | | | |
| 13 | | Internet | | | | |

**13**   Save the workbook.

# Using Math and Statistical Functions

## Using the SUM Function

**Objective 4.1.2**

Typing cell addresses and plus signs is a good method when you are adding the contents of a small number of cells. However, if you need to sum up a column of 50 numbers, this method is time-consuming and will soon exceed the maximum limits on cell contents. It would be very inefficient to enter something like "=B1+B2+B3+B4+...B50" for each cell you want to include.

Excel provides a large library of built-in functions to facilitate this and other types of mathematical and data operations. These functions enable the calculation of long or complex formulas to be simplified by using a specialized function. Generally, all Excel functions follow this format:

**FUNCTION(arguments)**

At first, it may appear that the number and variety of Excel functions is intimidating. The most commonly used ones are similar to each other, and very easy to use.

The SUM function is an example of a commonly used function. In fact it is so prevalent that you will find it in most workbooks. As its name implies, its purpose is to calculate the sum of all numeric values in a range of cells.

A function is not the same as a formula. As described at the start of this Lesson, a formula always has a "=" as the very first character. Functions do not need the "=". Just be aware that most descriptions include the "=" character before the function name as a reminder that it is part of a formula. But after the "=" character, you can construct your formula using as many values, operators, and functions as you want: for example, =A10+5+SUM(F2:F9)+B3+SUM(G2:G9)

The function uses arguments as input values to perform its calculations. There are some general rules to understand about arguments:

- Arguments can be values (numeric, text or date, depending on the type of function) or cell references. Each function has specifications for its arguments but the most common type of argument is a cell range. The format of the cell range is as follows:

    <first cell address>:<last cell address>
    Examples:
    A10:B15
    D25:B5
    C5:C25

- Many functions allow you to enter a variable number of arguments. For example:

    =SUM(C6:C18) – calculates the sum of the numbers in all cells from C6 to C18

    =SUM(C6:C18,D6:D18,F6:F18) – calculates the sum of the numbers in all cells from C6 to C18, and D6 to D18, and F6 to F18

    =SUM(C6:C18,C20) – calculates the sum of the numbers in all cells from C6 to C18, and cell C20

You can enter a cell range either by typing the cell reference(s) directly, or by using the pointing method. To use the pointing method, simply use the mouse to click on the first cell and drag to the last cell to select the cell range. The latter method has the advantage of visually identifying the cell range, which reduces the possibility of entering incorrect cell references.

An alternative to manually typing the SUM function into a cell is to use the AutoSum button in the Ribbon. Because the SUM function is so commonly used, Excel provides three ways of activating it:

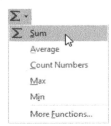

- on the Formulas tab, in the Function Library group, click **AutoSum** ( Σ AutoSum ), or

- on the Home tab, in the Editing group, click **AutoSum** ( Σ AutoSum ), or

  Notice that there is an arrow next to AutoSum in the Ribbon. When you click the arrow, it will display other summary functions that you can use in your formulas.

**Note:** If the Excel window is Maximized, this command appears as AutoSum. If the window is in a Restored state, the command may appear as just an icon because the window is not wide enough to display the entire command button.

When using AutoSum, be sure to verify that you have selected the correct cell range. Excel will automatically select the range of cells immediately above or to the left of the selected cell, and display it for you to accept or change.

# Learn to calculate the sum total

This exercise demonstrates how to calculate the sum total of a row and column of numbers.

1   In the *Quarterly Income Statement - Student* workbook click the *Quarter 1* worksheet tab and select cell **C19**.

2   On the Home tab, in the Editing group, click **AutoSum**.

Notice that the cell now shows *=SUM(C11:C18)*, with the cell range **C11:C18** highlighted, and a marquee around that cell range. Excel also reminds you of other ways to enter this formula using individual data values.

| ▲ | A | B | C | D | E | F |
|---|---|---|---|---|---|---|
| 1 | Tolano Adventures | | | | | |
| 2 | Department Budget | | | | | |
| 3 | | | | | | |
| 4 | | | Jan | Feb | Mar | Total |
| 5 | Revenues: | | | | | |
| 6 | | Sales | 6000 | 6100 | 6000 | 18100 |
| 7 | | Other Revenues | 125 | 50 | 80 | 255 |
| 8 | | Total: | 6125 | 6150 | 6080 | 18355 |
| 9 | | | | | | |
| 10 | Expenses: | | | | | |
| 11 | | Rent | 5000 | 5000 | 5000 | |
| 12 | | Telephone | 150 | 150 | 150 | |
| 13 | | Internet | 125 | 125 | 125 | |
| 14 | | Photocopier | 80 | 80 | 80 | |
| 15 | | Supplies | 250 | 250 | 250 | |
| 16 | | Courier | 65 | 65 | 65 | |
| 17 | | Advertising | 250 | 250 | 250 | |
| 18 | | Utilities | 325 | 325 | 325 | |
| 19 | | Total: | =SUM(C11:C18) | | | |
| 20 | | | SUM(**number1**, [number2], ...) | | | |
| 21 | | | | | | |

3   Press ENTER to accept the formula as displayed.

Excel always includes the cell immediately above the active cell, even if it is blank, and extends up the current column until it finds a blank cell. There are still numbers in the cells above the selected range, but they are not automatically included because there is at least one blank cell between them. You can manually extend the range to include additional cells.

4   Select cell **C19** again and copy it to cells **D19** to **E19**.

5   Select cell **F11** and type: =SUM( but do not press ENTER yet.

**Note:** You may enter cell references and the function name in lower or upper case characters. Excel will convert them all to upper case.

6   Use the mouse to select the cell range **C11** to **E11.** Then press ENTER.

In this case, Excel permits you to omit entering the last parenthesis for this function. However, Excel does not always permit this, and it is poor practice.

7   Select cell **F11** again and copy it to cells **F12** to **F19**.

Other arithmetic operations can be performed in a formula such as multiplication. If a cell contains a formula that is different from the cells around it (if any), Excel displays a marker symbol.

8   Select cell **F14**.

9   Enter: =C14+D14+E14.

The worksheet should look similar to the following example:

|   | A | B | C | D | E | F |
|---|---|---|---|---|---|---|
| 1 | Tolano Adventures | | | | | |
| 2 | Department Budget | | | | | |
| 3 | | | | | | |
| 4 | | | Jan | Feb | Mar | Total |
| 5 | Revenues: | | | | | |
| 6 | | Sales | 6000 | 6100 | 6000 | 18100 |
| 7 | | Other Revenues | 125 | 50 | 80 | 255 |
| 8 | | Total: | 6125 | 6150 | 6080 | 18355 |
| 9 | | | | | | |
| 10 | Expenses: | | | | | |
| 11 | | Rent | 5000 | 5000 | 5000 | 15000 |
| 12 | | Telephone | 150 | 150 | 150 | 450 |
| 13 | | Internet | 125 | 125 | 125 | 375 |
| 14 | | Photocopier | 80 | 80 | 80 | 240 |
| 15 | | Supplies | 250 | 250 | 250 | 750 |
| 16 | | Courier | 65 | 65 | 65 | 195 |
| 17 | | Advertising | 250 | 250 | 250 | 750 |
| 18 | | Utilities | 325 | 325 | 325 | 975 |
| 19 | | Total: | 6245 | 6245 | 6245 | 18735 |

Note the ⊢ symbol in cell **F14**. This marker is a reminder that this cell contains a formula that is different from the cells around it (in this case above and below it). It is not an error symbol because the different formula may be intentional. To remove the symbol, click on the smart tag.

The formula in this cell differs from the formulas in this area of the spreadsheet.

10   Select cell **F14** again, position the mouse over the smart tag, click the arrow and select **Ignore Error**.

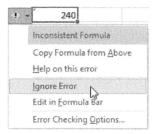

11  Select cell **C19** again and copy it to cells **C19** to **E19** in the *Quarter 2*, *Quarter 3*, and *Quarter 4* worksheets.

12  Select cell **F11** in the *Quarter 1* worksheet again and copy it to cells **F11** to **F19** in the *Quarter 2*, *Quarter 3* and *Quarter 4* worksheets.

13  Save and close the workbook.

There is no need to be concerned about the look of your worksheet. At this point, it is important to make sure the data is accurate. Enhancing the look of the worksheet can take place later. We will look at formatting in the next lesson.

## Using Statistical Functions

**Objective 4.1.3**

All Excel functions are grouped into one of 13 categories. The SUM function is in the Math & Trig (trigonometry) category.

There are also several commonly used math-related functions but are found in the Statistical category:

**=AVERAGE** – Calculates the arithmetic mean average of the numbers in the specified range (sum total of the cell range, divided by the total of the number of cells containing a number).

**=MIN** – Finds and displays the lowest numeric value in the specified range.

**=MAX** – Finds and displays the largest numeric value in the specified range.

**=COUNT** – Counts the number of cells in the specified range that contain numeric or date values.

**=COUNTA** – Counts the number of cells in the specified range that contain any value (numeric, date, or text).

**=COUNTBLANK** – Counts the number of empty (do not contain any value) cells in the specified range.

# Learn to use the statistical functions

This exercise demonstrates how to use several statistical functions.

1  Open the *Weekly Expense Report Statistics* workbook and save it to the student data files folder as: Weekly Expense Report Statistics - Student.

Use the standard SUM function to calculate the subtotal values in column **C**.

2  Select cell **C6** and then, on the Home tab, in the Editing group, click **AutoSum**. Verify that only cell **C5** is selected as the argument for the SUM function and press ENTER.

3  Select cell **C9** and then, on the Home tab, in the Editing group, click **AutoSum**. Verify that only cell **C8** is selected as the argument for the SUM function and press ENTER.

4  Select cell **C13** and then, on the Home tab, in the Editing group, click **AutoSum**. Verify that both expense values in the cells above are selected and press ENTER.

**5**  Repeat either step 3 or 4 (depending on whether there is one or two values to add together) for each of the remaining subtotal cells in cells **C17**, **C21**, **C24**, **E6**, **E9**, **E13**, **E17**, **E21**, and **E24**.

| | A | B | C | D | E | F | G |
|---|---|---|---|---|---|---|---|
| 1 | Tolano Adventures | | | | | | |
| 2 | Weekly Expense Report | | | | | | |
| 3 | | | SUM | | SUM + | | SUBTOTAL |
| 4 | Office | Travel Director | Expenses | | Expenses | | Expenses |
| 5 | Cape Town | Jamie Gibson | 122.05 | | 122.05 | | 122.05 |
| 6 | Subtotal for Cape Town | | 122.05 | | 122.05 | | |
| 7 | | | | | | | |
| 8 | London | Andrew McSweeney | 234.62 | | 234.62 | | 234.62 |
| 9 | Subtotal for London | | 234.62 | | 234.62 | | |
| 10 | | | | | | | |
| 11 | New York | Madison Cowell | 178.92 | | 178.92 | | 178.92 |
| 12 | New York | Nick Klassen | 199.25 | | 199.25 | | 199.25 |
| 13 | Subtotal for New York | | 378.17 | | 378.17 | | |
| 14 | | | | | | | |
| 15 | Sydney | Curtis Gorski | 82.54 | | 82.54 | | 82.54 |
| 16 | Sydney | Lawrence Jang | 101.76 | | 101.76 | | 101.76 |
| 17 | Subtotal for Sydney | | 184.30 | | 184.30 | | |
| 18 | | | | | | | |
| 19 | Tokyo | Christie Akira | 287.92 | | 287.92 | | 287.92 |
| 20 | Tokyo | Kanda Yamoto | 274.10 | | 274.10 | | 274.10 |
| 21 | Subtotal for Tokyo | | 562.02 | | 562.02 | | |
| 22 | | | | | | | |
| 23 | Toronto | Toby Belanger | 164.29 | | 164.29 | | 164.29 |
| 24 | Subtotal for Toronto | | 164.29 | | 164.29 | | |
| 25 | Grand Total - All Offices | | | | | | |
| 26 | Average | | | | | | |
| 27 | Count | | | | | | |
| 28 | Highest | | | | | | |
| 29 | Lowest | | | | | | |
| 30 | Count of Directors | | | | | | |
| 31 | Count of Blanks | | | | | | |

Up to this point, both columns C and E have been identical. The subtotal values have been calculated for each travel office. You will now try to calculate the grand total for all offices.

To do this, you will deliberately create an incorrect grand total for column C, which you will use for comparative purposes.

**6**  Select cell **C25** and then, on the Home tab, in the Editing group, click **AutoSum**. Select cells **C5:C24** and press ENTER.

**7**  Enter the following formulas:

| Cell | Formula |
|---|---|
| C26 | =AVERAGE(C5:C24) |
| C27 | =COUNT(C5:C24) |
| C28 | =MAX(C5:C24) |
| C29 | =MIN(C5:C24) |

Enter two more formulas to count the number of cells containing text (names of travel directors) and the number of cells without any data in column B.

**8**  Enter the following formulas:

| Cell | Formula |
|---|---|
| B30 | =COUNTA(B5:B24) |
| B31 | =COUNTBLANK(B5:B24) |

Now enter the correct formulas for column E. The grand total of =SUM(E6,E9,E13,E17,E21,E24) calculates based only on the subtotal values.

**9**    Select cell **E25** and then, on the Home tab, in the Editing group, click **AutoSum**.

To select individual cells instead of the full range as you did in step 6, you must use the CTRL key.

**10**   Select cell **E6**, hold down the CTRL key, and then click on each of cells **E9**, **E13**, **E17**, **E21**, and **E24**. Release the CTRL key and press ENTER.

Notice that the grand total in column E is half of the grand total in column C. This demonstrates that the latter value is double-counting everything in column C.

Now calculate the average weekly expense for all employees using the AutoSum button in the Ribbon.

**11**   Select cell **E26** and then, on the Home tab, in the Editing group, click the arrow next to **AutoSum** and click **Average** to select this function.

**12**   Select cell **E5**, hold down the CTRL key, and then click on each of cells **E8**, **E11**, **E12**, **E15**, **E16**, **E19**, **E20**, and **E23**. Release the CTRL key and press ENTER.

Note that the cells in this AVERAGE function are not the same as for the SUM function above. The average is calculated using each individual person's expense amount, not the subtotal for the office.

**13**   Enter the rest of the summary formulas (either by entering the full formula or by using the mouse to select the cells):

**Cell      Formula**
E27        =COUNT(E5,E8,E11,E12,E15,E16,E19,E20,E23)
E28        =MAX(E5,E8,E11,E12,E15,E16,E19,E20,E23)
E29        =MIN(E5,E8,E11,E12,E15,E16,E19,E20,E23)

| | A | B | C | D | E | F | G |
|---|---|---|---|---|---|---|---|
| 1 | Tolano Adventures | | | | | | |
| 2 | Weekly Expense Report | | | | | | |
| 3 | | | SUM | | SUM + | | SUBTOTAL |
| 4 | Office | Travel Director | Expenses | | Expenses | | Expenses |
| 5 | Cape Town | Jamie Gibson | 122.05 | | 122.05 | | 122.05 |
| 6 | Subtotal for Cape Town | | 122.05 | | 122.05 | | |
| 7 | | | | | | | |
| 8 | London | Andrew McSweeney | 234.62 | | 234.62 | | 234.62 |
| 9 | Subtotal for London | | 234.62 | | 234.62 | | |
| 10 | | | | | | | |
| 11 | New York | Madison Cowell | 178.92 | | 178.92 | | 178.92 |
| 12 | New York | Nick Klassen | 199.25 | | 199.25 | | 199.25 |
| 13 | Subtotal for New York | | 378.17 | | 378.17 | | |
| 14 | | | | | | | |
| 15 | Sydney | Curtis Gorski | 82.54 | | 82.54 | | 82.54 |
| 16 | Sydney | Lawrence Jang | 101.76 | | 101.76 | | 101.76 |
| 17 | Subtotal for Sydney | | 184.30 | | 184.30 | | |
| 18 | | | | | | | |
| 19 | Tokyo | Christie Akira | 287.92 | | 287.92 | | 287.92 |
| 20 | Tokyo | Kanda Yamoto | 274.10 | | 274.10 | | 274.10 |
| 21 | Subtotal for Tokyo | | 562.02 | | 562.02 | | |
| 22 | | | | | | | |
| 23 | Toronto | Toby Belanger | 164.29 | | 164.29 | | 164.29 |
| 24 | Subtotal for Toronto | | 164.29 | | 164.29 | | |
| 25 | Grand Total - All Offices | | 3290.90 | | 1645.45 | | |
| 26 | Average | | 219.39 | | 182.83 | | |
| 27 | Count | | 15 | | 9 | | |
| 28 | Highest | | 562.02 | | 287.92 | | |
| 29 | Lowest | | 82.54 | | 82.54 | | |
| 30 | Count of Directors | 9 | | | | | |
| 31 | Count of Blanks | 11 | | | | | |

As you can see, entering these sum, average, count, maximum, and minimum functions was painful — they were tedious and error-prone because you had to individually pick each of the subtotal numbers in the column.

**Tip:** Experienced Excel users would know that step 13 could have been accomplished more easily by converting the cell references in the AVERAGE formula to absolute cell references. You can then copy this formula from cell E26 to these cells, and just change the function name. Absolute cell references are covered later in this lesson.

**14** Save and close the workbook.

## Using the Subtotal Function

The SUM function calculates an arithmetical total of the selected cell range. In most situations, it is the appropriate function for automatically adding together the value in multiple cells.

In some worksheets, you may already have SUM functions included in the data to calculate the subtotals for subgroups of data. In these situations, it may be more appropriate to use the SUBTOTAL function.

The SUBTOTAL function does more than calculate a sum total for a range of cells. It actually performs a variety of statistical operations, depending on which function number is used. The general format of the SUBTOTAL function is:

   **=SUBTOTAL(Function #, Cell Range)**

The most commonly used function numbers are:

| Function # | Function |
|---|---|
| 1 | AVERAGE—mean average of the cell range |
| 2 | COUNT—number of cells containing numeric values |
| 3 | COUNTA—number of non-blank cells |
| 4 | MAX—highest value in the cell range |
| 5 | MIN—lowest value in the cell range |
| 9 | SUM—sum total of the cell range |

Other function numbers that are also available for SUBTOTAL are:

| Function # | Function |
|---|---|
| 6 | PRODUCT (all numbers multiplied together) |
| 7 | STDEV.S (standard deviation based on a sample) |
| 8 | STDEV.P (standard deviation based on entire population) |
| 10 | VAR.S (variance based on a sample) |
| 11 | VAR.P (variance based on entire population) |

The primary advantage of SUBTOTAL over SUM is that it will not include any other SUBTOTAL calculations within its range. As a result, you can insert subtotal, total, and grand total calculations into a table—without any risk of accidentally double-counting a subtotal—by simply including the entire range of cells.

To insert the SUBTOTAL function, use one of the following methods:

- click **Insert Function** and then, in the Or select a category field, click **Math & Trig**, or
- on the Formulas tab, in the Function Library group, click **Math & Trig**, or
- type the formula directly into the cell.

# Learn to use the SUBTOTAL function

This exercise demonstrates the use of the SUBTOTAL function.

**1** Open the *Weekly Expense Report* workbook and save it to the student data files folder as: Weekly Expense Report - Student.

Now use the SUBTOTAL function and see how it works.

**2** Select cell **G6** and enter: =SUBTOTAL(9,G5).

**3** Now enter the remaining subtotal formulas:

| Cell | Formula |
|---|---|
| G9 | =SUBTOTAL(9,G8) |
| G13 | =SUBTOTAL(9,G11:G12) |
| G17 | =SUBTOTAL(9,G15:G16) |
| G21 | =SUBTOTAL(9,G19:G20) |
| G24 | =SUBTOTAL(9,G23) |

Note that you can select the cell or cell range instead of typing the cell reference addresses into the function, if that is easier for you.

**4** Select cell **G25** and enter: =SUBTOTAL(9,G5:G24).

Enter the remaining statistical functions using SUBTOTAL.

**5** Enter the following formulas:

| Cell | Formula |
|---|---|
| G26 | =SUBTOTAL(1,G5:G24) |
| G27 | =SUBTOTAL(2,G5:G24) |
| G28 | =SUBTOTAL(4,G5:G24) |
| G29 | =SUBTOTAL(5,G5:G24) |

Step 5 here was much easier to do than using the AVERAGE, COUNT, MIN, and MAX functions used in column E because you simply selected a continuous range of cells in the column. The SUBTOTAL function simply ignored the presence of any other SUBTOTAL function within that cell range. As a result, column G shows the same results as column E. If you used the continuous range of cells with the SUM, AVERAGE, and other functions as shown in column C to enter those formulas, the results would be incorrect.

| | | | | | |
|---|---|---|---|---|---|
| 25 | Grand Total - All Offices | | 3290.90 | 1645.45 | 1645.45 |
| 26 | Average | | 219.39 | 182.83 | 182.827778 |
| 27 | Count | | 15 | 9 | 9 |
| 28 | Highest | | 562.02 | 287.92 | 287.92 |
| 29 | Lowest | | 82.54 | 82.54 | 82.54 |
| 30 | Count of Directors | 9 | | | |
| 31 | Count of Blanks | 11 | | | |

**6** Save and close the workbook.

## Using the IF Function

**Objective 4.2.1**

The ability to perform different calculations based on changing values is one of the most powerful and useful features of spreadsheets. The primary function used for this is the IF function. This function makes an evaluation or logical test and performs one of two different calculations based on the result. This automatic evaluation provides "on the fly" conditional worksheet calculations.

The format of the IF function is as follows:

=IF(logical test,value if true,value if false)

**Logical Test** – Specify what the IF statement will evaluate.

**Value if True** – If the Logical Test is found to be true, then the result of the IF function will be whatever is in this section of the formula.

**Value if False** – If the Logical Test is found to be false, then the result of the IF function will be whatever is in this section of the formula.

The Logical Test section of the function often uses comparison operators that will help you obtain the desired result. Qualifiers are punctuation marks used to identify or define different types of data. For example, text used in a formula requires double quotes as qualifiers.

Some of the comparison operators you can use are:

- = Equal to
- > Greater than
- < Less than
- >= Greater than or equal to
- <= Less than or equal to
- <> Not equal to

The Value if True/False sections can contain a text string, values or even other functions. In fact, you can nest or embed up to 64 IF functions within one IF function. An example of a nested IF function would appear as follows:

=IF(A1=10, "text A",IF(A1=20, "text B", "text C"))

In this example, Excel will display the following values when the conditions are met:

| If A1 contains | Then this will display |
| --- | --- |
| 10 | text A |
| 20 | text B |
| Any other value | text C |

# Learn to use the IF function

This exercise demonstrates how to use the IF function and nest a function within another function.

You will use a worksheet that will calculate the number of travel points given to customers based on the amount they spend. For every dollar a customer spends, the program awards 100 AirKm points. In addition, the program awards customers an additional 20 points for every dollar if the total amount is over $500.

1    Open the *AirKm Awards Points* workbook and save it to the student data files folder as: AirKm Awards Points - Student.

First, calculate the number of points per dollar.

2   Select cell **D5**, enter: =C5*100

3   Select cell **D5** again and copy it down to cells **D6** to **D20**.

Now calculate the bonus points per dollar, but only do this where the amount is greater than 500.

4   Select cell **E5**, and click **Insert Function**.

5   In the Or select a category list, click **Logical**.

6   In the Select a function list, click **IF** and click **OK**.

Excel displays the Function Arguments dialog box to help you enter the correct arguments for this function. You will base the logical test on the cost of travel, which is in cell C5, and must be over 500.

7   In the Logical_test field, type: C5>500 but do not press ENTER.

The next section is the Value_if_true section. If the result of the conditional test (C5 > 500 in this case) is true, Excel will return the value in this box to the worksheet cell. In this case, the value has to be calculated.

8   In the Value_if_true field, type: C5*20.

The last part of the function is the Value_if_false section. If the result of the conditional test is false, Excel will return this value. In this case, the value would be zero.

9   In the Value_if_false field, type: 0.

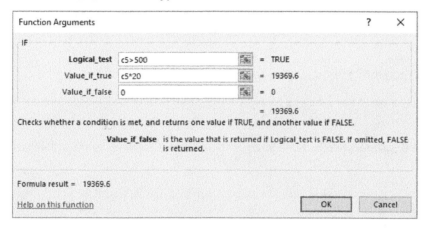

10  Click **OK**.

Note that the resulting formula is =IF(C5>500,C5*20,0).

Since the calculated value could result in a decimal value, you can use an additional rounding function to round the value up or down to the nearest whole number. You can accomplish this by embedding the IF function inside the ROUND function.

11  In cell **E5**, press F2.

12  Move the cursor inside the cell to the left, to a position between the  =  and  IF, and type: ROUND(.

13  Press the END key, type: ,0) and press ENTER.

=ROUND(IF(C5>500,C5*20,0),0)

This technique of using a function inside of another function is known as *nesting*. When you nest functions, Excel will perform the inner-most functions first and use those results as arguments for the next outer level of functions until the entire formula is calculated. You can nest up to seven levels of functions.

14  Copy the formula from cell **E5** to cells **E6:E20**.

Bonus points are now calculated only if the amount in column B is greater than $500.

| | A | B | C | D | E |
|---|---|---|---|---|---|
| 1 | Tolano Adventures | | | | |
| 2 | AirKm Points Awarded | | | | |
| 3 | | | | | |
| 4 | Passenger Name | Type | Amount | Points | Bonus Pts |
| 5 | Chan, A | Personal | 968.48 | 96848 | 19370 |
| 6 | Chan, H | Personal | 968.48 | 96848 | 19370 |
| 7 | Cox, T | Corporate | 315.58 | 31558 | 0 |
| 8 | Cox, W | Personal | 315.58 | 31558 | 0 |
| 9 | Dali, P | Corporate | 548.27 | 54827 | 10965 |
| 10 | Dali, S | Personal | 548.27 | 54827 | 10965 |
| 11 | Koehn, J | Personal | 370.82 | 37082 | 0 |
| 12 | Koehn, P | Personal | 370.82 | 37082 | 0 |
| 13 | Moore, M | Personal | 366.03 | 36603 | 0 |
| 14 | Noire, N | Personal | 464.78 | 46478 | 0 |
| 15 | Singh, G | Corporate | 835.69 | 83569 | 16714 |
| 16 | Smith, A | Corporate | 528.28 | 52828 | 10566 |
| 17 | Smith, B | Corporate | 492.44 | 49244 | 0 |
| 18 | Smith, T | Personal | 528.28 | 52828 | 10566 |
| 19 | Williams, M | Personal | 441.44 | 44144 | 0 |
| 20 | Wong, K | Personal | 578.28 | 57828 | 11566 |

15  Save the workbook.

You can modify your IF function if you want a more presentable worksheet. For example, if you want the IF formula to show a blank cell instead of zeros or dashes when the amount is $500 or less, modify the formula to appear as follows:

    =IF(C5>500,ROUND(C5*20,0)," ")

The set of double quotes will cause Excel to insert a blank in any cell that proves FALSE based on the argument in the Logical_test.

To have either example work properly, remember to copy the changed formula to the other cells on the worksheet.

When using the Insert Function, Excel will insert the quotes for you when entering text in the Value if True/False fields. When you want either of these fields to be blank, you must type both quotation marks or the word True or False will appear in the cell.

## Using Conditional Summary Functions

**Objective 4.2.2**

The summary functions AVERAGE, COUNT, and SUM will simply perform the calculations on a range of cells. The conditional function IF allows you to perform one of two different calculations, depending on the results of a logical test. These two can be combined together into what are known as conditional summary functions: AVERAGEIF, COUNTIF, and SUMIF.

**AVERAGEIF** – Calculate the average value of all cells in a range which meet the logical test. The format of this function is as follows:

    AVERAGEIF(criteria_range, logical_test, average_range)

    AVERAGEIF(criteria_range, logical_test)

The average range is optional. If it is not specified, then the average calculation is performed on the criteria range.

**COUNTIF** – Count the number of cells in a range that contain a non-blank value and meet the logical test.

COUNTIF(criteria_range, logical_test)

**SUMIF** – Calculate the sum total of all cells in a range which meet the logical test.

SUMIF(criteria_range, logical_test, sum_range)

SUMIF(criteria_range, logical_test)

The sum range is optional. If it is not specified, then the sum calculation is performed on the criteria range.

An example of a conditional summary function is:

=SUMIF(D4:D207,"Visa",F4:F207)

In this function, the criteria range is D4 to D207, the sum range is F4 to F207, and the logical test is "Visa". Therefore, Excel will examine each of the cells in the range D4 to D207. If the cell contains the value "Visa," the corresponding numeric value in the cell range F4 to F207 will be included in the sum total.

These functions are different from the IF function in that a more flexible logical test is used. With an IF function, you can only specify one logical test which must result in a TRUE or FALSE value, and this generally requires the use of a comparison operator.

A conditional summary function will apply the logical test to <u>each</u> and <u>every</u> cell in the range you specify (D4 to D207 in the example above). And if you do not specify a comparison operator, Excel will assume you want to use the "=" operator, for example:

=SUMIF(D4:D207,"=Visa",F4:F207) is the same as =SUMIF(D4:D207,"Visa",F4:F207).

The logical test may be a fixed value or a cell reference. The SUMIF formula above is an example of a fixed value test by comparing each cell in the range D4 to D207 to determine if it is equal to the value of "Visa". An example of a cell reference is =SUMIF(E4:E207,">"&B2). Notice that only the comparison operator is inside double-quotes, and the cell reference must be preceded by the & symbol.

The average_range and sum_range are optional. For the AVERAGEIF and SUMIF functions, you can perform the logical test on one cell range, and perform the AVERAGE or SUM calculation on a different cell range. This option makes these functions more flexible to use.

# Learn to use conditional summary functions

This exercise demonstrates the use of conditional summary functions.

**1**   In the *AirKm Awards Points - Student* workbook, enter the following text into cells:

| Cell | Text |
| --- | --- |
| G5 | Sales Over $500 |
| G6 | Total Sales Over $500 |
| G7 | Avg Sales Over $500 |

Now enter the conditional summary formulas.

**2**   Enter the following formulas into cells:

| Cell | Text |
| --- | --- |
| H5 | =COUNTIF(C2:C20,">500") |
| H6 | =SUMIF(C2:C20,">500") |
| H7 | =AVERAGEIF(C2:C20,">500") |

If you want to enable an advanced feature of these conditional summary functions, you can enter the logical test into worksheet cells instead of into each of the formulas. For example, suppose cell H5 has the formula =COUNTIF(C2:C20,G15), and cell G15 contained the text string >500. Referencing a cell that contains the test criteria makes it easier to change the logical test and avoid forgetting to change a function that contains the test criteria.

Notice that the SUMIF and AVERAGEIF conditional formulas used here perform their calculations on the same column in which the test criteria are applied. In other words, these formulas select only those cells that meet the stated criteria and then perform the COUNT, SUM, and AVERAGE on only those cells. The significance of this will become clearer as you examine the next set of conditional formulas.

Now enter conditional summary formulas that pertain only to rows where the sales type is "Corporate."

3  Enter the following text into cells:

| Cell | Text |
| --- | --- |
| G9 | Corporate Sales |
| G10 | Total Corporate Sales |
| G11 | Average Corporate Sales |

4  Enter the following formulas into cells:

| Cell | Text |
| --- | --- |
| H9 | =COUNTIF(B2:B20,"Corporate") |
| H10 | =SUMIF(B2:B20,"Corporate",C2:C20) |
| H11 | =AVERAGEIF(B2:B20,"Corporate",C2:C20) |

These are the same conditional formulas as used previously, except that an additional argument has been added to the SUMIF and AVERAGEIF. In this variation, the test criteria are applied to the cells in column B (= "Corporate"), but the SUM and AVERAGE are applied to the corresponding cells in column C, which is where the sales amounts are located. The average value can be verified by dividing the sum value into the count value.

The worksheet should now appear as follows:

| | A | B | C | D | E | F | G | H |
| --- | --- | --- | --- | --- | --- | --- | --- | --- |
| 1 | Tolano Adventures | | | | | | | |
| 2 | AirKm Points Awarded | | | | | | | |
| 3 | | | | | | | | |
| 4 | Passenger Name | Type | Amount | Points | Bonus Pts | | | |
| 5 | Chan, A | Personal | 968.48 | 96848 | 19370 | | Sales Over $500 | 8 |
| 6 | Chan, H | Personal | 968.48 | 96848 | 19370 | | Total Sales Over $500 | 5504.03 |
| 7 | Cox, T | Corporate | 315.58 | 31558 | 0 | | Avg Sales Over $500 | 688.00375 |
| 8 | Cox, W | Personal | 315.58 | 31558 | 0 | | | |
| 9 | Dali, P | Corporate | 548.27 | 54827 | 10965 | | Corporate Sales | 5 |
| 10 | Dali, S | Personal | 548.27 | 54827 | 10965 | | Total Corporate Sales | 2720.26 |
| 11 | Koehn, J | Personal | 370.82 | 37082 | 0 | | Average Corporate Sales | 544.052 |
| 12 | Koehn, P | Personal | 370.82 | 37082 | 0 | | | |
| 13 | Moore, M | Personal | 366.03 | 36603 | 0 | | | |
| 14 | Noire, N | Personal | 464.78 | 46478 | 0 | | | |
| 15 | Singh, G | Corporate | 835.69 | 83569 | 16714 | | | |
| 16 | Smith, A | Corporate | 528.28 | 52828 | 10566 | | | |
| 17 | Smith, B | Corporate | 492.44 | 49244 | 0 | | | |
| 18 | Smith, T | Personal | 528.28 | 52828 | 10566 | | | |
| 19 | Williams, M | Personal | 441.44 | 44144 | 0 | | | |
| 20 | Wong, K | Personal | 578.28 | 57828 | 11566 | | | |

5  Save and close the workbook.

# Using Text Functions

**Objective 4.3.1, 4.3.2, 4.3.3**

Excel includes several text-oriented functions that are useful for handling text strings. They are often used to manipulate data imported from other sources. Some of the most useful text functions include:

**LEFT** – Extract the specified number of characters starting from the left side of the text string. The format of this function is: LEFT(text_string, number_of_characters)

The text_string can be a cell range. If number is greater than the total length of the text string, then the shorter text string is returned and extra blank characters will not be padded on the right.

**RIGHT** – Extract the specified number of characters starting from the right side of the text string. The format of this function is: RIGHT(text_string, number_of_characters)

The text_string can be a cell range. If number is greater than the total length of the text string, then the shorter text string is returned and extra blank characters will not be padded on the left or right.

**MID** – Extract the specified number of characters starting from any position in the text string. The format of this function is:

MID(text_string, starting_position, number_of_characters)

The text_string can be a cell range. If number is greater than the number of characters available, then the shorter text string is returned and extra blank characters will not be padded on the right.

**UPPER** – Convert all characters in a text string to uppercase. The format of this function is:
UPPER(text_string)

**LOWER** – Convert all characters in a text string to lowercase. The format of this function is:
LOWER(text_string)

**PROPER** – Convert the first letter of the text string and any letter following a non-alphabetic character to uppercase. All other characters are set to lowercase. The format of this function is: PROPER(text_string)

**CONCATENATE** – Join two or more text strings together to create one text string. Alternatively, the & operator can be used instead of the CONCATENATE function. The format of this function is:
CONCATENATE(text_string_1, text_string_2, text_string_3, ...)

**TRIM** – Remove any blanks from the text string.

When spreadsheets are used for lists or as a database, these often overlooked functions can save many hours of manually entering data.

**Tip:** The Excel Flash Fill feature may also do many of the text conversions for you without having to use these text functions.

## Learn to use text functions

This exercise is designed to demonstrate how text functions can be used to change character strings.

**1** Create a new, blank workbook.

**2** Enter the following values (be sure to use the upper and lower characters as specified here):

| Cell | Value |
|---|---|
| A1 | JaNe |
| B1 | pArkER-smiTh |

3   Increase the width of columns **A**, **B**, and **C** to 22.

4   Select cell **C1** and enter: =CONCATENATE(A1," ",B1) and be sure to place one blank space between the quotation marks.

    The space between the quotation marks is required to separate first and last names.

5   Select cell **A2** and enter: =LOWER(A1).

6   Select cell **A3** and enter: =UPPER(A1).

7   Select cell **A4** and enter: =PROPER(A1).

8   Copy cells **A2:A4** to **B2:C4**.

    Notice that Excel inserts capitals in all the proper locations, including after the hyphen.

Now use other text functions to extract parts of text strings or join them together in different ways.

9   In cell **A6**, enter: BIRTHDAY.

10  In cell **B6**, enter: =LEFT(A6,5).

11  In cell **C6**, enter: =RIGHT(A6,3).

12  In cell **B7**, enter: =CONCATENATE(LEFT(A6,3),MID(A6,6,1)).

You will find the & operator to be easier to use than the CONCATENATE function, and it creates the same result.

13  In cell **C7**, enter: =LEFT(A6,3)&MID(A6,6,1).

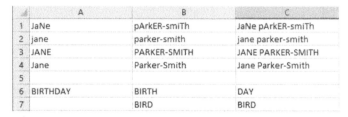

| | A | B | C |
|---|---|---|---|
| 1 | JaNe | pArkER-smiTh | JaNe pArkER-smiTh |
| 2 | jane | parker-smith | jane parker-smith |
| 3 | JANE | PARKER-SMITH | JANE PARKER-SMITH |
| 4 | Jane | Parker-Smith | Jane Parker-Smith |
| 5 | | | |
| 6 | BIRTHDAY | BIRTH | DAY |
| 7 | | BIRD | BIRD |

14  Save the workbook to the student data files folder as: Text Functions - Student and close it.

# Using Absolute and Relative Cell References

## Using Absolute Cell References

### Objective 4.1.1

Most formulas in an Excel worksheet use relative addressing for cells. If you copy a formula that contains a relative cell address and paste it to another cell, Excel automatically adjusts it for the new location. For example, suppose you have a formula that adds three rows together within one column. You can copy this formula to another column to add the adjusted set of three rows in the new column. The formula is relative to the column in which you place it.

This automatic adjustment feature is advantageous when you are creating sheets, such as budget sheets, which require the same formula to be repeated across many months or line items. However, in some cases you may not want this automatic adjustment feature.

Fortunately, Excel enables you to make cell addresses absolute or fixed. An absolute cell address refers to a fixed (non-moving) location on the worksheet.

To change a relative cell address to an absolute (fixed) cell address in a formula or function, enter a dollar sign before the row number and/or column letter (for example, $E$5). This ensures that when you copy a formula, Excel will not adjust the absolute cell addresses for the new location.

Another method to obtain the absolute signs in cell addresses is to press F4 once you have typed the cell address. You can also go back to formulas you have typed previously, edit them, position the insertion point in the cell address you wish to make absolute and press F4.

The number of times you press F4 determines which references become absolute:

- Press once to make both the column and row reference absolute.

- Press twice to make only row references absolute.

- Press three times to make only the column reference absolute.

- Press four times to remove the absolute references on both column and row.

## Using Mixed Absolute and Relative Cell References

### Objective 4.1.1

Cell addresses do not have to have both absolute column and row references. You can have mixed cell references. The column reference can be absolute and the row reference relative (for example, $E5). If a formula including this reference is copied to a new location, only the column reference ($E) is constant, and the row reference is adjusted for the new location.

Conversely, if you copy a formula including a cell reference with an absolute row reference and a relative column reference (for example, E$5) to a new location, Excel will adjust only the column reference for the new location. This adds flexibility for creating cell formulas, which will become increasingly important as your worksheets become more complex.

As a general rule of thumb: if you intend to copy the formula to other cells in the same row and keep the column reference locked, place the $ in front of the column letter. If you intend to copy the formula to other cells in the same column and keep the row reference locked, place the $ in front of the row number.

# Learn to use absolute cell references

This exercise demonstrates the use of absolute cell references.

1 Open the *Quarterly Income Statement - Student* workbook. If necessary, click the *Company* worksheet tab.

First create a new column of totals.

2 Select cell **G4** and enter: Total.

3 Select cells **C6** to **G8** and on the Home tab, in the Editing group, click **AutoSum**.

4 In cell **C11**, type: = then click the *Quarter 1* worksheet and select cell **F11** and press ENTER.

5   Repeat step 4 for other cells in this row:

**Cell**   **Source**

D11     Quarter 2 worksheet cell F11

E11     Quarter 3 worksheet cell F11

F11     Quarter 4 worksheet cell F11

6   Select cells **C11** to **G11** and on the **Home** tab, in the **Editing** group, click **AutoSum**.

7   Copy the contents of the cell range **C11** to **G11** down to cells **C12** to **G19**.

The relative addressing feature in Excel has saved you a lot of time in setting up these formulas.

8   Select cell **A21** and enter: Profit.

9   Select cell **C21** and enter: =C8-C19.

10  Copy cell **C21** across to cells **D21** to **G21**.

11  Select cell **A22** and enter: Quarterly Margin.

12  Select cell **C22** and enter: =C21/G8.

13  Copy cell **C22** across to cells **D22** to **G22**.

At first, it appears as if you can copy the formula into the other cells in row **22**. However, the result is as shown in the following:

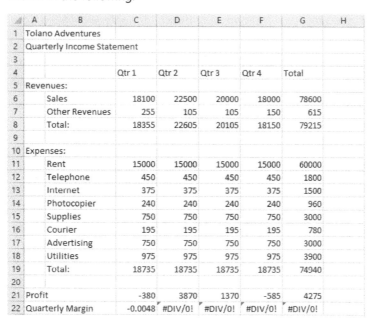

| | A | B | C | D | E | F | G | H |
|---|---|---|---|---|---|---|---|---|
| 1 | Tolano Adventures | | | | | | | |
| 2 | Quarterly Income Statement | | | | | | | |
| 3 | | | | | | | | |
| 4 | | | Qtr 1 | Qtr 2 | Qtr 3 | Qtr 4 | Total | |
| 5 | Revenues: | | | | | | | |
| 6 | | Sales | 18100 | 22500 | 20000 | 18000 | 78600 | |
| 7 | | Other Revenues | 255 | 105 | 105 | 150 | 615 | |
| 8 | | Total: | 18355 | 22605 | 20105 | 18150 | 79215 | |
| 9 | | | | | | | | |
| 10 | Expenses: | | | | | | | |
| 11 | | Rent | 15000 | 15000 | 15000 | 15000 | 60000 | |
| 12 | | Telephone | 450 | 450 | 450 | 450 | 1800 | |
| 13 | | Internet | 375 | 375 | 375 | 375 | 1500 | |
| 14 | | Photocopier | 240 | 240 | 240 | 240 | 960 | |
| 15 | | Supplies | 750 | 750 | 750 | 750 | 3000 | |
| 16 | | Courier | 195 | 195 | 195 | 195 | 780 | |
| 17 | | Advertising | 750 | 750 | 750 | 750 | 3000 | |
| 18 | | Utilities | 975 | 975 | 975 | 975 | 3900 | |
| 19 | | Total: | 18735 | 18735 | 18735 | 18735 | 74940 | |
| 20 | | | | | | | | |
| 21 | Profit | | -380 | 3870 | 1370 | -585 | 4275 | |
| 22 | Quarterly Margin | | -0.0048 | #DIV/0! | #DIV/0! | #DIV/0! | #DIV/0! | |

Clearly, the answers provided are incorrect—Excel displays a *#DIV/0!* (division by zero) error message in the other cells. Now examine the formulas you had copied in column **C**.

14  Select cell **D22** and examine the Formula Bar.

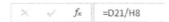

✗   ✓   *fx*   =D21/H8

As you can see, Excel has adjusted the cell address using relative addressing for each cell where you copied the formula. This adjustment process, which was so useful when you were creating and copying other formulas, is now causing a problem: dividing a value in cell D21 by the value in cell H8. The problem is that cell H8 is blank, which is interpreted as having the value of zero. If you divide any number by zero, you will get a "division by zero" error message.

You can resolve this problem by returning to cell C22 and editing the formula. The formula must use absolute cell referencing for the G8 cell reference. Thus, the formula in cell C22 should be =C21/$G$8 or =C21/$G8.

**15** Select cell **C22** and press F2 to activate the editing mode.

**16** Press F4 to put the absolute value signs around the nearest cell reference in the formula (G8).

**17** Press ENTER to accept this formula.

Note that the amount in cell **C22** does not change.

**18** Copy the formula from cell **C22** to cells **D22** through to **G22**.

Your worksheet should now look like the following example:

| | A | B | C | D | E | F | G |
|---|---|---|---|---|---|---|---|
| 1 | Tolano Adventures | | | | | | |
| 2 | Quarterly Income Statement | | | | | | |
| 3 | | | | | | | |
| 4 | | | Qtr 1 | Qtr 2 | Qtr 3 | Qtr 4 | Total |
| 5 | Revenues: | | | | | | |
| 6 | | Sales | 18100 | 22500 | 20000 | 18000 | 78600 |
| 7 | | Other Revenues | 255 | 105 | 105 | 150 | 615 |
| 8 | | Total: | 18355 | 22605 | 20105 | 18150 | 79215 |
| 9 | | | | | | | |
| 10 | Expenses: | | | | | | |
| 11 | | Rent | 15000 | 15000 | 15000 | 15000 | 60000 |
| 12 | | Telephone | 450 | 450 | 450 | 450 | 1800 |
| 13 | | Internet | 375 | 375 | 375 | 375 | 1500 |
| 14 | | Photocopier | 240 | 240 | 240 | 240 | 960 |
| 15 | | Supplies | 750 | 750 | 750 | 750 | 3000 |
| 16 | | Courier | 195 | 195 | 195 | 195 | 780 |
| 17 | | Advertising | 750 | 750 | 750 | 750 | 3000 |
| 18 | | Utilities | 975 | 975 | 975 | 975 | 3900 |
| 19 | | Total: | 18735 | 18735 | 18735 | 18735 | 74940 |
| 20 | | | | | | | |
| 21 | Profit | | -380 | 3870 | 1370 | -585 | 4275 |
| 22 | Quarterly Margin | | -0.0048 | 0.048854 | 0.017295 | -0.00738 | 0.053967 |

Check the formulas now entered in column **C**:

    C22 contains =C21/$G$8
    D22 contains =D21/$G$8
    E22 contains =E21/$G$8
    F22 contains =F21/$G$8
    G22 contains =G21/$G$8

When the reference to cell G8 is absolute, it is anchored to the total revenues cell.

**19** Save the workbook.

# Displaying Formulas

**Objective 1.4.8**

To see the formula in a cell, you must select that cell and examine the formula displayed in the Formula Bar, or press F2 to see the formula in the cell. In some circumstances, you may want to see all the formulas in all the cells at the same time, especially when you are verifying the accuracy of the spreadsheet. Excel has an option available to display all formulas in a worksheet at the same time. Cells that contain numeric or other values will simply display those data values.

Excel allows you to print the worksheet with the formulas displayed. This is an excellent technique for verifying that you have entered all the formulas correctly.

# Learn to display formulas

This exercise demonstrates how to display the formulas in worksheet cells, or to display the formula results.

1   In the *Quarterly Income Statement – Student* workbook, on the **Formulas** tab, in the Formula Auditing group, click **Show Formulas**.

**Hint:** An alternative way of activating this feature is to use the keyboard shortcut key sequence CTRL+` (Grave Accent).

2   If necessary, increase the size of the workbook window so that you can see columns A to G.

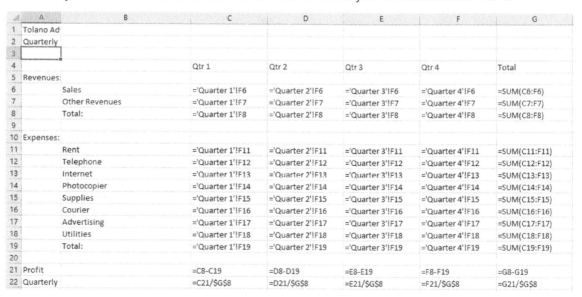

You can also print this worksheet with all of the formulas displayed.

To turn off the display of the formulas, simply click the Show Formulas button in the Ribbon again. An alternative method is to use the Excel Options screen.

3   Click the **File** tab, then click **Options**.

4   Click **Advanced** in the left pane of the Excel Options dialog box.

5   Scroll down to the Display options for this worksheet group of options and clear the **Show formulas in cells instead of their calculated results** check box. Click **OK**.

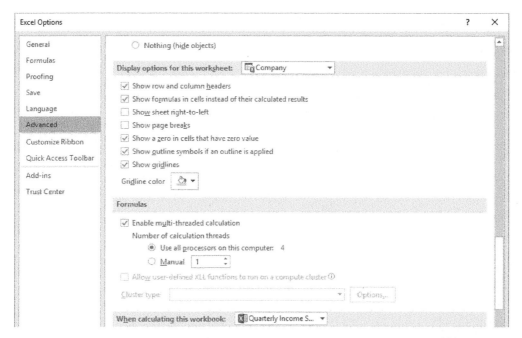

6    Close the workbook and discard any changes.

# Lesson Summary

Now that you have completed this lesson, you should be able to:

☑   what formulas are

☑   how to create and edit simple formulas

☑   how to use math operators and understand the precedent order of calculations

☑   how to reference other worksheets

☑   how to use common functions

☑   how to use the SUBTOTAL function

☑   how to use a conditional function

☑   how to use conditional summary functions

☑   how to use text functions

☑   how to use absolute and relative cell references

☑   how to use mixed absolute and relative cell addresses

☑   how to display and print formulas

# Review Questions

1.   What should you enter in a cell to find the difference between 9 and 5?

    a.   DIFF(9,5)          c.   =9-5

    b.   VAL(9-5)          d.   9-5

2.   Which of the following is the correct order of precedence for standard math operators?

    a.   Division, subtraction, multiplication, addition

    b.   Multiplication, division, addition, subtraction

    c.   Addition, subtraction, multiplication, division

    d.   Division, subtraction, addition, multiplication

3. Which of the following correctly identifies the different parts of the following reference: Tours!B4

    a. Tours is the name of the worksheet and B4 is the cell reference.

    b. Tours is the name of the workbook file and B4 is the cell reference.

    c. Tours is a named range in the worksheet, and B4 is the cell reference.

    d. Tours is the name of the column and B4 is the name of the row.

4. Which of the following are not valid formulas for calculating a statistical value using the data in several cells?

    a. b, c, and d

    b. =MAX(B5:B7,B8:B10,B11:B15)

    c. None – all are valid formulas.

    d. All of the above are invalid formulas.

    e. =AVERAGE(B5,B6,B7,B8,B9,B10,B11,B12,B13,B14)

    f. c

    g. =MAX(B1,B5:B8,B9:B15)

    h. =SUM(B5:B15)

5. Which of the following formulas says: if the value in cell B6 is greater than 500, then display a value equal to B6*20; otherwise, display a zero?

    a. =(B6>500,B6*20,0)

    b. =SUM(B6>500,B6*20,0)

    c. =MULT(B6>500,B6*20,0)

    d. =IF(B6>500,B6*20,0)

6. The LEFT and MID functions are fully interchangeable. In other words, can you always use the LEFT function instead of MID, as well as using MID instead of LEFT?

    a. True                          b. False

7. Which type of cell address will be adjusted in the new location based on the relative position of the original formula's input cells?

    a. A revolving cell address.        c. A fixed cell address.

    b. A relative cell address.         d. An absolute cell address.

8. Before submitting a worksheet full of accounting formulas to his boss, Ken wants to make sure that he has entered all of the formulas correctly. There are a lot of them. What is the easiest way to perform this check?

    a. Set the options for the worksheet to show the formula in every cell instead of the calculated results.

    b. Click on each formula in the worksheet in succession and read the formula input in the formula bar.

    c. Print the worksheet, then perform each mathematical operation in the worksheet on a calculator and compare the answers.

    d. Set the options for the worksheet to check each formula as it is entered.

Microsoft®

# Excel 2016

## Core Certification Guide

# Lesson 4: Formatting the Worksheet

## Lesson Objectives

In this lesson, you will learn how to use a variety of methods to format cells in a worksheet to emphasize different worksheet areas. Upon completion of this lesson, you should be able to:

☐ format numbers and decimal places

☐ change the alignment of cell contents

☐ merge and wrap cells

☐ change fonts and font size

☐ apply borders around cells

☐ apply background colors and patterns to cells

☐ use the Format Painter

☐ clear cell contents and formatting

☐ apply and modify themes

☐ apply and modify cell styles

☐ apply conditional formatting

## Formatting a Cell

How you present your worksheet is almost as important as the data it contains. Formatting is all about changing the appearance of the data. You are using the various features of Excel to draw attention to parts of the worksheet, or to make the data presented easier to understand. When you change the format of a cell, you do not alter its underlying value.

You should note the following important points:

- You can format a cell, or a range of cells, either before or after you enter the data. You can even format an entire row or column at one time.

- A cell remains formatted even after you clear the contents of the cell, unless you also clear the format or reformat a cell. When you enter new data in the cell, Excel displays the data in the existing format.

- When you paste or fill a cell from another cell, you copy the format and the contents of the originating cell. This feature enables you to save time, provided you apply the formatting before copying.

Some of the formatting features to change the appearance of your document include different fonts or sizes, bold and italic styles, borders around a cell or group of cells, and shading of cells. You will find the most commonly used formatting features displayed on the Home tab as well as on the Mini toolbar.

Certain types of formatting may not be compatible with the data values, and Excel will simply ignore that formatting until you enter the appropriate data type into that cell. For example, you may format a cell as numeric with commas and two decimal digits, but if the cell contains a word (such as "Total"), then Excel will only use the default cell formatting that pertain to text values.

Excel has a feature called Live Preview that temporarily changes the appearance of the selected cell(s) to the format that your mouse is currently pointing to on the Ribbon. If you click on that button on the Ribbon, Excel applies the formatting change. However, if you move your mouse away, the selected cell(s) revert to their current format. This useful feature allows you to preview a formatting change without having to click the Undo button if it turns out to be unsuitable. Be aware that only some formatting buttons on the Ribbon include Live Preview capability. Note that Live Preview does not function when you have a formatting dialog box in front of the worksheet.

## Formatting Numbers and Decimal Digits

### Objective 2.2.5

The formatting of numbers is usually the most common type of formatting applied to a spreadsheet. To meet a wide variety of needs, Excel provides a rich set of standard formats with changeable options. Except where you see it noted in each of the following sample screens, the underlying number in the active cell is 6798.52. As you select the formatting options, the sample box at the top of the dialog box shows what the number will look like with the selected options.

To format a cell, select the cell, and then use one of the following methods:

- on the Home tab, in the Font, Alignment or Number groups, click the appropriate button, or
- press CTRL+1, or
- right-click and click **Format Cells** on the shortcut menu, or
- right-click and click the appropriate number formatting from the Mini toolbar, or
- on the Home tab, in the Font, Alignment or Number groups, click the **Dialog box launcher** for the appropriate group.

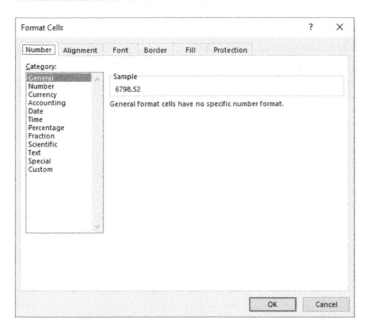

**General** – The General category is the default format for all cells. When you enter numbers into an unformatted cell, Excel displays them exactly as you entered them, except that it does not display trailing zeros after the decimal point. This can make the worksheet somewhat harder to read because the numbers in a column will not be lined up by their decimal points, as demonstrated in the example on the right. In addition, when you enter a number that is much larger than the width of the cell, Excel automatically changes the format to Scientific notation, adding another display format that is inconsistent with the other cells.

| |
|---:|
| 2432.635 |
| 1364 |
| 2656.316 |
| 1332.9 |
| 1177.82 |
| 1792.34 |
| 659.23 |
| 9.04E+09 |

**Number** – The Number category is a standard format for numbers with the option to show the comma (period in European countries) separator for values of 1,000 and higher. The number of digits after the decimal point must also be specified (the default is 2). If there are insufficient digits, the number will be right-filled with zeroes. Excel can show negative numbers with different options: in red, with a minus sign, or with parentheses.

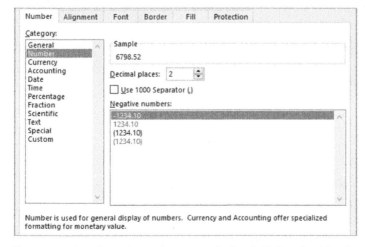

If any number has more than two decimal digits, the Number format will round it to the nearest second decimal digit. As with all formatting, this is for display purposes only—the actual number stored in the cell does not change.

One disadvantage with the Number format is that it does not display numbers with the comma separator.

**Currency** – The Currency format is similar to the Number format except that a currency symbol (for example, $ symbol) is shown and the comma separator is automatically displayed.

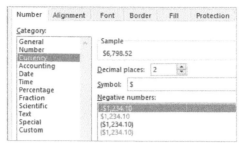

**Accounting** – The Accounting format is similar to the Currency format except that negative numbers appear in parentheses (you cannot change this) and the currency symbol appears at the far left side of the cell. Positive values include a space to the right of the value to ensure that decimal points always line up.

| Currency format | | $1,792.34 |
| Currency format | | -$528.45 |
| Accounting format | $ | 3,659.23 |
| Accounting format | $ | (248.10) |

**Date** – The Date format category displays date values in various ways. One complication is the region of the world to which your computer is set. For example, if you live in the United States, then your default date format would be m/d/yyyy. However, if your computer is set to the United Kingdom, your date format is dd/mm/yyyy. The d indicates that Excel will display single-digit day values as one digit—without filling in the left with a zero. A dd indicates a two-digit day value, with a leading zero for single digit values. The same format applies to the month and year values.

If you enter your date value with the month as a name (for example Sep 8, 2016, 8 Sep 2016, or September 8, 2016), then Excel will display it using the custom date format of d-mmm-yy where mmm indicates the first three characters of the month's name.

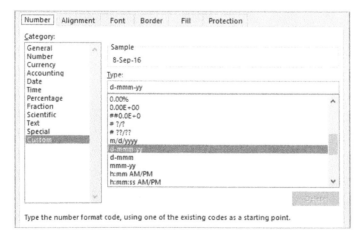

However, if you enter your date value with the month as a number (for example 9/8/16, 9-8-2016, or 2016-09-08), then Excel will display it using the date format that matches your region, as described above.

The Number tab in the Format Cells dialog box will display the alternate formats as follows:

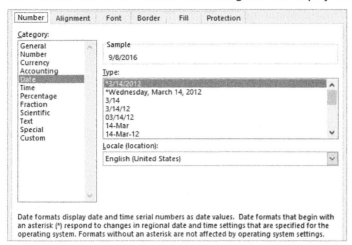

Note that the asterisk (*) indicates that this format changes with the computer's region setting, as described at the bottom of the dialog box.

**Time** – Because of the many different ways that time values may be entered, Excel will use a custom time format when you enter it.

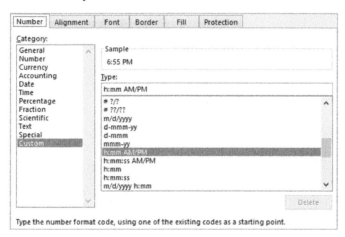

You can then select an alternate time format from the Number tab in the Format Cells dialog box or from the Number group in the Home tab of the Ribbon.

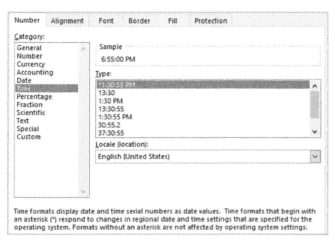

**Percentage** – The underlying cell value in this screen sample is 0.1234—Excel always shows percentage values as 100 times the number value. This format shows a percentage sign at the right side of the cell. You must also specify the number of decimal places (the default is 2).

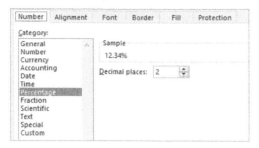

However, if you click the Percent Style button in the Number group of the Home tab in the Ribbon, Excel will use the Percentage format with a Decimal places value of 0 (zero).

**Fraction** – The Fraction format converts decimal digits to fractional values based on the fraction type that you select.

**Scientific** – You will usually use this format in scientific applications for very large and very small numbers. Excel shows only one digit to the left of the decimal point and you control the number of significant digits by specifying the number of decimal places.

**Special** – Use the Special format category for miscellaneous items such as phone numbers and zip codes.

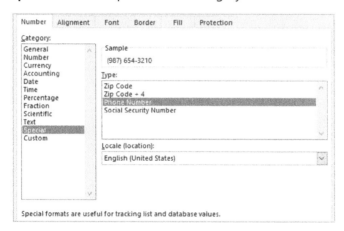

**Custom** – If you cannot find the exact format you want in the other categories, you can create a format of your own with the Custom category.

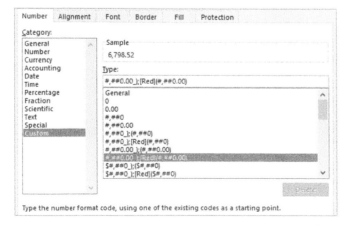

## Using the Ribbon

The Ribbon enables you to select the most frequently used formatting features from a convenient location. The number formatting options are found in the Number group on the Home tab.

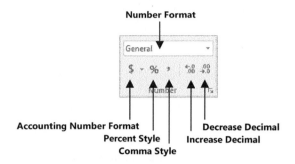

You can quickly format numeric cells using the Comma Style button. However, Excel interprets this formatting choice as the Accounting format with no currency symbol displayed. In addition, the Comma Style format displays negative numbers using parentheses instead of the minus sign, and positive numbers display with a slight indent to the left. The Number format is generally used more often than the Comma Style format.

Alternatively, you can display the mini-formatting menu by right-clicking on the cell.

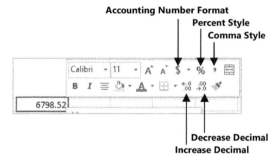

# Learn to apply numeric formats

In this exercise, you will examine some of the numeric formats available in Excel.

**1** Open the *Travel Itinerary* workbook and save it as: Travel Itinerary - Student.

Now format some of the cells containing numbers.

**2** Select the cell range **B19** to **B22**.

**3** On the Home tab, in the Number group, click the arrow for **Number Format**.

A list appears showing the most commonly used numeric formats for a cell. Below the title of each numeric format, Excel displays the number from the selected cell (or the top left cell, if you select a range) using that format. For example, the value of 3298 in cell B18 displays as 3298.00 under the Number format, and as $3,298.00 under the Currency format.

**4** Click **Number** on the list.

| 19 | Airfare: | 3298.00 |
|----|----------|---------|
| 20 | Hotel: | 2750.00 |
| 21 | Taxes & Fees: | 750.52 |
| 22 | Total: | 6798.52 |

Excel has applied a uniform format—two decimal digits—to all of the numbers.

**5** On the Home tab, in the Number group, click the **Dialog box launcher**.

In the Format Cells dialog box, the Category is already set to Number and 2 decimal places are specified. You only need to add the comma separator.

**6** Turn on the **Use 1000 Separator (,)** check box and click **OK**.

Now try the currency format.

**7** Select cell **B19**.

**8** On the Home tab, in the Number group, click the arrow for **Number Format** and then click **Currency**.

**9** Select cell **B22** and change this number format to Currency as well.

Using the Ribbon, you can also quickly change the number of digits appearing after the decimal point.

**10** With cells **B22** still selected, on the Home tab, in the Number group, click **Decrease Decimal** twice to remove all decimal digits.

   Notice that Excel has rounded the number up. You can also increase the number of decimal digits.

**11** On the Home tab, in the Number group, click **Increase Decimal** twice to show two decimal digits again.

**Hint:** You can also right-click and then click **Increase Decimal** or **Decrease Decimal** on the Mini toolbar.

You can also format cells containing date values.

**12** Select cell **B6**.

**13** On the Home tab, in the Number group, click the arrow for **Number Format** and click **Long Date**.

   The long date format is much too wide for this cell.

**14** On the Quick Access Toolbar, click the **Undo** button.

The cells containing the flight numbers are also numeric, but the General format is acceptable for them.

**15** Select cell **B4.**

**16** On the Home tab, in the Number group, click the **Dialog box launcher**.

**17** On the Number tab, click **Special** in the Category list.

**18** Click **Phone Number** in the Type list, and click **OK**.

   The customer's phone number now appears correctly formatted.

**19** Save the workbook.

# Changing Cell Alignment

## Cell Alignment and Indenting

**Objective 2.2.2**

Alignment refers to the position or placement of data within the cell. In Excel, you can align the cell contents horizontally as well as vertically, although you will most commonly use one of the horizontal alignment controls.

By default, Excel assigns General alignment to new values entered into a worksheet. This means that Excel aligns numbers and dates to the right, while it aligns text labels to the left, as shown in the example on the right. In most cases, you will not change the alignment of numbers and dates.

Also by default, cells are aligned on the bottom, which will only be noticed if you increased the row height. You can also change the vertical alignment to the top or middle of the cell.

Data can also be indented within the cell. In this example, the country names are displayed using normal cell alignment for text values with no indenting. The cells containing state and province names are indented to the right by one position, and the city names are indented by two positions.

As with the number formatting features, the most commonly used alignment options are readily available on the Home tab in the Ribbon:

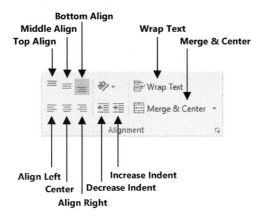

To change the alignment for the contents of a cell, after selecting the cell, use one of the following methods:

- on the Home tab, in the Alignment group, click the appropriate alignment button, or
- press CTRL+1 and then click the **Alignment** tab, or
- right-click, click **Format Cells**, and then click the **Alignment** tab, or
- on the Home tab, in the Alignment group, click the **Dialog box launcher**.

# Wrapping Text

**Objective 2.2.4**

As described in Lesson 1, you can enter very long text (up to 32,767 characters) into a cell. As long as the cells to the right are empty, the extra text that will not fit into the cell will overflow into the cells on the right.

Alternatively, you can use the wrap text feature to force the text label to stay within the left and right boundaries of the cell. Excel increases the height of that row to accommodate the full length of the text (in some cases, you may have to do this manually). If you turn off the wrap text feature for a cell, the text will revert back to displaying on one line. The example below demonstrates these two options.

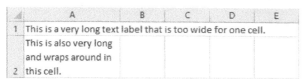

# Merging Cells

**Objective 2.2.1**

Merging cells is a feature commonly used on text labels to identify a group of cells together such as in the following example.

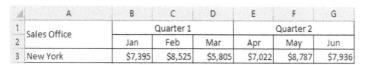

| Sales Office | Quarter 1 | | | Quarter 2 | | |
|---|---|---|---|---|---|---|
| | Jan | Feb | Mar | Apr | May | Jun |
| New York | $7,395 | $8,525 | $5,805 | $7,022 | $8,787 | $7,936 |

The months of January to March belong to Quarter 1. The months of April to June belong to Quarter 2. When you merge cells, Excel removes the edges separating the selected cells and treats the group as a single cell. It then becomes very easy to center text across these merged cells, as demonstrated in this example. You can also merge cells containing numeric and date values.

Excel offers a Merge & Center button on the Ribbon, which first merges the selected cells (whether you are merging horizontally or vertically) and then centers the text across these cells. This button actually has multiple options in it. By default, clicking it will perform the Merge & Center action, but you can click the arrow and choose any of the other options available.

The Merge Across option will only merge the selected cells, without centering the text. It will not allow you to merge cells vertically; instead, you can use the Merge Cells option to do this. In the example above, cells A1:A2 demonstrates how merging vertically is used.

If merged cells need to be split  apart again into their separate cells, simply click Merge & Center again in the Ribbon to turn it off, or select the Unmerge Cells option. Alternatively, you can also turn off the Merge cells check box in the Format Cells dialog box.

# Learn to modify cell alignment

This exercise demonstrates the most commonly used alignment options.

1    Make sure the *Travel Itinerary - Student* workbook is active on the screen.

At the top of the worksheet are two rows of text that you need to center across the width of the invoice document. To accomplish this, you will use the merge and center function.

2    Select cells **A1** to **H1**.

3    On the Home tab, in the Alignment group, click **Merge & Center**.

Notice that Excel has now merged the eight cells together and centered the title across these cells.

The merge and center function can only work on one row at a time. You will have to repeat the previous step for the next row.

4    Select cells **A2** to **H2** and on the Home tab, in the Alignment group, click **Merge & Center**.

Remember that, although you have merged cells together and therefore, centered the data contents across these cells, you entered the data in the original cell. Therefore, to make changes to those contents, you must go back to the original cell (A1 or A2).

You can force a number in a cell to align on the left.

5    Select cell **B4** and, on the Home tab, in the Alignment group, click **Align Left**.

Now align the text in some of the cells to the right.

6    Select cells **C7** to **C8** and, on the Home tab, in the Alignment group, click **Align Right**.

7    Select cells **C11** to **C12** and, on the Home tab, in the Alignment group, click **Align Right** again.

8    Select cell **E7** and hold down the CTRL key. Then select cell **E11** and release the CTRL key to select both cells.

9    On the Home tab, in the Alignment group, click **Align Right** again.

10   Select cells **G7** and **G11** using the CTRL key and, on the Home tab, in the Alignment group, click **Align Right** again.

Earlier, you tried to use the Long Date format, but there was not enough space in the cell to display it. You can now use it by merging across adjacent cells.

11   Select cell **B6** and, on the Home tab, in the Number group, click the arrow for **Number Format** and click **Long Date**.

12   Select cells **B6** to **D6** and, on the Home tab, in the Alignment group, click the arrow next to **Merge & Center.** Then click **Merge Across**.

13   On the Home tab, in the Alignment group, click **Align Left**.

14   Repeat steps 11 to 13 with cells **B10** to **D10**.

15   Select cells **B15** to **B16** and, on the Home tab, in the Alignment group, click **Align Left**.

16   With cells **B15** to **B16** still selected, on the Home tab, in the Alignment group, click **Increase Indent**.

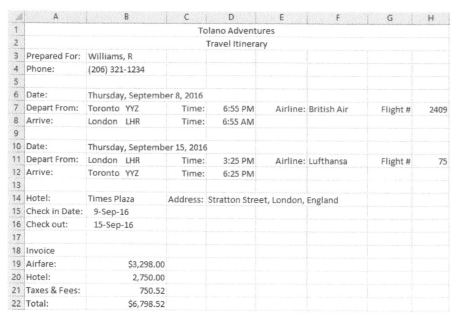

| | A | B | C | D | E | F | G | H |
|---|---|---|---|---|---|---|---|---|
| 1 | | | | Tolano Adventures | | | | |
| 2 | | | | Travel Itinerary | | | | |
| 3 | Prepared For: | Williams, R | | | | | | |
| 4 | Phone: | (206) 321-1234 | | | | | | |
| 5 | | | | | | | | |
| 6 | Date: | Thursday, September 8, 2016 | | | | | | |
| 7 | Depart From: | Toronto  YYZ | Time: | 6:55 PM | | Airline: | British Air | Flight # | 2409 |
| 8 | Arrive: | London  LHR | Time: | 6:55 AM | | | | |
| 9 | | | | | | | | |
| 10 | Date: | Thursday, September 15, 2016 | | | | | | |
| 11 | Depart From: | London  LHR | Time: | 3:25 PM | | Airline: | Lufthansa | Flight # | 75 |
| 12 | Arrive: | Toronto  YYZ | Time: | 6:25 PM | | | | |
| 13 | | | | | | | | |
| 14 | Hotel: | Times Plaza | | Address: | Stratton Street, London, England | | | |
| 15 | Check in Date: | 9-Sep-16 | | | | | | |
| 16 | Check out: | 15-Sep-16 | | | | | | |
| 17 | | | | | | | | |
| 18 | Invoice | | | | | | | |
| 19 | Airfare: | $3,298.00 | | | | | | |
| 20 | Hotel: | 2,750.00 | | | | | | |
| 21 | Taxes & Fees: | 750.52 | | | | | | |
| 22 | Total: | $6,798.52 | | | | | | |

**17** Save the worksheet.

# Changing Fonts and Sizes

### Objective 2.2.6

A font is a style of text. Changing fonts will alter how the text and numbers appear in the worksheet. As a general rule, you should not use more than three different fonts in a worksheet, as too many fonts on the worksheet can be distracting. You can apply font changes to any type of data displayed in the worksheet including numbers, text, and dates.

Generally, when you make changes to the font or size, Excel applies these changes to the entire cell or range of cells that you have selected. You can also select individual characters and numbers inside a cell and change the font or size.

To display the Font tab on the Format Cells dialog box, on the Home tab, in the Font group, click the Dialog box launcher. This tab enables you to select the many font-related formatting options available in Excel.

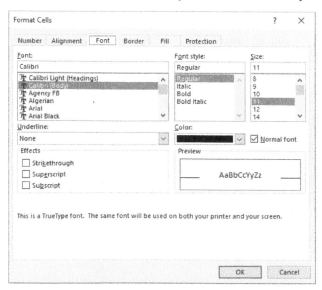

**Font** – This refers to the typeface of the text characters Excel displays. A set of characters in the same typeface is a font. A large selection of fonts is included with Microsoft Office.

**Font style** – Most fonts can be formatted bold, italicized, or both.

**Size** – Size refers to the height of a character, with a proportionate width. Most of the fonts are scalable. That is, they have a variety of sizes. A point is equal to a seventy-second of an inch. Thus, twelve-point type is twelve seventy-seconds of an inch high, or 1/6th of an inch high.

**Underline** – You can select various underline styles such as single, double, single accounting, or double accounting. Note that an underline is not the same as a cell border—if selected, the underline appears inside the cell, whereas borderlines appear along the selected edge(s) of the cell.

**Color** – You can select and change the color of the characters.

**Effects** – You can use special character effects, such as Strikethrough, Superscript and Subscript. Note that the latter two are mutually exclusive – you can use either one, but not both at the same time on the same cell.

As you select different options in this dialog box, the Preview box shows sample text with the options displayed.

The most commonly used font options (that is, font, point size, bold, italics, underline, and font color) can be changed directly on the Home tab, in the Font group of the Ribbon:

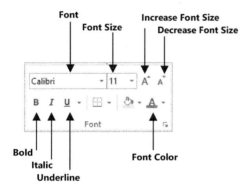

You can also select the text in editing mode to display the Mini toolbar and then click the appropriate option.

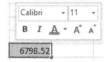

# Learn to change fonts and font styles

In this exercise, you will practice changing font options.

1    Make sure the *Travel Itinerary - Student* workbook is active on the screen.

First, change the font size and style for the document heading.

2    Select cell **A1**.

**Note:** You can actually select anywhere between A1 and H1 to select cell A1, as this whole range of cells has been merged.

3    On the Home tab, in the Font group, click the arrow next to **Font Size** and click **24**.

4    On the Home tab, in the Font group, click **Bold**.

**5**   Select cell **A2** and, on the Home tab, in the Font group, click the arrow next to **Font Size** to display the list of font sizes available.

**6**   Move the cursor down to point to various font sizes, but do not click on any of them yet.

**Note:** When you click the arrow and point to the new size (but do not click on it yet) Live Preview changes the appearance of the text.

Notice that the Live Preview feature temporarily changes the look of the active cell using the font size at which you are pointing.

**7**   Click on font size **14**.

**8**   On the Home tab, in the Font group, click **Bold**.

Live Preview does not work with the Bold, Italics, or Underline buttons.

Now bold all of the cell titles.

**9**   Select the cell range **A3** to **A22** and then, on the Home tab, in the Font group, click **Bold**.

**10**  Select all of the rest of the cell titles together by holding down the CTRL key until you have selected the last cell:

C7 to C8      Time (x 2)
C11 to C12   Time (x 2)
E7 to E11     Airline
G7 to G11     Flight #
C14           Address

**11**  On the Home tab, in the Font group, click **Bold** to bold all of these cells at the same time.

If you miss one or more cell(s), just select those cells and click the Bold button for those cells. If you accidentally bolded an incorrect cell, select those cells and click the Bold button again to reverse the setting. These formatting buttons in the Ribbon act as toggle switches to allow you to turn the feature on and off.

Now select a different font for a cell.

**Note:** Enable Live Preview by clicking **Font** on the Ribbon.

**12**  Select cell **A18** and, on the Home tab, in the Font group, click the arrow next to **Font**. Select **Arial Black**.

**13**  With cell **A18** still selected, on the Home tab, in the Font group, click the arrow next to **Font Size** and select **14**.

Now select another font for all of the data cells.

**14**  Hold down the CTRL key and click on the gray column headers for columns B, D, F, and H. Release the CTRL key.

**15**  With these columns selected, on the Home tab, in the Font group, click the arrow next to **Font** and select **Arial**.

**16**  Save the workbook.

# Applying Cell Borders

### Objective 2.2.6

Borders separate groups of data from each other to improve the readability of a worksheet, especially when it includes a large volume of numbers.

The border feature enables you to draw lines around any or all of the four edges of a cell or range of cells. The dialog box displays several presets, line thicknesses, color and style options, and allows you to specify where the lines will appear.

The Border tab in the Format Cells dialog box displays the various options and settings:

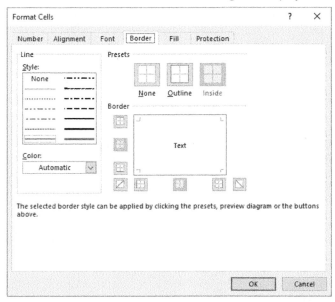

**Line** – Choose a line style or color for the border(s). If you want different lines or colors for specific borders, you have to select the style or color and then click in the Border area for the appropriate border.

**Presets** – Remove all borders, apply borders on all four outside edges or apply borders on all inside edges (only applicable when a range of cells is selected) for the selected cell or range of cells using the three preset configuration settings.

**Border** – Use the buttons to apply or remove borders on specific edges of the selected cell or range of cells. The graphics within each button help you see which borders you are applying or removing.

To apply a border, select the cell or range of cells and then use one of the following methods:

- on the Home tab, in the Cells group, click **Format**, click **Format Cells**, and click the **Border** tab, or
- on the Home tab, in the Font group, click the **Dialog box launcher** and click the **Border** tab, or
- on the Home tab, in the Font group, click the arrow for **Borders** and click **More Borders,** or
- right-click and then click **Format Cells** in the shortcut menu, and click the **Border** tab, or
- press CTRL+1 and click the **Border** tab.

These methods display the full borders options in the Format Cells dialog box.

Using the Borders button on the Ribbon is a faster method of applying borders to the selected cell(s): you can click on the button to apply the border using the current border settings for this button, or you can click the arrow for it to display a drop-down menu with commonly combined borders for a cell.

By default, when you start Excel, the Borders button on the Ribbon is set to Bottom Border. As you select different border options from the drop-down menu, the icon for the Borders button changes to show that new setting. This convenient feature allows you to minimize mouse clicks while applying borders to multiple cells throughout a worksheet.

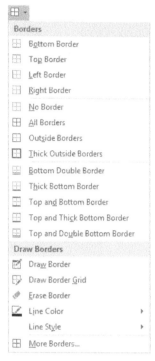

To apply a border from the Ribbon, select the cell or range of cells and then use one of the following methods:

- on the Home tab, in the Font group, click **Border** to apply the current border settings for this button, or
- right-click and then click **Border** on the Mini toolbar to apply the current border settings.

You can also select the border options from the Mini toolbar:

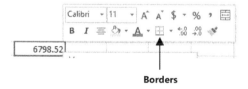

Borders

# Learn to apply borders

This exercise demonstrates how to apply borders to cells.

1   Make sure the *Travel Itinerary - Student* workbook is active on the screen.

First, place a border on all four outside edges of a range of cells.

2   Select cells **A6** to **H8**.

3   On the Home tab, in the Font group, click the arrow for **Borders** and select **Outside Borders**.

The Borders button in the Ribbon is now set to Outside Borders. Draw borders around the other two itinerary items.

4   Select cells **A10** to **H12**. On the Home tab, in the Font group, click **Outside Borders** directly from the Ribbon.

**5**   Select cells **A14** to **H16**. On the Home tab, in the Font group, click **Outside Borders** directly from the Ribbon.

Select a different border for the invoice section of the worksheet.

**6**   Select cells **A18** to **C23**.

**7**   On the Home tab, in the Font group, click the arrow for **Borders**.

**8**   Point to the **Line Color** option in the Borders menu, then click the **Dark Blue** color (second from the right) in the Standard Colors section of the menu.

**9**   On the Home tab, in the Font group, click the arrow for **Borders** again.

**10**   Point to **Line Style**, and then click the medium solid line style (sixth from the bottom).

Notice that when you select either of these two border options, the cursor changes to a pencil icon. This indicates that you can manually draw the border around any cell of your choosing. For this exercise, you want borders only around the currently selected cells. Note that with the cursor changed to a pencil icon, it appears that no cells are currently selected. However, the cells selected at step 6 are actually still selected.

**11**   On the Home tab, in the Font group, click the arrow for **Borders** once more and click **Outside Borders**.

**12**   Click in any other cell in the worksheet to see the results.

Now draw borders inside a range of cells, using the current line style and color.

**13**   Select cells **A18** to **C18**.

**14**   On the Home tab, in the Font group, click the arrow for **Borders** and select **Bottom Border**.

**15**   Select cells **A19** to **A23** and, on the Home tab, in the Font group, click the arrow for **Borders** and click **Right Border**.

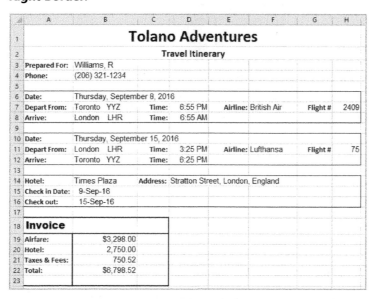

The Borders button is now set to a new style, color and position, which will continue to apply to all worksheets and workbooks until you exit Excel. Excel then resets these options back to the default settings.

**16**   On the Home tab, in the Font group, click the arrow for **Borders**.

**17**   Point to the **Line Color** option in the Borders menu and then click **Automatic**.

18  On the Home tab, in the Font group, click the arrow for **Borders** again.

19  Click **Line Style**, and then click the thin solid line style (second from the top).

20  Press ESC to deactivate the pencil, then save the workbook again.

# Using Colors and Patterns

**Objective 2.2.6**

You can also fill cells and ranges of cells with background colors to increase the visual appeal of the overall worksheet. Patterns and color can help draw a viewer's attention to particular parts of your worksheet, or serve to divide it off visually from the rest of the information. This can prove useful when trying to highlight the sum totals row or differentiate heading information from data.

Like the Borders button, the Fill Color button in the Ribbon begins with a default color (of no fill color), and then retains your last selected color until you select a new one. The Ribbon button also displays the current color setting.

If you click the arrow next to the **Fill Color** button, Excel presents a color palette which includes a No Fill option. You can choose from two sets of colors on the color palette: the bottom row of colors comprises the Standard Colors, while the Theme Colors section offers a wider range of tones based on the current selected document theme.

You can also click **More Colors** to access an even wider range of colors and tones up to the full color spectrum.

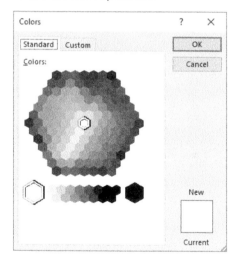
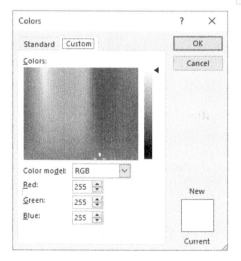

To select a fill color, select the cell or range of cells and then use one of the following methods:

*   on the Home tab, in the Font group, click the arrow for **Fill Color**, or
*   right-click the selection and, in the Mini toolbar, click the arrow for **Fill Color**.

If you click the **Fill Color** button, Excel applies the currently selected color to the selected range of cells.

In addition to filling a cell using color, you can also select different fill patterns. Excel offers several background patterns for cells. However, you should use them sparingly because the formatting can overwhelm the appearance of the worksheet. You need to open the Format Cells dialog box to access these settings.

To display the full set of options for filling a cell, select the cell or range of cells and then use one of the following methods:

- on the Home tab, in the Cells group, click **Format**, click **Format Cells**, and then click the **Fill** tab, or
- on the Home tab, in the Font group, click the **Dialog box launcher**, and then click the **Fill** tab, or
- right-click the selection, click **Format Cells**, and then click the **Fill** tab.

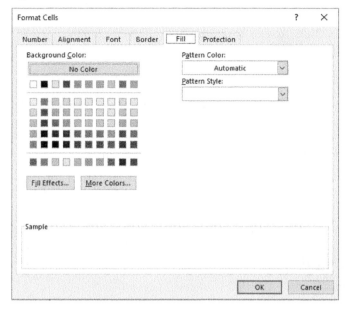

Patterns and background colors are distinctly different features. You can use either or both of them at the same time.

Dark colors and dense patterns may obscure the information in the cells. It is best to avoid them.

# Learn to apply colors and patterns

This exercise demonstrates how to apply patterns and background color to cells on a worksheet.

**1**   Make sure the *Travel Itinerary - Student* workbook is active on the screen.

Add a background color to the worksheet titles.

**2**   Select cells **A1** to **A2**.

**3**   On the Home tab, in the Font group, click the arrow for **Fill Color**.

Live Preview works with the fill colors. That is, the background of the selected cells temporarily changes to display that color until you move on to another color.

**4**   Point to various colors to see the different effects.

**5**   Click **Light Green** (fifth from the left) in the Standard Colors section of the palette.

Now add a pattern and a background color to a range of cells.

**6**   Select cells **A18** to **C23**.

**7**   On the Home tab, in the Cells group, click **Format** and then click **Format Cells**.

**8**   In the Format Cells dialog box, click the **Fill** tab and then click the **Pattern Style** arrow.

---

Pattern Style:

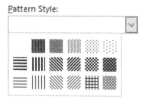

9   Click **6.25% Gray** (far right in the top row).

10  In the Background Color section, click **Blue, Accent 1, Lighter 80%** (fifth column from the left, second row from the top). Click **OK**.

Add a background color to the hotel section of the itinerary.

11  Select cells **A14** to **H16** and, on the Home tab, in the Font group, click the arrow for **Fill Color** and select **Yellow** from the Standard Colors section.

This color choice did not appear to fit with the rest of the worksheet, so remove the fill color.

12  With cells **A14** to **H16** selected, on the Home tab, in the Font group, click the arrow for **Fill Color** and then click **No Fill**.

The completed worksheet should look similar to the following example:

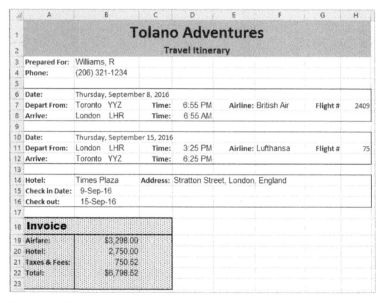

13  Save and close the workbook.

# Using the Format Painter

**Objective 2.2.3**

Once you have formatted a cell or range of cells, you may want to duplicate its formatting to the remaining parts of your worksheet. Excel provides a tool called the Format Painter that enables you to copy the cell formatting quickly from one area on the worksheet to another.

Before using the Format Painter, you must select the cell or range of cells that display the formatting you wish to copy. To activate the Format Painter, use either the one-click or the double-click method:

*   on the Home tab, in the Clipboard group, click **Format Painter** once, and then click the target cell you wish to format with the same features. The Format Painter turns off as soon as you click the target cell, or

- on the Home tab, in the Clipboard group, double-click **Format Painter** to keep the tool on while you continue applying the selected formatting to several cells. When you are finished formatting the cells, turn off the Format Painter by clicking the button again or pressing ESC.

# Learn to use the Format Painter

In this exercise, you will learn how to use the Format Painter feature.

1 Open the *RV Booking* workbook and save it as: RV Booking - Student.

Format the Invoice section first.

2 Select cells **B17** to **B20** and, on the Home tab, in the Number group, click the **Dialog box launcher**.

3 In the Number tab, select **Number** under Category, if necessary change the **Decimal places** to 2 and click the **Use 1000 Separator (,)** check box to turn it on and click **OK**.

4 On the Home tab, in the Font group, click the arrow next to **Font** and click **Arial**.

Change the first number to the currency format, and then use the Format Painter to copy the format down to the bottom number.

5 Select cell **B17** so that it is the only cell selected and, on the Home tab, in the Number group, click the **Dialog box launcher**.

6 In the Number tab, under Category, select **Currency** and click **OK**.

7 With cell **B17** still selected, on the Home tab, in the Clipboard group, click the **Format Painter** once.

The Format Painter button is now highlighted and a marquee appears around cell B17.

8 Select cell **B20** to apply the same formatting to that cell.

Notice that the Format Painter button has turned off and the marquee is no longer showing around cell B17.

Add a border for the bottom number.

9 Select cell **B20** and, on the Home tab, in the Font group, click the arrow next to the **Borders**, then click **Top and Double Bottom Border**.

Now format the field titles.

10 Select cell **A3** and, on the Home tab, in the Font group, click the arrow next to **Font**. Click **Times New Roman**.

11 With cell **A3** still selected, on the Home tab, in the Font group, click **Bold**.

The Format Painter can be set to apply the formatting to multiple sets of cells.

12 On the Home tab, in the Clipboard group, double-click **Format Painter**.

**13**  Click on each of the following cells or cell ranges to apply the same formatting:

A5 to A6
C5
A8 to A10
C9 to C10
A12 to A14
C13 to C14
A17 to A20

Now turn off the Format Painter.

**14**  On the Home tab, in the Clipboard group, click **Format Painter** again to turn it off.

Increase the font size of two cells containing text labels.

**15**  Select cell **A8** and, on the Home tab, in the Font group, click the arrow next to **Font Size**, then click **14**.

**16**  With cell **A8** still selected, on the Home tab, in the Clipboard group, click the **Format Painter** once.

**17**  Click cell **A12** to apply the same formatting there.

Now change the font for the cells containing data using the format painter.

**18**  Select cell **B3** and then, on the Home tab, in the Font group, click the arrow next to **Font**, and click **Arial**.

**19**  With cell **B3** still selected, on the Home tab, in the Clipboard group, double-click **Format Painter**.

**20**  Click on each of the following cells or cell ranges to apply the same formatting:

B5 to B6
D5
B9
D9
B13
D13

**21**  On the Home tab, in the Clipboard group, click **Format Painter** again to turn it off.

You could not use the format painter from cells containing text to cells containing dates and times—you will have to format these separately.

**22**  Select cell **B10** and change the Font to **Arial**.

**23**  Use the Format Painter to copy that format to cell **B14**.

**24**  Select cell **D10** and change the Font to **Arial**.

**25**  Use the Format Painter to copy that format to cell **D14**.

Your sheet should now look like the following:

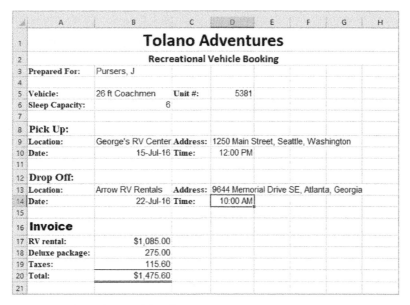

**26**   Save and close the workbook.

# Clearing Cell Contents and Formatting

The Clear feature can be used to remove the contents (or certain components that you choose) from the cell. Because you have not deleted the cell, the structure of the worksheet stays intact. You can choose from different options:

**All** – Remove all data, cell formats, and comments from the selected cell(s).

**Format** – Remove only the formatting from the selected cell(s) while the data and comments remain unchanged. Because the cell formatting reverts back to the default settings, Excel displays the data that way.

**Contents** – Remove only the data from the selected cell(s). Because the cell formatting is unchanged, any new data entered into the same cells afterward uses that formatting again.

**Comments** – Remove only the comments part of the selected cell(s).

**Hyperlinks** – Converts any hyperlinks in the selected cell(s) to text. The topic of hyperlinks will be covered in more detail in a later lesson.

In contrast, using **Delete**, found on the Home tab in the Cells group, removes the selected cells (or the entire row or column) from the worksheet. The remaining worksheet cells then shift over to replace the deleted cells.

**Hint:** A quick way to remove the contents of a cell without removing formatting is to select the cell or cells you want to clear and then use DELETE on the keyboard.

## Learn to use the Clear command

This exercise demonstrates the use of the Clear command on the three main types of data: numbers, dates, and text. To better illustrate this feature, you will use a worksheet containing random data.

**1**   Open the *Clear Formats* workbook and save as: Clear Formats - Student.

Use each of the different Clear commands to see how it affects the data.

**2** Select cells **B2** to **D2** and, on the Home tab, in the Editing group, click **Clear** and click **Clear All**.

**3** Select cells **B3** to **D3** and, on the Home tab, in the Editing group, click **Clear** and click **Clear Formats**.

**4** Select cells **B4** to **D4** and, on the Home tab, in the Editing group, click **Clear** and click **Clear Contents**.

**5** Select cells **B5** to **D5** and press DELETE.

The Clear Contents command and the DELETE key accomplish the same result.

**6** Select cells **B6** to **D6** and, on the Home tab, in the Editing group, click **Clear** and click **Clear Comments**.

By comparing row 1 to the other rows, you can see how the different clearing actions affected the cell contents.

Now re-enter different data into some of the cells.

**7** Enter the following values (do not use the copy and paste functions):

| Cell | Value |
|---|---|
| B2 | 9876.543 |
| B4 | 9876.543 |
| B5 | 9876.543 |
| C2 | Mar 1, 2016 |
| C3 | Mar 1, 2016 |
| C4 | Mar 1, 2016 |
| C5 | Mar 1, 2016 |
| D2 | label |
| D4 | label |
| D5 | label |

Notice the following:

- In rows **2** and **3**, the Clear command removes all cell formats to revert them to default.
- In cell **C3**, the date format temporarily reverts to a numeric format until replaced with a new date value, which is displayed in the default Excel date format instead of the date format that was cleared away.
- In row **2**, Excel deletes all of the original data, including formatting and the cell comment, whereas in row **3**, Excel retains all of the original data, even though the date value in cell **C3** initially looked odd.
- In both rows **4** and **5**, Excel deletes all of the original data except for the cell comments, but Excel retains the individual cell formats.
- In row **6**, Excel deletes only the cell comment.

The completed worksheet should look similar to the following example:

| | A | B | C | D |
|---|---|---|---|---|
| 1 | | 12,345.68 | June 15, 2016 | Sample text |
| 2 | | 9876.543 | 1-Mar-16 | label |
| 3 | | 12345.6789 | 1-Mar-16 | Sample text |
| 4 | | 9,876.54 | March 1, 2016 | label |
| 5 | | 9,876.54 | March 1, 2016 | label |
| 6 | | 12,345.68 | June 15, 2016 | Sample text |

**8** Save and close the workbook.

# Themes

## Using Themes

A document theme is a set of theme colors, theme fonts and display effects that you choose and apply to a document as a combination. By default, Excel (as well as Word and PowerPoint) uses the Office theme for all workbooks.

You can change the theme to any one of several built-in themes. You can also search for more themes on the Microsoft web site or you can create your own themes. To display the document themes, on the Page Layout tab, in the Themes group, click **Themes**.

Themes are very useful for creating a consistent look for all of your documents, whether they are letters, spreadsheets or slide presentations. By maintaining a consistent theme for these documents, you can create an identity that external customers, suppliers, and others can quickly recognize.

# Learn to use a theme

This exercise demonstrates how to change the theme in a workbook.

1   Open the *Monthly Sales* workbook and save as: Monthly Sales - Student.

Notice that this worksheet is already formatted with fonts, sizes and colors.

2   On the **Page Layout** tab, in the Themes group, click **Themes**.

3   Point to different theme buttons and note how the Live Preview feature changes the background and border colors on this worksheet.

**Hint:** The only colors changed on a worksheet are the ones selected from the Theme Colors section. Any colors selected from the Standard Colors section of the color palette remain unchanged when you select a different theme.

4   Click the **Metropolitan** theme.

All of the cells with the background colors are now changed to the newly selected theme.

Notice that not only the colors, but also the font changed as well. A Theme is actually a combination of a Color Theme with several colors and a Font Theme with two fonts. You can select a different color theme independently of the font.

5   On the Page Layout tab, in the Themes group, click **Colors**.

6   Point to different color themes in the drop-down list and observe the changes to the worksheet.

7   Click anywhere away from the color palette to close the drop-down list without selecting anything.

8   On the Page Layout tab, in the Themes group, click **Fonts**.

9   Point to different font selections in the drop-down list and observe the changes to the worksheet.

10  Click anywhere away from the font list to close it.

The completed workbook should look similar to the following example:

| | A | B | C | D | E | F |
|---|---|---|---|---|---|---|
| 1 | | Tolano Adventures | | | | |
| 2 | | Sales for July | | | | |
| 3 | | | | | | |
| 4 | Employee | Office | Units | Sales, Local Currency | Exchange Rate | Sales, US $ |
| 5 | Nick Klassen | New York, USA | 832 | 645,921 | 1.0000 | $645,921 |
| 6 | Madison Cowell | New York, USA | 743 | 712,732 | 1.0000 | $712,732 |
| 7 | Jamie Gibson | Cape Town, South Africa | 983 | 4,376,422 | 0.1089 | $476,592 |
| 8 | Toby Belanger | Toronto, Canada | 425 | 582,085 | 0.9868 | $574,398 |
| 9 | Andrew McSweeney | London, England | 782 | 562,493 | 1.5231 | $856,706 |
| 10 | Kanda Yamoto | Tokyo, Japan | 884 | 93,742,745 | 0.0104 | $973,237 |
| 11 | Christie Akira | Tokyo, Japan | 827 | 87,643,124 | 0.0104 | $909,911 |
| 12 | Lawrence Jang | Sydney, Australia | 542 | 651,952 | 1.0419 | $679,298 |
| 13 | Curtis Gorski | Sydney, Australia | 501 | 598,623 | 1.0419 | $623,732 |
| 14 | **Total** | | | | | **$6,452,527** |

11  Save the workbook.

# Modifying Themes

### Objective 1.3.6

Theme colors consist of four sets of text and background colors, six accent colors and two hyperlink colors. You can select any color for any of these settings, but you need to consider how they will appear when combined together.

When you modify the theme colors, the Sample pane of the Create New Theme Colors window shows your proposed changes. The left sample shows the Dark 2 background and Light 1 text combination, and the right sample shows the Light 2 background and Dark 1 text combination.

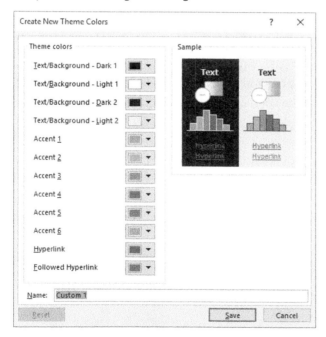

After you have made changes, save the theme colors with a name of your choice. You must also save the overall theme using a theme name of your choice.

# Learn to create a theme

This exercise demonstrates how to create a theme of your own.

**1**    Make sure the *Monthly Sales - Student* workbook is active on the screen.

**2**    On the Page Layout tab, in the Themes group, click **Colors** and then click **Customize Colors** at the bottom of the list.

**3**    Click the arrow for **Accent 1**.

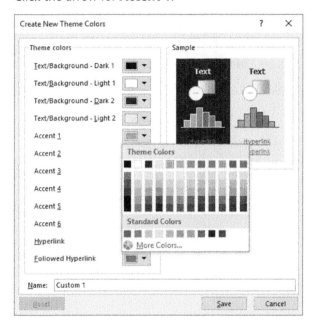

**4**    Click **More Colors** at the bottom of the color palette window.

**5**    In the Colors dialog box, click the **Standard** tab and select a bright green color of your choosing.

If the Standard tab does not contain the specific color shade that you want, you can select it from the Custom tab.

**6**    Click **OK**.

In the Sample section of the Create New Theme Colors dialog box, the left-most bar in the left and right sample bar charts are now displayed using the green color you selected.

**7**    In the **Name** field, replace the default name with: My colors.

**8**    Click **Save**.

The colors used on your worksheet now reflect your new selection.

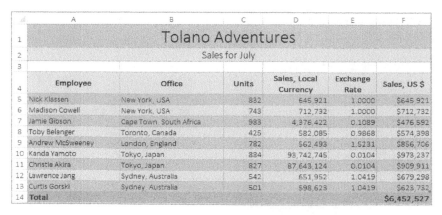

| | A | B | C | D | E | F |
|---|---|---|---|---|---|---|
| 1 | Tolano Adventures | | | | | |
| 2 | Sales for July | | | | | |
| 3 | | | | | | |
| 4 | Employee | Office | Units | Sales, Local Currency | Exchange Rate | Sales, US $ |
| 5 | Nick Klassen | New York, USA | 832 | 645,921 | 1.0000 | $645,921 |
| 6 | Madison Cowell | New York, USA | 743 | 712,732 | 1.0000 | $712,732 |
| 7 | Jamie Gibson | Cape Town, South Africa | 983 | 4,376,422 | 0.1089 | $476,592 |
| 8 | Toby Belanger | Toronto, Canada | 425 | 582,085 | 0.9868 | $574,398 |
| 9 | Andrew McSweeney | London, England | 782 | 562,493 | 1.5231 | $856,706 |
| 10 | Kanda Yamoto | Tokyo, Japan | 884 | 93,742,745 | 0.0104 | $973,237 |
| 11 | Christie Akira | Tokyo, Japan | 827 | 87,643,124 | 0.0104 | $909,911 |
| 12 | Lawrence Jang | Sydney, Australia | 542 | 651,952 | 1.0419 | $679,298 |
| 13 | Curtis Gorski | Sydney, Australia | 501 | 598,623 | 1.0419 | $623,732 |
| 14 | Total | | | | | $6,452,527 |

9   On the Page Layout tab, in the Themes group, click **Themes** and then click **Save Current Theme**.

10  In the Save Current Theme dialog box, replace the File name with: My  Theme.

11  Click **Save**.

You have now saved the new theme to this workbook. The new theme and set of theme colors are now available to all workbooks used on this computer. You can also copy them and make them available to other users.

12  On the Page Layout tab, in the Themes group, click **Themes** to display the drop-down list of all available themes.

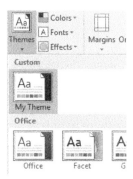

Notice your custom theme appears under the Custom heading at the top of the list of available themes.

When you no longer need your customized theme, you can delete it.

13  On the Page Layout tab, in the Themes group, click **Themes** to display the list of all available themes.

14  Right-click **My Theme** and click **Delete**.

A message box appears with the question: "Delete this theme?"

15  Click **Yes**.

16  On the Page Layout tab, in the Themes group, click **Colors** to display the list of available colors.

17  Right-click **My colors** and click **Delete**.

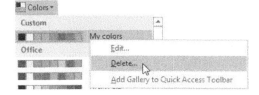

A message box appears with the question: "Delete these theme colors?"

18  Click **Yes**.

Notice that the workbook still uses the new customized color theme—until another theme is selected in the future—even though the theme has been deleted.

19  Save and close the workbook.

# Using Cell Styles

### Objective 2.2.7

You can use cell styles in Excel workbooks as a powerful formatting feature. Like Microsoft Word, a style is simply a grouping of specific format settings for a cell such as font, size, and color. Every time you apply this style to a cell, Excel formats it the same way. If the style is changed, Excel applies the changes to all cells with that style to maintain a consistent look throughout the worksheet with minimal effort.

Excel provides you with a set of prebuilt styles known as *Quick Styles* because you can access them easily from the Ribbon, on the Home tab in the Styles group:

Note the following restrictions:

- Styles are defined individually for each workbook. You cannot store them in a template file. The only way to copy any custom user-defined styles from one workbook to another is to copy the original workbook, delete any data not needed, and re-enter the data.

- If you change a style, Excel applies the changes to all cells using that style in every worksheet in that workbook.

- To see the style currently applied to a cell, you must select it and then click Cell Styles in the Ribbon. The name of the applied style will be highlighted with a border. If the cell has no style applied, the Normal style will be highlighted. Each cell must be checked individually to view the cell style assigned to it.

- Styles are based on the currently selected theme. If you change the theme or the formatting of the theme, the style also changes.

You can create new styles using one of the following three methods:

- use the formatting in a cell or cell range as an example, or

- display the Format Cells dialog box to specify the formatting, or

- merge the styles from another workbook into the current workbook.

## Learn to apply cell styles

This exercise demonstrates the cell styles feature.

1  Open the *Balance Sheet* workbook and save as: Balance Sheet - Student.

First, apply one of the built-in cell styles to a cell in the worksheet.

2  Select cell **B5**, then on the Home tab, in the Styles group, click **Cell Styles**. Alternatively, the Cell Styles button may not appear in the Ribbon; instead, a small sample of different styles with a vertical scroll bar may be displayed in its place in the Ribbon. If so, click the **More** button at the bottom of the scroll bar to see the full display of cell styles.

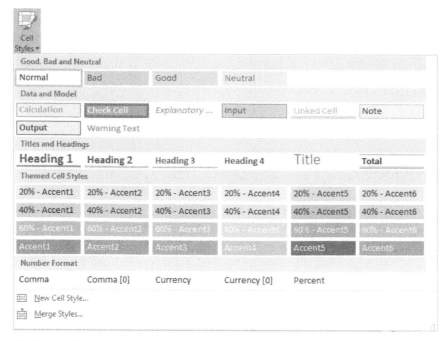

**3** Click **Heading 3** in the Titles and Headings section.

Apply this same style to another cell.

**4** Select cell **D5** and, on the Home tab, in the Styles group, click **Cell Styles** and click **Heading 3**.

**Hint:** Alternatively, you can use the Format Painter to copy a format from one cell to another.

**5** Click cell **D5** and, on the Home tab, in the Clipboard group, double-click **Format Painter.**

**6** Click on each of the following cells to copy the formatting to them: **A6**, **A13** and **A18**.

**7** On the Home tab, in the Clipboard group, click **Format Painter** to turn it off.

Set the first and last number in each cell range to the currency format with no decimal digits.

**8** Select cell **B7** and, on the Home tab, in the Styles group, click **Cell Styles**. Click **Currency [0]** in the Number Format section.

**9** Use the **Format Painter** to copy the style in cell **B7** to each of the following cells:

B11, B14, B16, B19, B21, B23
D7, D11, D14, D16, D19, D21, D23

**10** Turn off the **Format Painter**.

Set the remaining numbers in the worksheet to numeric format with commas and no decimal digits.

**11** Select cell **B8** and, on the Home tab, in the Styles group, click **Cell Styles**. Click **Comma [0]** in the Number Format section.

**12** Use the **Format Painter** to copy the style in cell **B8** to each of the following cells or cell ranges:

B9:B10, B15, B20
D8:D10, D15, D20

**13** Turn off the **Format Painter**.

Use the Total style for the totals in each major account group.

14 Select cell **B11** and, on the Home tab, in the Styles group, click **Cell Styles**. Click **Total** in the Titles and Headings section.

15 Use the **Format Painter** to copy the style in cell **B11** to each of the following cells: D11, B23 and D23.

16 Turn off the **Format Painter**.

Use the Heading 4 style for the row titles in each major account group.

17 Select cell **A11** and, on the Home tab, in the Styles group, click **Cell Styles**. Click **Heading 4** in the Titles and Headings section.

18 Use the **Format Painter** to copy the style in cell **A11** to each of the following cells: A16, A21 and A23.

19 Turn off the **Format Painter**.

The subtotal numbers need a new style with a single border at the top and bottom of the cell.

20 Select cell **B16**.

21 On the Home tab, in the Styles group, click **Cell Styles** and then click **New Cell Style**.

Excel displays the Style dialog box to allow you to create this new style. Because you had selected a cell with another style applied to it, this new style inherits the same settings. Any changes to the parent style automatically flow through to this style as well.

22 In the **Style Name** field, overtype the contents with: Subtotal.

23 Click **Format** in the Style dialog box.

Excel displays the Format Cells dialog box so that you can specify your formatting options.

24 Click the **Border** tab.

25 Click the arrow for the **Line Color**, select **Blue, Accent 1** (top row in the Theme Colors section, fifth from the left).

26 Click **Top Border** and **Bottom Border** to place the border at the top and bottom edges of the cell and click **OK**.

**Hint:** Alternatively, you can click on the top and bottom edges in the preview box.

You have now completed your formatting changes. The next step is to save the new style.

**27** Click **OK** to save and close the Style dialog box.

Apply this new style to the subtotal numbers.

**28** Select cell **B16**, then on the Home tab, in the Styles group, click **Cell Styles** and click **Subtotal** in the Custom section.

**29** Use the **Format Painter** to copy the style in cell **B16** to each of the following cells: D16, B21 and D21.

**30** Turn off the **Format Painter**.

Now see what the effect of changing themes will do to the formatting.

**31** On the **Page Layout** tab, in the Themes group, click **Themes**.

**32** Point the mouse cursor over some of the themes listed and note how the cell style changes again.

**33** Click on an empty part of the worksheet to close the Themes list.

Excel indents all the numbers a little to the left. You can change this by modifying the style.

**Note:** You do not have to select a particular cell to modify the formatting in a style—Excel does not automatically apply the style to the current cell.

**34** On the **Home** tab, in the Styles group, click **Cell Styles**, right-click **Comma [0]** and select **Modify**.

**35** Click **Format** in the Style dialog box.

Excel now displays the Format Cells dialog box to allow you to specify your formatting options.

**36** In the Format Cells dialog box, click the **Number** tab.

**37** Click **Number** in the Category list and click **-1,234** in the Negative numbers list.

**38** Click **OK** to close the Format Cells dialog box, and click **OK** to close the Style dialog box.

Notice that the change to the style affects _all_ the cells in the worksheet with that selected cell style. The numbers in cells such as B8, B9, B15, and others are now fully right-aligned. The other cells using the Currency [0] cell style are still indented a little to the left. You can change this by modifying the style as well.

**39** On the Home tab, in the Styles group, click **Cell Styles**, right-click **Currency [0]** and select **Modify**.

**40** Click **Format** in the Style dialog box.

Excel now displays the Format Cells dialog box to allow you to specify your formatting options.

**41** In the Format Cells dialog box, click the **Number** tab if necessary.

**42** Click **Currency** in the Category list, and click **-$1,234** in the Negative numbers list.

**43** Click **OK** to close the Format Cells dialog box and click **OK** to close the Style dialog box.

This change does not affect the cells using the Currency [0] style along with another style. You will have to apply that change manually.

44 Select cell **B11** and then, on Home tab, in the Styles group, click **Cell Styles** and click **Currency [0]**.

45 Use the Format Painter to copy this format to cells: B23, D11 and D23, and turn off the Format Painter.

46 Select cell **B16** and then, on Home tab, in the Styles group, click **Cell Styles** and click **Currency [0]**.

47 Use the Format Painter to copy this format to cells: B21, D16 and D21, and turn off the Format Painter.

| | A | B | C | D |
|---|---|---|---|---|
| 1 | Tolano Adventures | | | |
| 2 | Consolidated Balance Sheet | | | |
| 3 | As at June 30 | | | |
| 4 | | | | |
| 5 | | Current Year | | Previous Year |
| 6 | Assets | | | |
| 7 | Cash | $45,430 | | $44,536 |
| 8 | Customer Deposits | 85,930 | | 75,930 |
| 9 | Equipment, Net | 234,824 | | 235,924 |
| 10 | Buildings, Net | 1,927,245 | | 1,927,350 |
| 11 | Total Assets | $2,293,429 | | $2,283,740 |
| 12 | | | | |
| 13 | Liabilities | | | |
| 14 | Accounts Payable | $42,569 | | $36,096 |
| 15 | Mortgage Payable | 1,592,742 | | 1,592,850 |
| 16 | Total Liabilities | $1,635,311 | | $1,628,946 |
| 17 | | | | |
| 18 | Shareholders' Equity | | | |
| 19 | Share Capital | $100,000 | | $100,000 |
| 20 | Retained Earnings | 558,118 | | 554,794 |
| 21 | Total Shareholders' Equity | $658,118 | | $654,794 |
| 22 | | | | |
| 23 | Total Liabilities and Equity | $2,293,429 | | $2,283,740 |

48 Save and close the workbook.

# Conditional Formatting

## Using the Ribbon

**Objective 2.3.4**

You use cell formatting to enhance the visual appeal of a worksheet. However, highlighting certain cells to differentiate them from the rest of the worksheet also draws attention to them or conveys the data they contain in a visual manner.

Conditional formatting is a powerful tool you can use to display the data in cells one way for some values, but another way for others, without the additional effort of manually changing the formatting each time you modify data or add new data to a worksheet.

The Ribbon offers several choices for setting up conditional formats.

**Highlight Cell Rules** – Use this option to highlight cell values based on their relation to specific values you enter. In this example, you specified that Excel should highlight cell values of greater than 12000 with a green background, while cells with less than 9000 would be highlighted with a pink background, and cells with in-between values would be in dark yellow text with a light yellow background.

| | A | B |
|---|---|---|
| 1 | Sales By Customer, Year To Date | |
| 2 | | |
| 3 | Air Wing Fuels Inc. | 5,025.74 |
| 4 | Awesome Bikes Ltd. | 6,100.02 |
| 5 | Boat Brokerage Sales Corp. | 14,559.50 |
| 6 | Consolidated Amalgamated Corp. | 11,290.13 |
| 7 | Global Swimsuits Unlimited | 11,341.36 |
| 8 | Ecological Bicycles Ltd. | 6,346.47 |
| 9 | Exotic Flowers Inc. | 5,053.12 |
| 10 | Farley's Farm Supplies Inc. | 13,259.16 |
| 11 | Flaming Hot Skis Ltd. | 9,890.61 |
| 12 | Fraser Glen College | 10,296.38 |
| 13 | Gas Tank Wholesalers Inc. | 6,806.98 |
| 14 | Hole In The Wall Computers Inc. | 9,041.47 |
| 15 | Humongous Holdings Ltd. | 12,369.33 |
| 16 | Les's Tailors Ltd | 13,062.72 |
| 17 | Megatron Entertainment Corp. | 13,127.39 |
| 18 | Millennium Holdings Ltd. | 10,287.27 |
| 19 | Office Supplies Unlimited | 8,118.71 |
| 20 | Paint The World Ltd. | 8,628.84 |
| 21 | Pullemout Dental Suppliers Inc. | 10,020.39 |
| 22 | Sweet Stuff Manufacturing Corp. | 11,535.14 |
| 23 | The Potato Chipper Ltd. | 14,273.87 |

**Top/Bottom Rules** – Use this option to activate the conditional formatting on the top or bottom ranking cells in a range. In this example, the conditional formatting is set so that Excel highlights the top 10% of cells in red with a pink background, and the bottom 10% in dark green with a light green background. There are 21 cells selected in the range, so 10% is 2 cells each. If the range comprises 50 cells, the top and bottom 10% would be 5 cells each.

You can choose to highlight any percentage of cells for conditional formatting.

| | A | B |
|---|---|---|
| 1 | Sales By Customer, Year To Date | |
| 2 | | |
| 3 | Air Wing Fuels Inc. | 5,025.74 |
| 4 | Awesome Bikes Ltd. | 6,100.02 |
| 5 | Boat Brokerage Sales Corp. | 14,559.50 |
| 6 | Consolidated Amalgamated Corp. | 11,290.13 |
| 7 | Global Swimsuits Unlimited | 11,341.36 |
| 8 | Ecological Bicycles Ltd. | 6,346.47 |
| 9 | Exotic Flowers Inc. | 5,053.12 |
| 10 | Farley's Farm Supplies Inc. | 13,259.16 |
| 11 | Flaming Hot Skis Ltd. | 9,890.61 |
| 12 | Fraser Glen College | 10,296.38 |
| 13 | Gas Tank Wholesalers Inc. | 6,806.98 |
| 14 | Hole In The Wall Computers Inc. | 9,041.47 |
| 15 | Humongous Holdings Ltd. | 12,369.33 |
| 16 | Les's Tailors Ltd | 13,062.72 |
| 17 | Megatron Entertainment Corp. | 13,127.39 |
| 18 | Millennium Holdings Ltd. | 10,287.27 |
| 19 | Office Supplies Unlimited | 8,118.71 |
| 20 | Paint The World Ltd. | 8,628.84 |
| 21 | Pullemout Dental Suppliers Inc. | 10,020.39 |
| 22 | Sweet Stuff Manufacturing Corp. | 11,535.14 |
| 23 | The Potato Chipper Ltd. | 14,273.87 |

**Data Bars** – You can use conditional formatting to embed a bar chart into a selected range of cells based on the value in each cell.

This type of formatting offers a quick visual representation of each cell value in relation to the others.

| | A | B |
|---|---|---|
| 1 | Sales By Customer, Year To Date | |
| 2 | | |
| 3 | Air Wing Fuels Inc. | 5,025.74 |
| 4 | Awesome Bikes Ltd. | 6,100.02 |
| 5 | Boat Brokerage Sales Corp. | 14,559.50 |
| 6 | Consolidated Amalgamated Corp. | 11,290.13 |
| 7 | Global Swimsuits Unlimited | 11,341.36 |
| 8 | Ecological Bicycles Ltd. | 6,346.47 |
| 9 | Exotic Flowers Inc. | 5,053.12 |
| 10 | Farley's Farm Supplies Inc. | 13,259.16 |
| 11 | Flaming Hot Skis Ltd. | 9,890.61 |
| 12 | Fraser Glen College | 10,296.38 |
| 13 | Gas Tank Wholesalers Inc. | 6,806.98 |
| 14 | Hole In The Wall Computers Inc. | 9,041.47 |
| 15 | Humongous Holdings Ltd. | 12,369.33 |
| 16 | Les's Tailors Ltd | 13,062.72 |
| 17 | Megatron Entertainment Corp. | 13,127.39 |
| 18 | Millennium Holdings Ltd. | 10,287.27 |
| 19 | Office Supplies Unlimited | 8,118.71 |
| 20 | Paint The World Ltd. | 8,628.84 |
| 21 | Pullemout Dental Suppliers Inc. | 10,020.39 |
| 22 | Sweet Stuff Manufacturing Corp. | 11,535.14 |
| 23 | The Potato Chipper Ltd. | 14,273.87 |

**Color Scales** – Use this type of conditional formatting to show the relative value of each cell to each other cell using color gradients. This example shows the red-yellow-green option, with the lowest value highlighted with dark red, dark green for the highest value and yellow for the middle values.

| | A | B |
|---|---|---|
| 1 | Sales By Customer, Year To Date | |
| 2 | | |
| 3 | Air Wing Fuels Inc. | 5,025.74 |
| 4 | Awesome Bikes Ltd. | 6,100.02 |
| 5 | Boat Brokerage Sales Corp. | 14,559.50 |
| 6 | Consolidated Amalgamated Corp. | 11,290.13 |
| 7 | Global Swimsuits Unlimited | 11,341.36 |
| 8 | Ecological Bicycles Ltd. | 6,346.47 |
| 9 | Exotic Flowers Inc. | 5,053.12 |
| 10 | Farley's Farm Supplies Inc. | 13,259.16 |
| 11 | Flaming Hot Skis Ltd. | 9,890.61 |
| 12 | Fraser Glen College | 10,296.38 |
| 13 | Gas Tank Wholesalers Inc. | 6,806.98 |
| 14 | Hole In The Wall Computers Inc. | 9,041.47 |
| 15 | Humongous Holdings Ltd. | 12,369.33 |
| 16 | Les's Tailors Ltd | 13,062.72 |
| 17 | Megatron Entertainment Corp. | 13,127.39 |
| 18 | Millennium Holdings Ltd. | 10,287.27 |
| 19 | Office Supplies Unlimited | 8,118.71 |
| 20 | Paint The World Ltd. | 8,628.84 |
| 21 | Pullemout Dental Suppliers Inc. | 10,020.39 |
| 22 | Sweet Stuff Manufacturing Corp. | 11,535.14 |
| 23 | The Potato Chipper Ltd. | 14,273.87 |

**Icon Sets** – You can use this type of conditional formatting to highlight values using icons. In this example, a 5-bar strength meter (similar to the wireless network strength indicator on mobile computers and devices) indicates the relative value of each cell to all other cells in the range. The cells with the lowest values have no bars filled, while the highest values have all bars filled.

In all of these examples, you see the same conditional format applied to the entire cell range. If you change a value in any of these cells, the conditional format is automatically re-evaluated and the highlighting may change.

A cell may have both a manual format and a conditional format. If the cell contains a value that does not meet any of the specified conditions, the cell uses the manual format.

| | A | | B |
|---|---|---|---|
| 1 | Sales By Customer, Year To Date | | |
| 2 | | | |
| 3 | Air Wing Fuels Inc. | | 5,025.74 |
| 4 | Awesome Bikes Ltd. | | 6,100.02 |
| 5 | Boat Brokerage Sales Corp. | | 14,559.50 |
| 6 | Consolidated Amalgamated Corp. | | 11,290.13 |
| 7 | Global Swimsuits Unlimited | | 11,341.36 |
| 8 | Ecological Bicycles Ltd. | | 6,346.47 |
| 9 | Exotic Flowers Inc. | | 5,053.12 |
| 10 | Farley's Farm Supplies Inc. | | 13,259.16 |
| 11 | Flaming Hot Skis Ltd. | | 9,890.61 |
| 12 | Fraser Glen College | | 10,296.38 |
| 13 | Gas Tank Wholesalers Inc. | | 6,806.98 |
| 14 | Hole In The Wall Computers Inc. | | 9,041.47 |
| 15 | Humongous Holdings Ltd. | | 12,369.33 |
| 16 | Les's Tailors Ltd | | 13,062.72 |
| 17 | Megatron Entertainment Corp. | | 13,127.39 |
| 18 | Millennium Holdings Ltd. | | 10,287.27 |
| 19 | Office Supplies Unlimited | | 8,118.71 |
| 20 | Paint The World Ltd. | | 8,628.84 |
| 21 | Pullemout Dental Suppliers Inc. | | 10,020.39 |
| 22 | Sweet Stuff Manufacturing Corp. | | 11,535.14 |
| 23 | The Potato Chipper Ltd. | | 14,273.87 |

Formatting options include only the font styles (regular, bold, italics, or bold and italics), font colors, borders and background fill colors and patterns. You may not choose different font names or font sizes in a conditional format.

# Learn to apply conditional formatting

This exercise demonstrates how to apply conditional formats to a range of cells.

You have been asked to prepare a report for your manager, identifying your best corporate customers based on the amount of sales this year. In addition, you need to identify mid-level corporate customers because the Marketing department may want to work closely with them during the latter half of the year.

You will identify the best customers as having generated more than $12,000 of sales this year, and the mid-level customers as having generated more than $9,000 but less than $12,000.

**1** Open the *Sales By Customer* workbook and save as: Sales By Customer - Student.

Add a conditional format to identify the mid-level customers.

**2** Select cells **B3:B23**. On the Home tab, in the Styles group, click **Conditional Formatting**.

---

**3** Click **Highlight Cells Rules** and then click **Between**.

**4** In the Between dialog box, replace the value in the left-most text box with: 9000.

**5** Press **TAB** and replace the value in that text box with: 12000.

**6** Click the arrow for the right-most list box and click **Yellow Fill with Dark Yellow Text**.

**7** Click **OK**.

Now add another conditional format to identify the best customers.

**8** With cells **B3:B23** still highlighted, on the Home tab, in the Styles group, click **Conditional Formatting**, click **Highlight Cell Rules** and click **Greater Than**.

**9** In the Greater Than dialog box, replace the value on the left with: 12000.

**10** Click the arrow for the right-most list box and click **Custom Format**.

Excel displays the Format Cells dialog box to allow you to select from a wide variety of formatting options.

**11** Click the **Fill** tab.

**12** Click the light green color (fifth from the left, bottom row) in the Background Color section and click **OK**.

**13** Click **OK** in the Greater Than dialog box.

**14** Click in an empty cell outside of the cell range to view the data.

Now observe what happens when you change data values. Assume that two of the cell values are incorrect.

**15** Select cell **B3** and enter: 13,000.

**16** Select cell **B10** and enter: 2,000.

Even though the formatting has not changed for any of these cells, the highlighting has changed based on the new cell values.

**17** Save the workbook.

# Using the Rules Manager

### Objective 2.3.4

When you use the Ribbon to set up conditional formatting in your worksheet, Excel creates the conditional formatting rules in the background.

You can use the Rules Manager directly to create new rules that are more customized to your needs. The Rules Manager can also be used to modify existing rules or delete rules that are no longer needed.

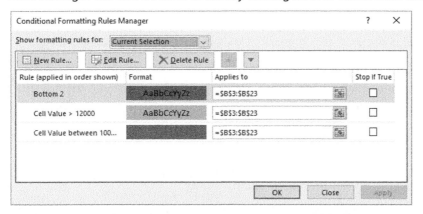

## Learn to use the Rules Manager

This exercise demonstrates how to add, modify, and delete conditional formats for a range of cells using the Rules Manager.

**1** Make sure the *Sales By Customer - Student* workbook is active on the screen.

Use the Rules Manager to display the existing conditional formatting rules.

**2** Select cells **B3:B23**.

**3** On the Home tab, in the Styles group, click **Conditional Formatting**, and click **Manage Rules**.

Change one of the existing conditional formatting rules.

**4** Click on the bottom rule (**Cell Value between 9000 and 12000**) to select it, then click **Edit Rule**.

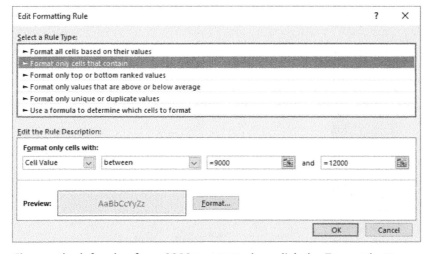

**5** Change the left value from 9000 to 10000, then click the **Format** button.

The Format Cells dialog box is displayed. Use this dialog box to make changes to the cell formatting.

**6** Click the **Fill** tab, then select blue (third from the right in the Standard Colors section) as the fill color, and click **OK**.

**7** In the Edit Formatting Rule dialog box, click **OK** to close it.

**8** In the Conditional Formatting Rules Manager dialog box, click **Apply** to see the changes take effect on the worksheet.

Add a new conditional formatting rule using the Rules Manager.

**9** In the Conditional Formatting Rules Manager dialog box, click **New Rule**.

**10** In the New Formatting Rule dialog box, click on each of the options in the **Select a Rule Type** section and observe the options available in the lower half of the dialog box.

**11** Select the **Format only top or bottom ranked values** option, then select **Bottom 2** (do not choose **% of the selected range**) in the Edit the Rule Description section.

**12** Click **Format**, click the **Fill** tab and select dark red (far left) in the Standard Colors section. Click **OK**.

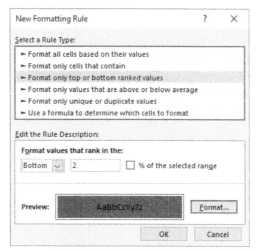

**13** Click **OK** to close the New Formatting Rule dialog box, and click **OK** to close the Conditional Formatting Rules Manager dialog box.

**14** Click on an empty cell to view the worksheet data.

Delete one of the formatting rules using the Rules Manager dialog box.

**15** Select cells **B3:B23**, then on the Home tab, in the Styles group, click **Conditional Formatting**, and click **Manage Rules**.

**16** Select the bottom rule (Cell Value between 10000 and 12000), and click **Delete Rule**.

**17** Click **OK** in the Conditional Formatting Rules Manager dialog box.

**18** Save and close the workbook.

# Lesson Summary

Now that you have completed this lesson, you should be able to:

☑ format numbers and decimal places

☑ change the alignment of cell contents

☑ merge and wrap cells

☑ change fonts and font size

☑ apply borders around cells

☑ apply background colors and patterns to cells

☑ use the Format Painter

☑ clear cell contents and formatting

☑ apply and modify themes

☑ apply and modify cell styles

☑ apply conditional formatting

# Review Questions

1.  Which feature temporarily changes the appearance of selected cell(s) to the format that your mouse is currently pointing to on the Ribbon?

    a.  Live Preview

    b.  Gallery View

    c.  Format Manager

    d.  Format Painter

2.  Which number format does not allow you to control how negative numbers display?

    a.  Currency

    b.  Accounting

    c.  Fixed

    d.  Custom

3.  When the alignment is set to General, text values align to the _____ in a cell.

    a.  Right

    b.  Left

    c.  Center

    d.  Top

4.  When the alignment is set to General, numeric, date and time values align to the _____ in a cell.

    a.  Right

    b.  Left

    c.  Center

    d.  Top

5. What is the difference between clicking the Format Painter once and clicking it twice?

   a. When you click it once, you can apply formatting attributes to only one other cell or cell range, whereas when you click it twice, you replace the contents of the target cell with the contents of the source cell.

   b. When you click it once, you can apply formatting attributes to only one other cell or cell range, whereas when you click it twice, you clear all the formatting from the target cell or cell range.

   c. When you click it once, you clear the formatting attributes of the cell, whereas when you click it twice, you restore the formatting attributes of the cell to their original state.

   d. When you click it once, you can apply the formatting attributes to only one other cell or range, whereas when you click it twice, you can apply the formatting attributes to as many cells or cell ranges as you want until you turn it off.

6. Carol has inherited a large worksheet which contains accurate data, but the data has been entered in various fonts, colors, and alignments. Carol's manager has asked her to give the worksheet a more business-like appearance – one or two typefaces is okay, and so are a few colors, but they need to be more unified. Her manager has asked Carol to complete this task in ten minutes so that the worksheet will be ready for an upcoming meeting. What should Carol do?

   a. Clear all existing formatting and then apply a theme to the worksheet.

   b. Clear all existing formatting and then apply a few attributes using the Format Painter.

   c. Tell her manager that it is not possible to complete the task within ten minutes.

   d. Use the Paste Special command to copy only the cell contents to a new, blank worksheet.

7. A group of cell format settings (such as font, size and color) which can be applied to a cell is called a(n):

   a. Cell group

   c. Cell style

   b. Format group

   d. Format tab

8. Ed has created a worksheet of sales projections, and the numbers change daily. He would like all projected sales figures over 25,000 to display in purple. What is the easiest way to accomplish this?

   a. Apply conditional formatting to the projected sales figures.

   b. Sort the range of sales figures every day to see which are the highest, then apply formatting manually.

   c. There is no easy way; Ed must look at each figure and manually apply formatting as appropriate.

   d. Use the AutoFilter feature to only display sales over 25,000 and manually apply formatting to these rows.

Microsoft®

# Excel 2016
Core Certification Guide

# Lesson 5: Viewing and Printing Workbooks

## Lesson Objectives

In this lesson, you will learn how to change the views in preparation for printing worksheets, print and preview worksheets and customize the page setup for printing worksheets. Upon completion, you should be able to:

☐ create worksheet windows

☐ arrange worksheet windows

☐ split panes

☐ freeze panes

☐ zoom in and out of worksheets

☐ print and preview worksheets

☐ use different workbook views

☐ add and preview page breaks

☐ change printing margins, orientation, paper size and scale

☐ print column and row titles or selected ranges of cells

☐ add and modify headers and footers

☐ print selected worksheets

## Changing Worksheet Views

Worksheets can become very large with a lot of data. On the other hand, computer monitors can vary in size from small netbooks with 10 inches to large desktops with 24 inches (measured diagonally) or more. The newer monitors have very good screen resolution to enable you to view large worksheets even on the smaller monitors.

Nevertheless, you will have many situations when you need to work with worksheets that are much larger than your monitor, even if your monitor is 24 inches in size. To overcome this limitation, Excel provides you with the ability to change how Excel displays the worksheet. If you are doing some "What-if" evaluations, for example, you may want to see distant parts of a large worksheet on the screen at the same time. On the other hand, you may wish to have more than one workbook on the screen to cut and paste from one worksheet to another. Alternatively, you may experience difficulty working on your large worksheet because you cannot see the row and column headings when making entries.

The View tab offers a number of tools to facilitate different ways of viewing your worksheet:

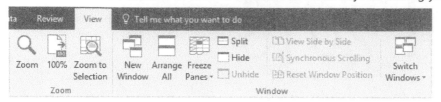

**Zoom** – Change the magnification percentage to zoom closer or further away from the worksheet.

**100%** – Force the zoom back to 100% immediately.

**Zoom to Selection** – Zoom into the selected block of cells on the worksheet.

**New Window** – Create a new window containing a copy of the workbook.

**Arrange All** – Arrange all of the windows on the screen in one of several layouts: tiled, horizontal, vertical, or cascade.

**Freeze Panes** – Lock in place the rows above and the columns to the left of a selected cell while you scroll in the worksheet. This option is useful to keep the headings on the screen when you are working in cells remote from those headings.

**Split** – Split the worksheet into two or four panes.

**Hide** – Hide the active window from the screen. This is useful when you are working with multiple windows and you want Excel to display only specific windows.

**Unhide** – Display a dialog box listing the windows you have hidden so that you can select individual windows and redisplay them.

**View Side by Side** – Place two open workbooks side by side in the Excel document window. You can place the two side by side in a vertical or horizontal position.

**Synchronous Scrolling** – Scroll through the worksheets in each pane simultaneously.

**Reset Window Position** – Reset the displayed worksheets to equal sizes.

**Switch Windows** – Present a list of the documents currently open in Excel. You can then bring a workbook to the front by clicking on it.

Even though you may have multiple workbooks open at the same time, only one workbook can be active at a time. That is, you can only work on one workbook at a time. If you need to update two of them at essentially the same time, you must switch back and forth between workbooks to do the entries.

To increase the amount of display area available to view all of your document windows, you can also minimize the Ribbon temporarily.

# Creating and Arranging Worksheet Windows

**Objective 1.4.5**

The New Window button enables you to open another view of the active workbook. You can then arrange the workbook windows to view different parts of the workbook (either the same worksheet, or different worksheets of the same workbook) at the same time without having to scroll around the worksheet continuously to view cells that are far from each other.

For example, you may want to do some "What-if" evaluations on a workbook. These evaluations may require that you make changes at the top of your worksheet while you view the effects on the totals at the bottom of the worksheet. Using at least two windows on the same workbook facilitates this process.

Every open workbook will have its own window in the Excel screen. If you use the New Window feature to create a second (or more) view of any of the workbooks, you will quickly run out of available space on the screen to display all of these windows.

The Arrange All button in the Ribbon enables you to quickly reposition all open workbook views on the screen at the same time. When arranging the windows on the screen, you can choose from several options:

**Tiled** – Re-arrange worksheet windows on the screen so that all windows are as square as possible and positioned next to each other.

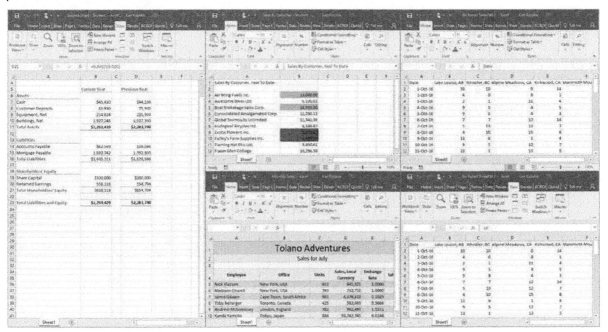

**Horizontal** – Re-arrange worksheet windows on the screen so that each window stretches across the entire width of the Excel screen. Excel lays them horizontally so that you can see as many columns as possible in each worksheet.

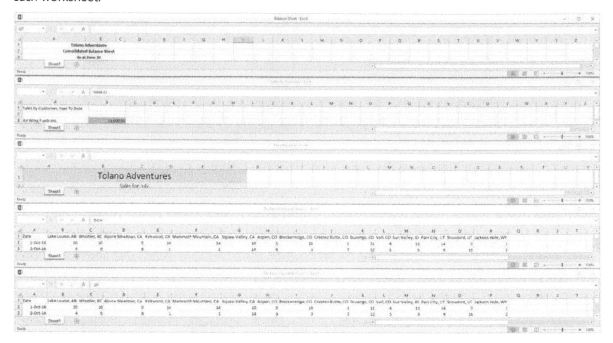

**Vertical** – Re-arrange worksheet windows on the screen so that each window stretches from the top to the bottom of the Excel screen. Excel lines up these windows vertically so that you can see as many rows as possible in each worksheet.

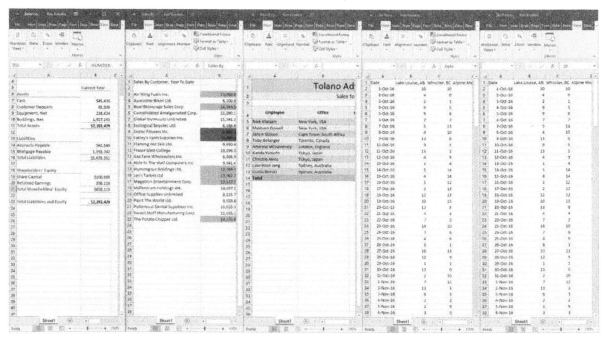

**Cascade** – Re-arrange worksheets so that each one is on top of the next and slightly offset to give you a three-dimensional view of all open workbooks. This kind of arrangement is best when you do not want to reduce the size of each worksheet window, and you can flip between the open windows as needed.

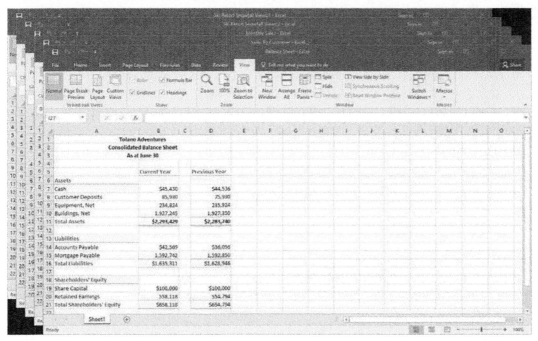

In all of these view options, the active workbook is the one with the thin green border around the window edges and the workbook's filename displayed in bright white in the title bar. The other open workbooks have the workbook name displayed in a lighter shade of gray in the title bar, and the border around the window edges is light gray.

There is no limit to the number of Excel windows open at the same time, however, the size of your computer monitor will limit how many – and how much of each – you can view at the same time. Another way to work around this problem is to connect a second (or more) monitor and extend your Windows display across to it.

# Learn to use multiple workbooks

In this exercise, you will practice creating another window for a workbook, moving between workbooks and arranging workbooks.

1   Open the *Ski Resort Snowfall* workbook.

2   On the View tab, in the Window group, click **New Window**.

Note that if the workbook was maximized to the full screen, nothing seems to happen when you select this option. But if you take a closer look at the title bar, the workbook is now identified as *Ski Resort Snowfall2*. At the same time, you will notice that the Excel taskbar icon now shows a shadow, indicating that there are two workbooks currently open.

The original window is still open and identified as *Ski Resort Snowfall1*. If the original workbook was displayed as a window, then the second copy will appear as another workbook window in front of – and offset a little to the right and down from – the original one.

You can change the arrangement of these windows to view both at the same time.

**3**   On the View tab, in the Window group, click **Arrange All**.

Excel displays the Arrange Windows dialog box.

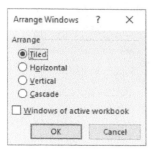

**4**   With the Tiled option selected, click **OK**.

Excel arranges the two workbook windows on your screen side by side. If you had more than two windows or had other files open, Excel would tile them in several same-sized rectangles.

In this exercise, both of these workbooks appear identical on the screen, but only one of them is the active one. The active window is the one with the workbook name displayed in bright white in the title bar. The inactive window(s) display the workbook name in a light gray color.

Both of these windows are views of the same workbook. If you change a cell value in one window, the view in the other window is updated at the same time.

**5**   Select cell **B3**, and enter: 5

You can move around the worksheet in each of these windows independently of each other, allowing you to view different parts of the same worksheet (or even different worksheets) at the same time.

**6**   Drag the horizontal scroll bar of the active window (the one on the left) to move to the right of the worksheet.

**7**   Click anywhere in the other window to make it the active worksheet.

**8**   Drag the vertical scroll bar to move down the worksheet.

This demonstrates that you can scroll through the two windows independently of each other, even though they are both showing the same worksheet.

**9**   Close all of the workbook windows and discard all changes made to the workbook.

## Splitting Panes

### Objective 1.4.5

The split feature enables you to have just one instance of your workbook open, but be able to view the current active worksheet using two or four window panes. In each of the split window views, you can move around to see different (or even the same) parts of the worksheet without having to continuously shift from one end of the worksheet to the other, or move rows and columns around to see the related data closer together. The operation is similar to using four different cameras simultaneously, with the ability to manipulate each one semi-independently of one another – you can point to any part of the worksheet whether they are close or far away from each other.

On the View tab, in the Window group, click **Split** to split the worksheet:

- into two horizontal panes if the active cell is in column A, and the split will be just above this row, or

- into two vertical panes if the active cell is in row 1, and the split will be to the immediate left of this column, or

- into four panes if the active cell is any other cell, and the worksheet will split into four panes immediately above and on the left of this cell.

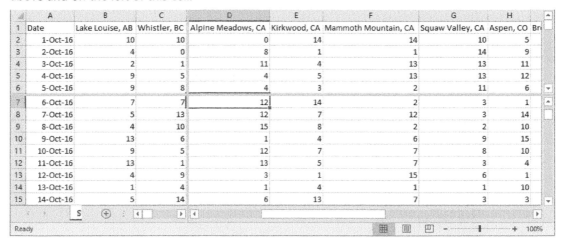

After splitting the window, the split will stay at that location even as you move around the worksheet. The panes will scroll if you try to move to a cell outside of the current window.

You can only alter the position of either the horizontal or vertical split bar by using the mouse. To move a split bar, position your mouse pointer over the bar. When the double-headed arrow appears, press and hold the mouse button and move the bar to the new location.

To remove the split:

- click the **Split** button in the Ribbon again to remove both split bars, or

- drag the vertical split bar to the far left or far right of the worksheet, or

- drag the horizontal split bar to the top or bottom of the worksheet, or

- double-click on either of the split bars.

# Learn to split panes

In this exercise, you will use the split bars to view separate parts of a worksheet.

1   Open the *Ski Resort Snowfall* workbook and save it as: Ski Resort Snowfall - Student.

2   Select cell **D7**.

3   On the View tab, in the Window group, click **Split**.

4   Drag the horizontal split bar down so that it is in the middle of the screen.

5   Use the vertical scroll bar in the upper right pane to scroll down the worksheet.

    Notice how the upper two panes in the window scroll down together.

6   Drag the horizontal scroll bar in the bottom left and bottom right panes to observe how the windows change.

Notice how the two panes in the window scroll left or right together.

7   Drag the scroll bars so that cell **H10** is visible in the middle of each of the four panes.

8   Select cell **H10** in any one of the panes.

9   Type: 9 to begin entering this value into cell H10.

The worksheet should now appear as shown in the following example:

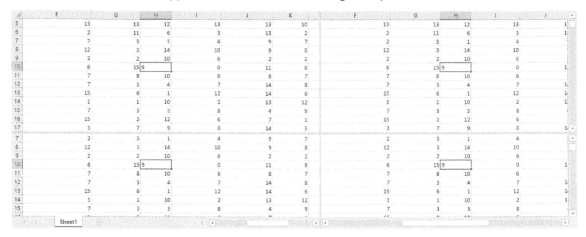

10  Press ENTER to save the new value into cell H10.

11  On the View tab, in the Window group, click **Split** to remove the split bars.

12  Save the workbook.

## Freezing Panes

**Objective 1.4.5**

As your worksheet grows in size, it will become increasingly difficult to view all of the data on the screen at the same time. More importantly, you will reach a point when you can no longer keep the row and column headings on the screen as you scroll down or across your large worksheet. It can become difficult to determine, for example, whether you are entering data in the February or March column, or in the Taxes or Travel row. To help you overcome this, Excel allows you to lock the titles on the screen while you scroll to a remote part of the worksheet.

Freezing panes refers to the feature that enables you to lock the top row(s) or left-most column(s). This feature provides you with three options from which to choose:

**Note:** Excel does not allow you to freeze and split panes at the same time.

**Freeze Panes** – In this option, the active cell serves as an anchor—when the feature is activated, all rows above and all columns to the left of the active cell remain in view until the feature is turned off. You may freeze more than one row or column in place. You can also freeze just the top row(s) or just the leftmost column(s).

**Freeze Top Row** – When you select this option, the selection of the active cell is not important. Excel will always freeze only the one row currently displayed at the top of the worksheet window. Note that if the top row currently displayed on the screen is not row 1 (for example, row 20), Excel will freeze that row, even though your column titles may be in row 1.

**Freeze First Column** – When you select this option, the selection of the active cell is not important. Excel will always freeze only the one column currently displayed at the far left of the worksheet window. Like the Freeze Top Row option, be sure to verify that the left column currently displayed is the correct one to freeze.

When freezing panes using the current cell, Excel locks *all* rows above and *all* columns to the left so that they will not move. Therefore, you should not freeze a block of rows and columns in the middle of the worksheet as you will not have much space to move the rest of your worksheet.

# Learn to freeze panes

In this exercise, you will practice freezing panes.

1   Make sure the *Ski Resort Snowfall - Student* workbook is active on the screen.

2   Select cell **B2**.

3   On the View tab, in the Window group, click **Freeze Panes**, and then click **Freeze Panes**.

4   Scroll to the right of the worksheet so that columns **M** and **N** are displayed.

Note that the dates in column **A** remain in view.

5   Scroll down the worksheet.

Note that row **1** remains in place.

The worksheet should now appear as shown in the following example:

| | A | J | K | L | M | N | O | P |
|---|---|---|---|---|---|---|---|---|
| 1 | Date | Crested Butte, CO | Durango, CO | Vail, CO | Sun Valley, ID | Park City, UT | Snowbird, UT | Jackson Hole, WY |
| 29 | 28-Oct-16 | 1 | 0 | 5 | 1 | 14 | 3 | 14 |
| 30 | 29-Oct-16 | 10 | 13 | 7 | 7 | 3 | 14 | 11 |
| 31 | 30-Oct-16 | 13 | 12 | 5 | 5 | 7 | 13 | 11 |
| 32 | 31-Oct-16 | 10 | 13 | 4 | 11 | 14 | 14 | 11 |
| 33 | 1-Nov-16 | 9 | 5 | 3 | 1 | 2 | 10 | 1 |
| 34 | 2-Nov-16 | 11 | 2 | 7 | 9 | 6 | 2 | 13 |
| 35 | 3-Nov-16 | 6 | 6 | 13 | 6 | 8 | 4 | 13 |
| 36 | 4-Nov-16 | 11 | 3 | 5 | 6 | 11 | 13 | 5 |
| 37 | 5-Nov-16 | 14 | 3 | 11 | 11 | 13 | 8 | 13 |
| 38 | 6-Nov-16 | 4 | 1 | 8 | 9 | 1 | 13 | 9 |
| 39 | 7-Nov-16 | 2 | 10 | 12 | 10 | 13 | 2 | 13 |
| 40 | 8-Nov-16 | 10 | 12 | 11 | 5 | 1 | 2 | 11 |
| 41 | 9-Nov-16 | 13 | 5 | 7 | 14 | 14 | 9 | 12 |
| 42 | 10-Nov-16 | 9 | 11 | 8 | 13 | 8 | 2 | 5 |

If you need to change the location of the titles, unfreeze the panes, relocate the cell marker and then freeze the panes again.

6   On the View tab, in the Window group, click **Freeze Panes** and then click **Unfreeze Panes**.

7   Select cell **D6**.

8   On the View tab, in the Window group, click **Freeze Panes**, and then click **Freeze Panes**.

9   Scroll to the right of the worksheet so that columns **M** and **N** are displayed.

Notice that the top 5 rows and the 3 left-most columns remain locked while you scroll around the worksheet.

10  On the View tab, in the Window group, click **Freeze Panes** and then click **Unfreeze Panes**.

11  Save the workbook.

## Changing the Zoom

**Objective 1.4.7**

The Zoom feature changes the display magnification of the worksheet on the screen. A higher magnification level is useful for looking at small objects close up or to highlight an area. A lower magnification level helps you to see the format and structure of the overall worksheet.

Several preset magnification levels are available using one of the following methods:

- on the View tab, in the Zoom group, click the appropriate zoom option, or

- on the Status bar, click **Zoom Out** or **Zoom In**, or drag the Zoom slider to the desired zoom percentage.

Alternatively, you can launch the Zoom dialog box - which enables you to select different magnification levels – using one of the following methods:

- on the View tab, in the Zoom group, click **Zoom,** or

- on the Status bar, click **Zoom Level**.

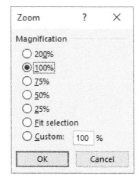

A quick way of having Excel calculate the right zoom level is to use the **Fit selection** option: select a range of cells and this option will magnify this group to fill the window.

You can also type a value in the **Custom** box if you want a different percentage than what is listed in the Zoom dialog box.

## Learn to change the zoom

In this exercise, you will practice changing the zoom setting for the worksheet.

1  Make sure the *Ski Resort Snowfall - Student* workbook is active on the screen.

Select a magnification level to see more of the worksheet.

2  On the View tab, in the Zoom group, click **Zoom**.

3  In the Zoom dialog box, click **50%** and then click **OK**.

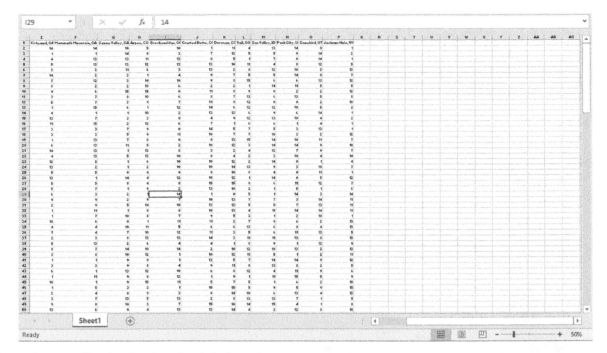

Reset the magnification level to the default setting.

**4**  On the Status bar, click **Zoom level**, click **100%** and then click **OK**.

**Hint:** You can also quickly set the zoom to 100%: on the View tab, in the Zoom group, click **100%**.

Choose a block of cells and zoom into that block.

**5**  Select cells **E17** to **G23**. On the View tab, in the Zoom group, click **Zoom to Selection**.

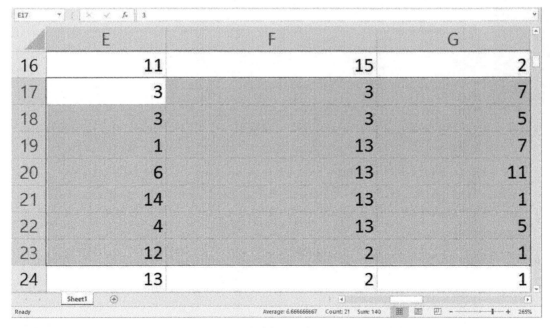

**6**  On the View tab, in the Zoom group, click **100%**.

**7**  Save the workbook.

# Printing and Previewing the Workbook

To print your workbook, use one of the following methods:

- click **File** and then click **Print,** or

- press CTRL+P.

Excel will display the Print pane in the Office Backstage:

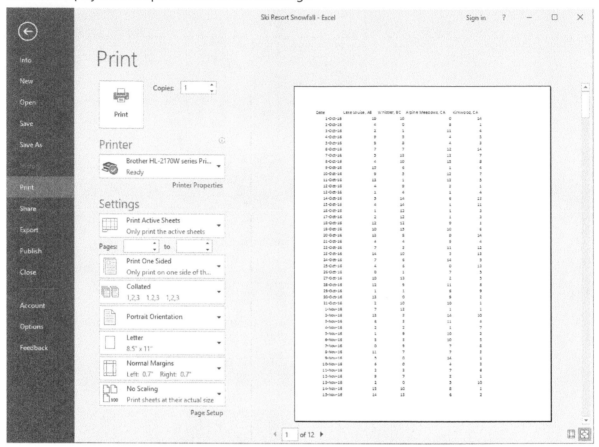

By default, Excel will only print the current active worksheet(s) of the workbook. You can also choose to print all worksheets in the workbook, a selected group of pages, or only a selected range of cells.

Excel takes advantage of a printer's ability to produce presentation quality work. Whether you are printing on an inkjet or laser printer, Excel uses the special fonts, borders and shading to their maximum potential. Excel takes the WYSIWYG (What You See Is What You Get) screen display and delivers it to the printer for a very professional presentation.

**Note:** You can customize the Quick Access Toolbar to display the Quick Print button. Clicking this button will print the worksheet immediately using the current page layout settings.

Prior to sending your worksheet to the printer, you should look at the preview area of the screen because the printer output will look almost exactly as it appears. Previewing a worksheet before printing is cost-effective and environmentally sound because it can reduce the paper waste that often results from page layout mistakes.

# Changing the Workbook Views

### Objective 1.4.4

Excel allows you to select different ways of viewing your workbook on the screen:

**Normal** – You will see this view by default. In this view, only the worksheet rows, columns, and headers appear. The page break lines only appear if you activate a print-related feature such as inserting page breaks or seeing a print preview of the workbook.

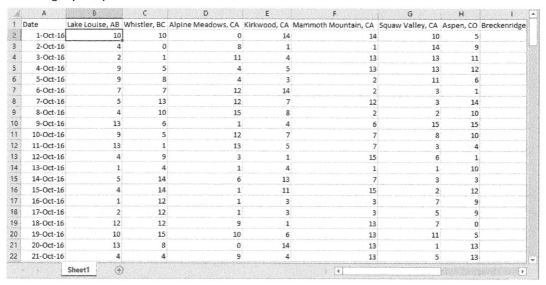

**Page Break Preview** – Display watermarks on your worksheet to identify which rows and columns will appear on which pages, with the page break lines to mark the boundaries.

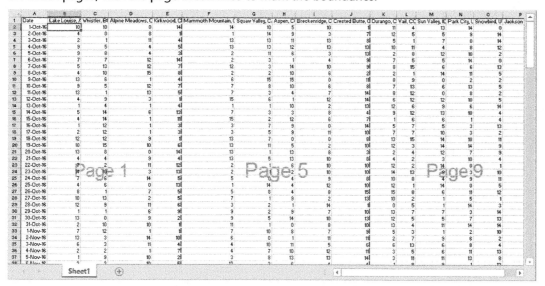

**Page Layout** – Display the workbook as it will appear on the printer. For example, you can see which rows and columns will appear on which page, how wide the margins are, and the contents of the header and footer on each page. The vertical and horizontal rulers are also displayed to show the placement of all output on the page.

Note that this view is only a mockup without considering the capabilities of your printer. The print preview view (on the File tab, under the Print option) previews your worksheet on the screen more accurately because Excel can then identify what type of printer you are using.

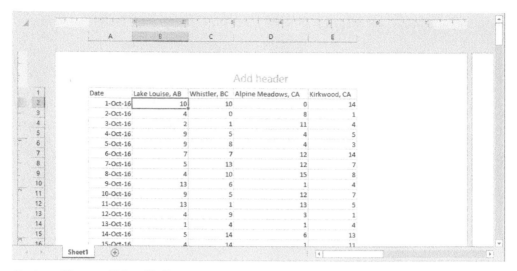

**Custom Views** – This will allow you to save your current page layout settings with a name so that you can re-activate them later at any time.

Another window view option that does not appear in the Workbook Views group in the Ribbon is the full screen view. At the upper right of the Excel window, click the ⊞ **Ribbon Display Options** button then click **Auto-hide Ribbon** to enable this view. This option maximizes the Excel window to the screen, turns off the Ribbon, Quick Access Toolbar and Status Bar to give you more space to view the worksheet data.

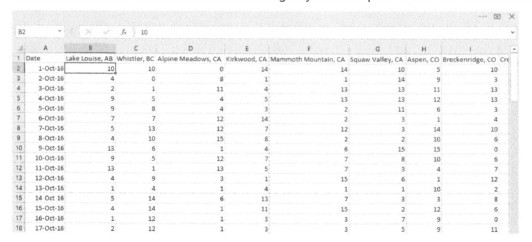

To return to normal Ribbon view click the **Ribbon Display Options** button then click **Show Tabs and Commands**.

These different views are very useful to help you format your workbook prior to printing.

# Learn to change the view

This exercise will demonstrate how to access each of the different workbook views as well as the print feature in Excel.

1   Make sure the *Ski Resort Snowfall - Student* workbook is active on the screen.

2   Press CTRL+HOME.

Go to the Office Backstage and display the worksheet in the print preview mode.

3   Click **File** and then click **Print**.

4   Click the **Zoom to Page** toggle switch at the bottom right corner of the print preview section to zoom in closer to the page.

5   Click the **Zoom to Page** toggle switch again to zoom back out to view the whole page again.

6   Click the **Next Page** and **Previous Page** buttons at the bottom of the print preview section to scroll through the different pages of the workbook.

Now switch to the Page Layout view to compare how this view displays the worksheet.

7   Click the ⊙ **Back** button, then on the View tab, in the Workbook Views group, click **Page Layout**.

8   Use the horizontal and vertical scroll bars to scroll up and down, and to the left and right to view different parts of the worksheet.

9   On the View tab, in the Workbook Views group, click **Page Break Preview**.

10  At the upper right of the Excel window, click the ⊡ **Ribbon Display Options** button then click **Auto-hide Ribbon**.

Since the last view was the Page Break Preview, this view now occupies the entire screen.

11  Scroll up and down the worksheet to view the rest of the worksheet.

12  Click the ⋯ menu display button to display the Quick Access Toolbar and Ribbon.

The Ribbon and Quick Access Toolbar will hide again when you click anywhere outside of the Ribbon.

13  Click anywhere on the worksheet.

Now change the Ribbon display options back to normal.

14  At the upper right of the Excel window, click the ⊡ **Ribbon Display Options** button then click **Show Tabs and Commands**.

15  On the View tab, in the Workbook Views group, click **Normal**.

16  Click **Restore Down** to reduce the worksheet to a window.

17  Close the workbook and discard any changes.

# Customizing the Page Layout

By default, Excel creates every new workbook with the same print settings:

- The top and bottom margins are set to 0.75", and the left and right margins to 0.7".
- The orientation is portrait (vertical) rather than landscape (horizontal).
- The paper size is set to letter or A4, depending on the regional setting.
- The scaling is set to 100% (no zoom).
- There is no header or footer.
- There are no gridlines, or row and column headings.
- If the worksheet prints on more than one page, the page order sequence is set to top-down, and then left-to-right.

If you find the page order sequence confusing at first, visualize it as dividing the worksheet into vertical strips. Excel prints down each consecutive strip, starting from the left-most strip, and then starts at the top of the next strip, and the next, until the entire worksheet is printed. A nine-page worksheet, therefore, prints in this sequence:

| Page 1 | Page 4 | Page 7 |
|--------|--------|--------|
| Page 2 | Page 5 | Page 8 |
| Page 3 | Page 6 | Page 9 |

Before printing your worksheet, you will likely want to customize the page layout options to make it more presentable.

## Setting Page Breaks

It is common to have worksheets that are too large to fit on a single sheet of paper. In those situations, Excel automatically inserts page breaks where one or more rows or columns do not fit within the printable area of the page. In many cases, these page breaks do not coincide with the natural grouping of the data. You can overcome this by manually inserting page breaks where you want them in the worksheet.

**Note:** You can also try other techniques to fit more data onto a single page, such as reducing the page margins or reducing the print scale.

When you manually insert a page break, Excel positions it in the upper left corner of the active cell. This is important to understand because the page break applies to both the current row and the current column. Not only does Excel force the current row to the next page, it also forces all data in the current column and to its right to the next strip of the printed pages. When you need to remove a manually inserted page break, you must do so in the cell into which you inserted it. In the following example, a manual page break has been inserted in cell **D23**:

| | A | B | C | D | E |
|---|---|---|---|---|---|
| 22 | 21-Oct-16 | 4 | 4 | 9 | 4 |
| 23 | 22-Oct-16 | 7 | 2 | 11 | 12 |
| 24 | 23-Oct-16 | 14 | 10 | 3 | 13 |

In the Normal view, this manual page break is barely visible with the slightly thicker and darker gray lines marking it. Therefore, finding these cells to remove the manual page break will be somewhat difficult using the Normal view. However, the Page Break Preview view will clearly mark the location of all page breaks.

The positioning of page breaks is often a trial-and-error process. The Page Break Preview layout is an excellent tool that greatly simplifies this task. In this mode, you can drag the page breaks to a new position. If necessary, Excel will automatically scale the print output to fit the information within the page breaks you have set.

The default page breaks appear as dotted lines in the Page Break Preview view. Whereas, manually inserted page breaks appear as solid lines.

**Note:** If you select the Fit to option, Excel ignores all manual page breaks when you print the worksheet.

# Learn to adjust the page layout

In this exercise, you will practice manually inserting page breaks into a worksheet in order to group similar columns together on the same page.

**1**   Open the *Ski Resort Snowfall – Student* workbook.

**2**   Select cell **D23**.

**3**   On the **Page Layout** tab, in the Page Setup group, click **Breaks** and then click **Insert Page Break**.

Notice that the page break lines now appear in the worksheet to indicate where the page breaks are. However, in this view it is difficult to distinguish between a manual page break and an automatic one.

**4**   Click **File**, and then click **Print**.

**5**   Click **Next Page** and **Previous Page** to view the different pages of the worksheet.

Notice that the first page has only three short columns of data with a lot of empty space on lower area of the page and to the right. This is the result of inserting a page break too high and too far to the left by selecting cell D23. It is in the wrong location, so remove this manual page break.

| Date | Lake Louise, AB | Whistler, BC |
|---|---|---|
| 1-Oct-16 | 10 | 10 |
| 2-Oct-16 | 4 | 0 |
| 3-Oct-16 | 2 | 1 |
| 4-Oct-16 | 9 | 5 |
| 5-Oct-16 | 9 | 8 |
| 6-Oct-16 | 7 | 7 |
| 7-Oct-16 | 5 | 13 |
| 8-Oct-16 | 4 | 10 |
| 9-Oct-16 | 13 | 6 |
| 10-Oct-16 | 9 | 5 |
| 11-Oct-16 | 13 | 1 |
| 12-Oct-16 | 4 | 9 |
| 13-Oct-16 | 1 | 4 |
| 14-Oct-16 | 5 | 14 |
| 15-Oct-16 | 4 | 14 |
| 16-Oct-16 | 1 | 12 |
| 17-Oct-16 | 2 | 12 |
| 18-Oct-16 | 12 | 12 |
| 19-Oct-16 | 10 | 15 |
| 20-Oct-16 | 13 | 8 |
| 21-Oct-16 | 4 | 4 |

**6**   Click the ⊙ **Back** button to return to the worksheet.

**7**   With cell D23 selected, on the Page Layout tab, in the Page Setup group, click **Breaks** and then click **Remove Page Break**.

Go to the Page Break Preview to see what it looks like.

**8**   On the **View** tab, in the Workbook Views group, click **Page Break Preview**.

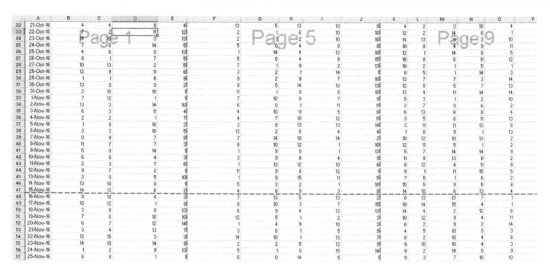

In this view, Excel displays the page numbers as a watermark on each section of data to identify which rows and columns it will print on each page. All of the page break lines are dotted which indicates that none of them are set manually.

9   Position the mouse pointer over the page break line between pages 1 and 5 until an ↔ arrow appears. Click the mouse button and drag the page break to the left by one column.

You have now set a manual page break to the left side of column E. Notice that the page break between pages 1 and 5 is now a solid line instead of a dotted line – this indicates that this is a manual page break.

Also notice that the automatic page break between pages 5 and 9 (and the pages below them) has moved from the left side of column K to column J because of your manual page break.

10  Drag the page break line at the left side of column **J** to the left by two columns.

You can also set a manual page break between rows.

11  Drag the horizontal page break line at the top of row 48 up to the top of row 33.

If you want to remove a manual page break, you can do so in this view.

12  Select any cell on the right side of the page break on page 11 (any cell in the range **H1:H32**).

13  On the **Page Layout** tab, in the Page Setup group, click **Breaks** and then click **Remove Page Break**.

You can also remove all manual page breaks.

14  On the Page Layout tab, in the Page Setup group, click **Breaks** and then click **Reset All Page Breaks**.

Excel allows you to add more columns to print on a page. It accomplishes this by changing the scaling.

15  Drag the vertical page break line at the left side of column F to the left side of column H.

16  Drag the vertical page break line at the left side of column P to the right by one column (the end of the data).

17  Drag the horizontal page break line at the top of row 62 down to the top of row 63.

The worksheet should look similar to the following:

Scroll down the worksheet and verify that the next horizontal page break is set at a natural break between months, not partway into a month.

**18** Scroll down the worksheet and confirm that the next horizontal page break is set at the top of row 125.

**19** On the Page Layout tab, look at the **Scale** setting in the Scale to Fit group.

Excel has automatically adjusted it down from 100% to about 75% to fit all of the data on each page.

**20** Click the File tab and click **Print**.

**21** Click the **Next Page** and **Previous Page** buttons to view each of the pages.

Now go back to the normal page view and remove all page breaks.

**22** Click the ⊖ **Back** button, then on the **View** tab, in the Workbook Views group, click **Normal**.

**23** On the **Page Layout** tab, in the Page Setup group, click **Breaks** and then click **Reset All Page Breaks**.

**24** Save the workbook.

# Page Formatting

### Objective 1.3.4, 1.5.4

The formatting of printed worksheets can be changed using the settings located in three different areas:

- using the Page Layout tab in the Ribbon, or
- using the Page Setup dialog box, or
- using the Print pane in the Office Backstage.

## Page Formatting Using the Ribbon

The Page Layout tab has several page formatting settings that you can modify.

**Margins** – The Top, Bottom, Left, and Right settings are the amount of white space (measured in inches) from the edge of the page. Many printers—especially laser printers—require a minimum page margin because they are not able to print to the edges of the paper. This is reasonable because reports are not visually appealing when data appears up to the edges of the paper. You also need to allow space on the left or right margin if you are going to insert the pages into a notebook or ring binder. A wider margin is needed where the paper is held in place by the binding mechanism.

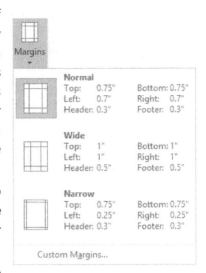

The Header margin sets the distance between the Header and the top edge of the page, and the Footer margin between the Footer and the bottom edge of the page to allow space for the page header and footer to appear.

If you select Custom Margins, the Page Setup dialog box is displayed to show all Margin options available.

**Orientation** – The page orientation options are Portrait (vertical) or Landscape (horizontal).

**Size** – This option lets you specify what size of paper to use for printing. You must choose options that are within the print capabilities of your printer and you must remember to load the appropriate paper or select the correct tray from which to print.

If you select More Paper Sizes, the Page Setup dialog box is displayed showing the various page options.

**Scale, Width, Height** – The Scale option enables you to magnify or shrink the size of the worksheet proportionally on the page. The Zoom feature only affects the display of the workbook on the screen. Scale is the equivalent for printing.

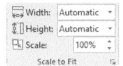

You can use the Width and Height options to calculate the correct scale value to fit the worksheet into the specified number of pages automatically. For example, you can scale down a worksheet that requires nine pages to fit into a width of two pages and a height of three pages so that it will print on six pages.

**Gridlines, Headings** – The Gridlines option causes lines to display around each cell. By default, they are turned on for the screen (View) and turned off for printing.

Similarly, the Headings option is turned on by default on the screen and turned off for printing. This option identifies columns to be labeled as A, B, C, and so on, and rows are labeled as 1, 2, 3, and so on.

## Page Formatting Using Page Setup

The Page Setup dialog box has been the traditional way of formatting worksheets pages since the very first version of Excel. Therefore, long-time Excel users are accustomed to using this method to format their worksheets before printing them.

On the other hand, the Page Layout tab described above is a relatively new feature that allows you to access most of the formatting features from the Ribbon. If you need a page formatting option that is not available in the Ribbon, you will need to access it in the Page Setup dialog box.

Page is the tab in Page Setup that allows you to change the characteristics of your printed output page.

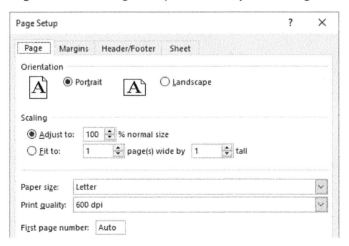

The following items can be changed using the Page tab of your Page Setup dialog box but are not found or labeled differently in the Ribbon:

**Scaling** – The Adjust to option is labeled as Scale in the Page Layout tab on the Ribbon. You can specify a specific percentage to magnify or shrink the size of the worksheet proportionally. The Fit to option is labeled as Width and Height in the Page Layout tab to force automatic scaling feature to "fit" the worksheet into the specified number of pages.

**Print quality** – This option determines the density of the print characters. Generally, the higher the print quality, the more time it will take your printer to form the print output on the paper. This option made a significant difference with the now-obsolete dot matrix printers. With the current efficiencies of inkjet and laser printers, changing this setting does not affect the speed of the printing.

**First page number** – You can use this option to specify the starting page number for the printed worksheet. This may be useful if you are fitting some Excel output into another printed document and you want the page numbering to follow properly. Note that this is only effective if you include a page number in a header or footer.

The Margins tab in the Page Setup dialog box can be used to specify the following options or print parameters:

* how much white space (measured in inches or centimeters, depending on your region) to leave on each side of the page,

* the distance between the Header and the top edge of the page, and between the Footer and the bottom edge of the page, if they are present,

* whether to center the worksheet on the page horizontally or vertically, or both.

The Header/Footer and Sheet tabs will be explained in more detail later in this Lesson.

## Formatting Using the Office Backstage

Just as the Ribbon contains most of the page formatting features, the Print pane in the Office Backstage contains even fewer options (but include the most commonly used settings).

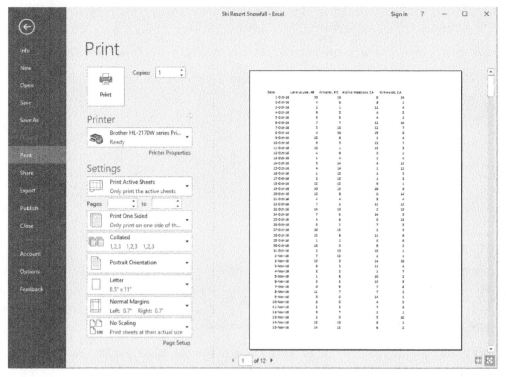

The Print pane displays a page of your worksheet in Print Preview mode. As you change your page formatting settings, the print preview adjusts to show those changes immediately.

You can also open the Page Setup dialog box directly from this pane to access any page formatting setting that is not available in this pane.

# Learn to use page formatting

In this exercise, you will examine the effects of changing some of the page formatting settings.

1   Make sure the *Ski Resort Snowfall - Student* workbook is active on the screen.

2   On the Page Layout tab, in the Page Setup group, click **Orientation** and click **Landscape**.

3   On the Page Layout tab, in the Page Setup group, click **Size** and click **Legal** (or **A4 Long** or **A4 Plus**, if this is the page size for your region).

**Note:** For some types of printers, Excel may only display paper sizes (8.5 x 11) or the paper size name (Letter or Legal).

4   Click the File tab and click **Print**.

5   Click the **Next Page** and **Previous Page** buttons to view each of the pages.

Note that the worksheet now appears sideways and the page is wider at 14 inches (legal size paper). More columns now fit onto each page, but some columns still need to overflow to additional pages. Make note of the total number of pages.

6   Click the ⊕ **Back** button, then on the Page Layout tab, in the Scale to Fit group, click the arrow next to **Width** and click **1 page**.

7   Click the File tab and click **Print**.

8   Click the **Next Page** and **Previous Page** buttons to view each of the pages.

Excel has automatically scaled the data down to fit all columns onto one page. Again, make note of the number of pages and compare against the number of pages before scaling.

Many of the same page layout options can also be modified directly in the Office Backstage.

9   In the Office Backstage, click **Fit All Columns on One Page** to view the options displayed.

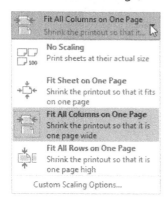

10  Click in a blank area of the Excel window to close this pop-up list.

11  Click **Landscape Orientation** and then click **Portrait Orientation**.

The entire worksheet now fits onto two pages but the size of the text is very small. You can enter your own scale value to find a better compromise.

12  Click **Fit All Columns on One Page** and then click **Custom Scaling Options**.

13  On the Page tab, click **Adjust to** and replace the number in the text box with: 65. Click **OK**.

14  Click the **Zoom to Page** button in the lower right corner of the window to zoom in closer.

15  Click **Zoom to Page** to zoom out again.

**Hint:** You can also set the Adjust to value by entering it into the Scale field, on the Page Layout tab, in the Scale to Fit group.

16  Click the **Show Margins** button in the lower right corner of the window to display the margin markers in the preview.

The margin markers are useful to show the amount of white space reserved as the page margins. Excel has three predefined margins and the ability to specify your own custom margins.

17  Click **Normal Margins** and then click **Narrow**.

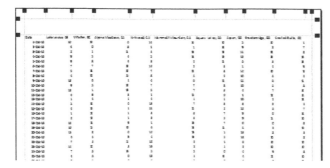

If you print this worksheet, the page will appear cramped because of the narrow margins and the amount of data. Now revert to the default page settings: scale at 100%, letter page size, and normal margins.

**18**  Click **Show Margins** again to remove the margin markers in the preview.

**19**  Click **Custom Scaling** and then click **No Scaling**.

**20**  Click **Legal** then click **Letter** (or **A4** if that is your standard paper size).

**21**  Click **Narrow Margins** then click **Normal**.

Now print the worksheet with the row and column headings. Print only the first page to see how it looks.

**22**  Click the ⬅ **Back** button, then on the Page Layout tab, in the Sheet Options group, click the **Print** check box under Headings to turn it on.

**23**  Click the File tab and click **Print**.

**24**  Enter: 1 in both text boxes for **Pages** so that only page 1 of the worksheet is printed.

**Hint:** After you have finished printing, remember to go back to the Office Backstage Print screen to remove or change the first and last page numbers. The page number selections will remain there until the workbook is closed.

**25**  Click **Print** to print this page.

The worksheet is displayed again after printing.

**26**  On the Page Layout tab, in the Sheet Options group, click the **Print** check box under Headings to turn it off.

**27**  Save the workbook.

# Adding a Header or Footer

### Objective 1.3.8

A *header* is the text you insert to be printed at the top of every page. A *footer* is the text you insert to be printed at the bottom of every page of a worksheet. If you do not insert text into the header and footer, they remain blank.

Every printed worksheet should have a header and footer to help readers identify the data presented on the pages. As a minimum, you should add a header and footer to your worksheet displaying the current page number, print date and workbook name, whether or not the worksheet requires one or more pages to print. Whenever possible, you should enter a descriptive heading label instead of using the workbook name. Workbook names sometimes do not describe the data contents. To illustrate this point, ask yourself if you have created workbooks named as data.xlsx or Book1.xlsx. By entering a heading label such as Daily Snowfall Readings, your printed pages will be more meaningful and appear more professional.

Any header or footer that you set up will only apply to the active worksheet. Therefore, if two or more worksheets in a workbook have data that you need to print, you must set up the header and footer for each of the worksheets even if they all contain the same information.

To add or modify a worksheet header or footer using the Page Setup dialog box, use one of the following methods:

- on the Page Layout tab, in the Page Setup group, click **Print Titles** and then click the **Header/Footer** tab, or

- on the Page Layout tab, in the Page Setup group, click the **Dialog box launcher** and then click the **Header/Footer** tab.

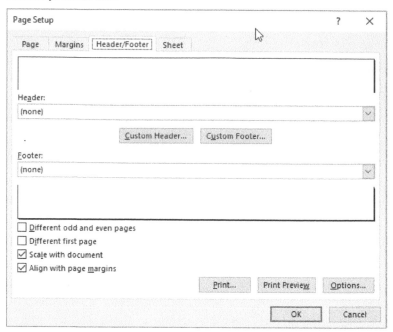

In the Page Setup dialog box, click **Custom Header** or **Custom Footer** to create your own header or footer for the worksheet. The header or footer consists of three sections: left, center, and right.

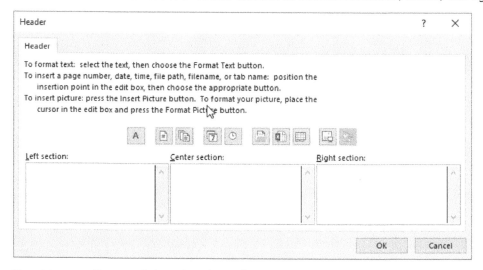

To add or modify a worksheet header or footer using the Ribbon, use one of the following methods:

- on the Insert tab, in the Text group, click **Header & Footer**, or
- on the View tab, in the Workbook Views group, click **Page Layout** and then click in the header or footer section of the worksheet.

These methods use the Page Layout view. You can then select any of the header or footer sections and enter your changes directly.

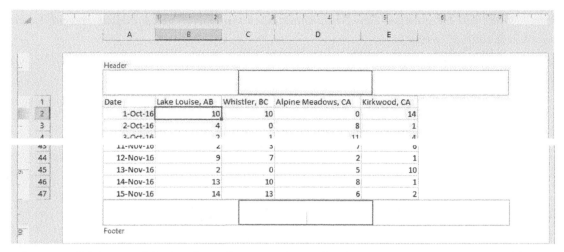

When you click in any of the header or footer sections while in the Page Layout view, the Ribbon displays the Design tab under Header & Footer Tools:

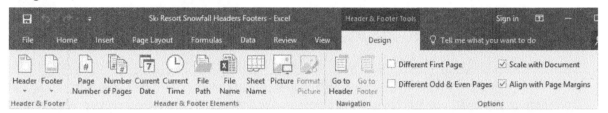

The Header & Footer section of this tab has several predefined standard header or footer options to choose from:

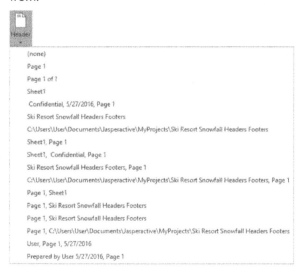

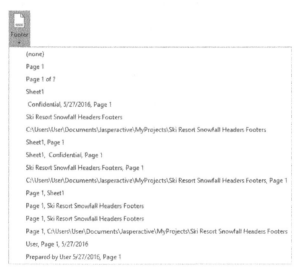

The Header & Footer Elements section of the tab contains nine command buttons that can be used to insert commonly used variables into the header or footer:

**Page Number** – Click this button to display the code &[Page] in the selected section of the header or footer. The page number will start at 1 by default. You can change this in the Page Setup dialog box.

**Number of Pages** – Click this button to display the code &[Pages]. This calculates the total number of pages in the selected worksheet(s) to be printed. This is often used with the Page number code to show each page number as one among the total of all the pages (for example, Page 1 of 4).

**Current Date** – Insert the current date (from the computer) into the report, displayed as the code &[Date].

**Current Time** – Insert the current time (from the computer) into the report, displayed as the code &[Time].

**File Path** – Insert the current path (drive and folder location) and file name into the header or footer, displayed as the code &[Path]&[File].

**File Name** – Insert the name of the file into the header or footer, displayed as the code &[File].

**Sheet Name** – Insert the name of the tab for the current worksheet, displayed as the code &[Tab].

**Picture** – Insert a picture into the header or footer, displayed as the code &[Picture].

**Format Picture** – Provide options to change the properties for the picture.

The Options group in the Ribbon gives you more flexibility with the headers and footers such as creating a different header and footer for the first page, and different headers and footers for odd and even pages.

# Learn to add headers and footers

In this exercise, you will create headers and footers on your printed output.

1   Make sure the *Ski Resort Snowfall - Student* workbook is active on the screen.

2   Click the **File** tab and click **Print**.

3   Click the **Next Page** and **Previous Page** buttons to view each of the pages.

Notice that each of the pages has a lot of data on it but there are no page numbers to indicate in what sequence they are printed. If you inadvertently mix up your pages (such as accidentally dropping your report on the floor), you will have a hard time reassembling them in the correct sequence. You can insert a header or footer containing the page number to prevent this from happening.

4   Click the ⊖ **Back** button, then on the **Insert** tab, in the Text group, click **Header & Footer**.

Excel automatically displays the Page Layout view with the cursor in the middle section of the header.

**Hint:** Another way to insert or modify a header is on the View tab, in the Workbook Views group, click Page Layout and then click in the header section of the worksheet.

5   On the Header & Footer Tools Design tab, in the Header & Footer group, click **Header** and then click the preformatted header that appears as *Ski Resort Snowfall - Student*.

By selecting this predefined header, the header is now closed and the cursor is back in the active cell of the worksheet.

The header may not change immediately – it may take up to a minute before the label "Ski Resort Snowfall - Student" is actually displayed in the header.

6   Click on the middle section of the header again.

The header shows a code: &[File] instead of the file name. When you print the workbook, the code is automatically translated to show the workbook file name. By using a code instead of the text label ("Ski Resort Snowfall - Student" in this case), the header will always show the correct file name even if you save the workbook with a different name.

| Header | | | | |
| --- | --- | --- | --- | --- |
| | | &[File] | | |
| Date | Lake Louise, AB | Whistler, BC | Alpine Meadows, CA | Kirkwood, CA |
| 1-Oct-16 | 10 | 10 | 0 | 14 |
| 2-Oct-16 | 4 | 0 | 8 | 1 |

**7** On the Header & Footer Tools Design tab, in the Navigation group, click **Go to Footer**.

The cursor is now in the center section of the footer.

**Hint:** Alternatively, you can manually scroll down the worksheet and click in the footer area.

**8** On the Header & Footer Tools Design tab, in the Header & Footer group, click **Footer** and then click the preformatted footer second from the top of the list (*Page 1*).

Again, it may take up to a minute before the footer is updated to display the selected footer text labels.

Now add the company logo to the header.

**9** Scroll up the worksheet and click in the left section of the page header.

**10** Click the Header & Footer Tools **Design** tab.

**11** On the Header & Footer Tools Design tab, in the Header & Footer Elements group, click **Picture**.

The Insert Pictures dialog box is displayed. This dialog box allows you to select a source from which to obtain the picture from your local computer or from the Internet:

**12** In the Insert Pictures dialog box, click **Browse** in the From a file option.

A second Insert Picture dialog box is displayed to find the picture file from your local computer.

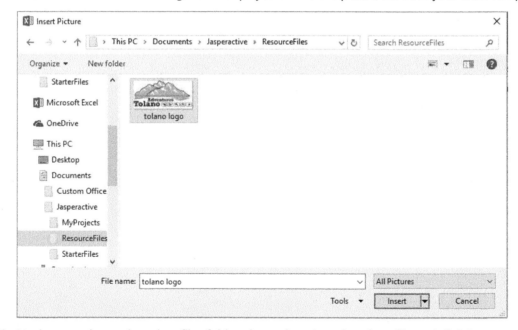

**13** Navigate to the student data files folder, then select the *tolano logo* file and click **Insert**.

**14** Click on any cell in the worksheet area.

Note that the logo is too big and is covering some of the data.

**15** Click in the left section of the header again. Then, on the Header & Footer Tools Design tab, in the Header & Footer Elements group, click **Format Picture**.

16  Ensure that the Lock aspect ratio box is checked and then reduce the **Scale Height** or **Scale Width** to 33%.

17  Click **OK** and then click anywhere in the worksheet.

Now view the results of adding the header and footer to this worksheet.

18  Click the **File** tab and click **Print**.

19  Click the **Next Page** and **Previous Page** buttons to view each of the pages.

Note the preformatted header and footer entries on each page. The screen should look similar to the following example:

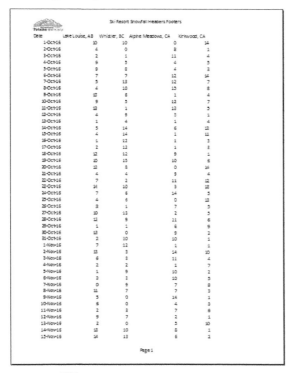

20  Click the  **Back** button to return to your worksheet.

21  Save the workbook.

# Printing Titles and Ranges of Cells

### Objective 1.5.1, 1.5.5

With large worksheets, you have the ability to freeze row and column titles so that you can always relate any cell to their descriptions. However, the Freeze Panes feature only applies to the screen. The equivalent feature when printing is to set *Print Titles*. By printing titles, you designate specific data rows or data columns or both to print on every page of the printed worksheet. Typically, these rows and columns contain the text labels that identify the purpose of the data in those rows or columns.

Excel also provides an option to specify a range of cells as the Print Area, which will ensure that only this section of the worksheet is always selected for printing. This feature is very useful when you may want to only print a range of cells instead of the entire worksheet.

Alternatively, you can select just a range of cells to print as a one-time event. To do so, select the range of cells on the worksheet, then change the print settings to **Print Selection**.

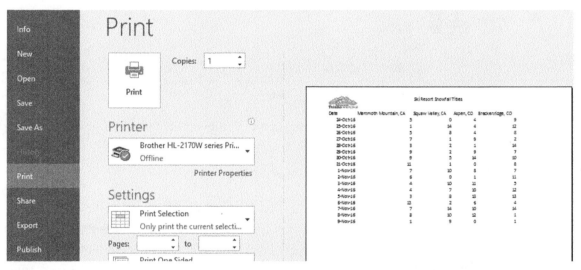

Before deciding to set only a range of cells for printing, you should take another look at your data. In most cases, you should expect to print the entire contents of a worksheet. If you are setting the print area because you have more than one group of data, you should consider separating the different groups into different worksheets. The real problem is that these different groups of data just happen to be on the same worksheet. Once separated, you can then print the entire worksheet without being confused by the print range setting.

# Learn to print titles and a cell range

In this exercise, you will display the column and row titles on every page and select a range of cells for printing.

1   Make sure the *Ski Resort Snowfall - Student* workbook is active on the screen.

2   Click the **File** tab and click **Print**.

3   Click the **Next Page** and **Previous Page** buttons to view each of the pages.

While looking at each of the pages, you will notice that some of the pages are just rows and columns of numbers. As a result, you are unable to relate these numbers to dates and locations. This can be resolved by displaying row and column titles.

**4** Click the ⊖ **Back** button, then on the Page Layout tab, in the Page Setup group, click **Print Titles**.

Excel displays the Page Setup dialog box. Alternatively, you can also display the Page Setup dialog box on the Page Layout tab, in the Page Setup group, and clicking the Page Setup dialog box launcher. This dialog box has four tabs; the titles options are in the Sheet tab.

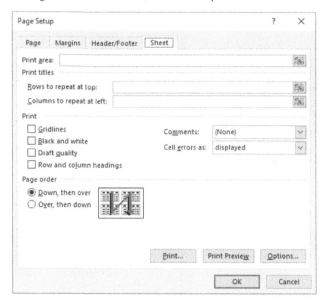

You can now select column or row headers or the range of cells you want to print by selecting these cells directly from the worksheet.

**5** Click the **Collapse** button for the Rows to repeat at top field.

**6** Click the row **1** header on the worksheet behind the Page Setup - Rows to repeat at top dialog box.

**Note:** You must access the Page Setup dialog box from the Ribbon to be able to make these changes. If you had clicked Page Setup in the Print screen, the Print area and Print titles selection boxes will be grayed out and you can't change them.

Excel enables you to select any number of rows to display at the top of every page provided they are contiguous (all rows are together).

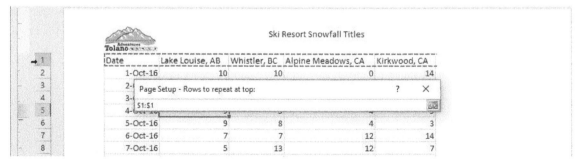

**7** Click the **Expand** button in the Page Setup - Rows to repeat at top window.

**Hint:** You can also press ENTER to expand this dialog box.

Instead of shrinking the Page Setup dialog box, you can simply move it aside before selecting the rows or columns.

**8** In the Page Setup dialog box, click in the **Columns to repeat at left** field.

**9**   If necessary, move the Page Setup dialog box so that it is not blocking your view of column A in the worksheet.

**10**  Click the column **A** header on the worksheet, collapse the window, then press ENTER to close the Page Setup dialog box.

**11**  Scroll down and across the worksheet in Page Layout mode to view each of the pages.

The worksheet now has row 1 and column A repeated on every page. With this change, it is much easier to relate every cell value to the date and ski resort.

Suppose you only want to print the data for Oct. 24 to Nov. 9 for a small group of ski resorts. You can do this by designating a range of cells as a Print Area.

**12**  Select the cell range **F25** to **I41**.

**13**  Click the **File** tab and click **Print**.

**14**  Click **Print Active Sheets** under Settings, then click **Print Selection**.

There will only be one page to print in this case, and only this cell range will be printed.

**15**  Click the ⊖ **Back** button.

To demonstrate that this limited cell range printing is temporary, you will select another small group of cells.

**16**  On the worksheet select the cell range **G36** to **G37**, then click the **File** tab and click **Print**.

The print preview now shows these two selected cells will be printed.

You can also restrict Excel to only print a selected range of cells so that you do not have to use the Print Selection option.

**17**  Click the ⊖ **Back** button, then select the cell range **F25** to **I41**.

**18**  On the Page Layout tab, in the Page Setup group, click **Print Area** and click **Set Print Area**.

**19**  Click the **File** tab and click **Print**.

**20**  Click **Print Selection** under Settings, then click **Print Active Sheets**.

Even though you have specified to print the entire worksheet, Excel is limited to only print the selected range of cells. This print range restriction remains even if you close the workbook or you temporarily select a different range for printing.

**21**  Save and close the workbook, then open the *Ski Resort Snowfall - Student* workbook again.

**22**  On the worksheet select the cell range **I42** to **I46**, then click the **File** tab and click **Print**.

**23**  Click **Print Active Sheets** under Settings, then click **Print Selection**.

Excel will now print the currently selected range of cells only.

**24**  Click **Print Selection** under Settings, then click **Print Active Sheets**.

Excel is once again limited to printing the cell range that you defined as a print area.

If you want to switch back to printing the entire worksheet, you can temporarily disable the print area setting.

**25**  Click **Print Active Sheets** under Settings, then click **Ignore Print Area**.

The print preview now shows 16 pages for the worksheet.

26   Click **Print Active Sheets** again, and then click **Ignore Print Area** to re-enable the print area for printing.

The print area setting can be removed easily if it is no longer needed.

27   On the Page Layout tab, in the Page Setup group, click **Print Area** and click **Clear Print Area**.

28   Save and close the workbook.

## Printing Selected Worksheets

**Objective 1.5.3**

The Office Backstage Print Settings allow you to select one of three options for printing:

• print the current active worksheet(s),

• print all worksheets in the entire workbook, or

• print the currently selected range of cells in the current active worksheet.

You will usually have only one worksheet as your active worksheet. When you print the active sheet, Excel will only print the contents of that worksheet.

If you want to print more than one worksheet (but not the entire workbook) at the same time, then you must select all of these worksheets as a group first, and then print them. Use the CTRL key to add the worksheets to the group of active worksheets. You can also use the SHIFT key to select a range of worksheets as the active group.

# Learn to print select worksheets

In this exercise, you will print a selected group of worksheets in a workbook.

1   Open the *Quarterly Income Statement Printing* workbook.

2   Click the **Quarter 1** worksheet tab.

3   Hold down the CTRL key and click the **Quarter 3** and **Quarter 4** worksheet tabs to select them as part of the group.

Notice the label [Group] appearing in the title bar of the workbook.

4   Click the **File** tab and click **Print**.

5   Verify that Print Active Sheets is currently selected.

6   Click the **Next Page** and **Previous Page** buttons to view each of the worksheets you have selected for printing. Three pages are currently selected.

You can also print all the worksheets in this workbook.

7   Click **Print Active Sheets** under Settings, then click **Print Entire Workbook**.

8   Click the **Next Page** and **Previous Page** buttons to view each of the worksheets that have been selected for printing. Five pages are now selected.

9   Close the workbook and discard any changes.

# Lesson Summary

Now that you have completed this lesson, you should be able to:

☑  create worksheet windows                ☑  use different workbook views

☑  arrange worksheet windows               ☑  add and preview page breaks

☑  split panes                             ☑  change printing margins, orientation, paper size and scale

☑  freeze panes                            ☑  print column and row titles or selected ranges of cells

☑  zoom in and out of worksheets           ☑  add and modify headers and footers

☑  print and preview worksheets            ☑  print selected worksheets

# Review Questions

1.  The open windows in the following figure are arranged in which configuration?

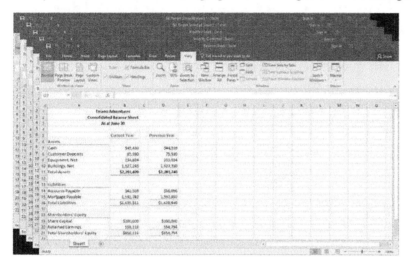

  a.  Horizontal                c.  Cascade

  b.  Tiled                     d.  Vertical

2.  How do you open another view of the active workbook?

  a.  Press Ctrl+N.             c.  Click the View Side by Side button.

  b.  Press Ctrl+V.             d.  Click the New Window button.

3.  Sarah is entering weekly sales data for week 37 of the current year; however, when she moves down to the cells where she needs to enter the data, the column headings scroll out of view and sometimes she loses track of which column she is working in. What can Sarah do to keep the column headings visible even while she is working in a distant portion of the worksheet?

  a.  Freeze the panes.

  b.  Reset the window position.

  c.  Cascade the window.

  d.  Adjust the zoom so that she can see the entire worksheet on screen.

4. What of the following are benefits of previewing a worksheet prior to printing?

   a. You can easily see formulas that contain circular references.

   b. You can see how many pages your printed output will require.

   c. You can avoid wasting paper due to page layout settings.

   d. You can easily correct grammar errors because grammar check is part of the print preview process.

5. Which view is shown in the following figure?

   a. Normal
   
   c. Page Break Preview

   b. Watermark
   
   d. Page Layout

6. Denise needs to print a report that will be inserted into a larger report, and therefore needs the page numbering to begin at 312. In which tab of the Page Setup dialog box can she specify this beginning page number?

   a. Margins
   
   c. Sheet

   b. Header/Footer
   
   d. Page

7. Which code inserts the name of the tab for the current worksheet into an Excel footer?

   a. &[Tab]
   
   c. &[File]

   b. &[Page]
   
   d. &[Path]&[File]

8. Andrea needs to print a 7-page report of inventory figures. The column headings print only on the first page of the report. What should she do to ensure the column headings print on every page?

   a. Add the column headings into the report header.

   b. There is no way to ensure that column headings print on every page of a report.

   c. Set the row with the column headings as a print title.

   d. Repeat the column headings at the page break locations throughout the report.

Microsoft®

# Excel 2016

Core Certification Guide

# Lesson 6: Working with Charts and Graphics

## Lesson Objectives

In this lesson you will learn to work with charts. You will also learn to work with different types of graphic images including shapes and pictures. Upon completion of this lesson, you should be able to:

☐ create charts

☐ move a chart to a different location on a worksheet or its own chart sheet

☐ resize a chart to a different size or shape

☐ change the chart type

☐ work with pie charts

☐ change the chart design

☐ add new data to the chart

☐ create, customize, and remove a sparkline chart

☐ print a chart

☐ use the Quick Analysis Tool

☐ draw different types of shapes on a worksheet

☐ move, resize, and format shapes

☐ insert clip art and pictures

☐ use the Image Editor tools

☐ use the Format Shape pane

☐ resize, reshape, and rotate graphics objects

# Creating a Basic Chart

**Objective 5.1.1**

A chart is a pictorial representation of the data you enter in a worksheet. Often, a chart can be a more descriptive way of representing your data. As a result, those viewing the information provided by your spreadsheets may find it easier to examine and understand a chart rather than many rows and columns of numbers. A pictorial representation of the data will often help identify trends or patterns in the data.

Charts can be easily created using the Ribbon. On the Insert tab, in the Charts group, there are several buttons to select the chart that you want to create:

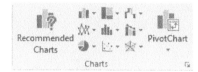

After selecting the data to be charted and then clicking the **Recommended Charts** button, this dialog box will appear with a set of charts that are commonly used for the data you have selected:

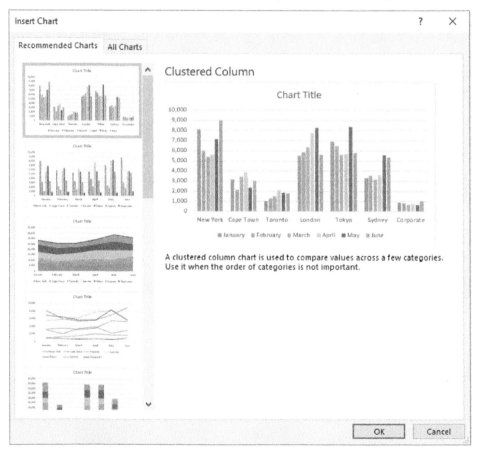

If this set of charts does not meet your needs, the full set of chart types and layouts are available in the All Charts tab:

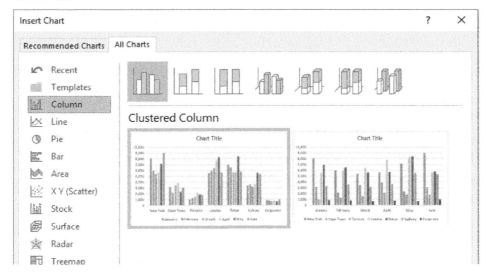

Alternatively, each of the chart types can be selected directly from the Ribbon on the Insert tab, in the Charts group.

Excel can display worksheet information in a variety of ways. Incorporating fonts, patterns, symbols, graphics and 3-D (three-dimensional) effects, Excel's charting feature is an extremely professional presentation tool.

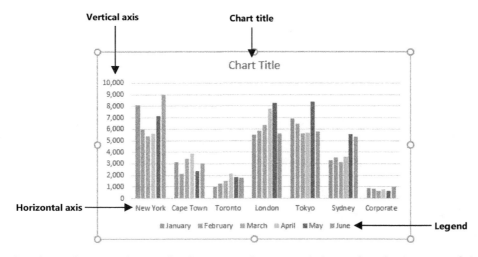

The chart's horizontal axis (also known as the *X axis*) is located at the bottom of the chart and the vertical axis (also known as the *Y axis*) is located at the left or right side of the chart. You will have the opportunity to apply labels for both axes. Excel will automatically include a legend with the chart to explain the meaning of each line in a line chart or column in a column chart. Although you can remove the legend, it may be helpful to others to retain it if your chart has more than one data series.

To create a chart, simply select the cells containing the data you want to chart and click the desired chart type. Once the chart appears in the worksheet, you will also see two different tabs for the Chart Tools that you can use to create or modify chart elements. You will learn about many of these tools as you progress through this lesson.

# Learn to create a chart

This exercise demonstrates how to create a chart in seven (or fewer) easy steps using the Ribbon.

**1**   Open the *Website Hits* workbook and save it as: Website Hits - Student.

This worksheet shows the number of times that potential customers of Tolano Adventures are accessing their website.

**2**   Select the range of cells from **A4** to **G11**.

Note that the row and column titles were included in this range, but the total values were not. If you wish, you can include the totals in the chart. In many cases, however, the purpose of creating a chart is to show any patterns in the data. Including the totals will actually reduce the visibility of the pattern because their presence causes the rest of the data to shrink in size.

**3**   On the **Insert** tab, in the Charts group, click **Insert Column or Bar Chart**.

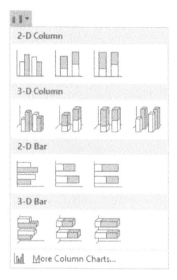

**4**   Point to each of the icons in the drop-down menu.

A live preview of the selected chart is displayed. If none of them meets your requirement, you can click on a different chart type from the Ribbon.

**5**   Click the **Clustered Column** option (left-most item in the 2-D Column set).

The column chart now displays. Note that whenever you select the chart, the cells containing the source data are marked and two new tabs display under Chart Tools.

In the default chart, each row of data has been set up as the categories (appearing in the X-axis), and each column is a series (as shown in the legend). Assume that you need to exchange their positions so that each month is a category, you can do this very easily.

**6**   Under Chart Tools, on the Design tab, in the Data group, click **Switch Row/Column**.

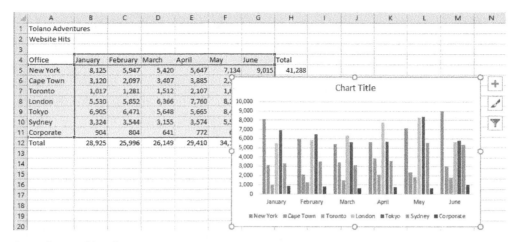

**7**   Save the workbook.

If the Total column (column H) and Total row (row 12) were included, then the chart would look like this example:

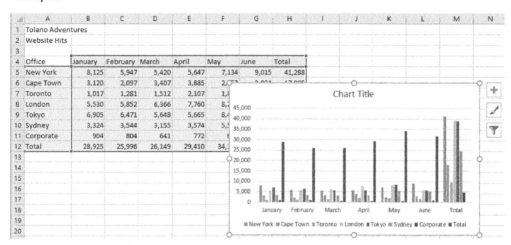

For the Total category (the right-most group of bars in the chart), you can clearly see the difference in total hits between the different offices. However, the presence of the Total category overwhelms the patterns that emerge in the individual months. In addition, having the Total included for each month also overwhelms the individual offices. If you included the Total column and Total row in your chart by mistake, you can redraw the chart by deleting it, selecting the correct range of cells, and creating the chart again.

# Moving and Resizing Charts

**Objective 5.2.1**

You can move charts to any location on a worksheet. Typically, you place a chart next to its source data so that users can see both at the same time. To move a chart around a worksheet, simply use the mouse to drag it to its new location. While moving a chart, take care when placing the cursor to ensure that you are not moving a single component within the chart by mistake. To move an entire chart, you must click on a blank area of the chart where no chart components are located.

You can also make charts larger or smaller, or change their shape. To resize a chart, click and drag any of the handles located around the border of the chart. Every chart has eight of these handles: four in the corners and four at mid-points between the corners. The mid-point handles are used to change either the width or the height of the chart. The corner handles can be used to make the chart larger or smaller in two directions at the same time by changing the width and height at the same time. Whenever you change the size or shape of a chart, the internal components will generally resize proportionately.

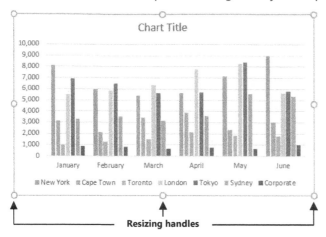

**Resizing handles**

You can also move charts to their own chart sheets. If you do this, the chart will automatically resize itself to fill the entire sheet.

# Learn to move and resize a chart

This exercise demonstrates how to move and resize a chart and its components.

1   Make sure the *Website Hits - Student* workbook is active on the screen.

2   If necessary, click in any blank area of the worksheet to take the chart out of editing mode.

To move a chart right after creating it, you may have to click outside of the chart before you are permitted to move it.

3   Click in any blank area of the column chart to put it back into editing mode.

4   Under Chart Tools, click the **Format** tab.

5   Look in the **Chart Elements** box in the Current Selection group, which displays the name of the chart component that you selected.

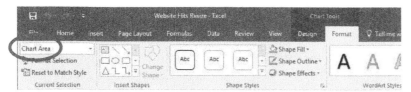

**Hint:** You can also identify components of a chart by positioning the mouse cursor over that part of the chart. A screen tip will display the name.

6   If the Chart Elements box displays a name other than Chart Area, click another blank area of the chart until it does. Generally, any of the four corners of the chart are the best choices.

**Hint:** You can also select Chart Area from the list box in the Current Selection group.

Use that spot to drag the chart to a new location of your choice on the worksheet.

**7** Click that spot on the chart again and drag the chart so that it is directly below the data.

Make the chart bigger.

**8** Point to each of the four corners of the chart to view how the mouse cursor changes.

**9** Click and drag the bottom right corner down and outwards to make the chart bigger.

**10** Point to each of the mid-points of the chart corners to view how the mouse cursor changes.

**11** Click the middle handle at the bottom of the chart and drag it down to make the chart bigger.

You can also resize and move the components inside the chart. Imagine a square box around each of these components of the chart. To move the component, you click inside the box and move it to a new location.

**12** Click in a blank area inside the legend, then drag the legend to another location in the chart such as in the middle of the column bars.

**13** Click **Undo** in the Quick Access Toolbar.

**14** Save the workbook.

# Changing Chart Types

You can easily change the type of chart you have selected if it does not display the worksheet information appropriately.

The type of chart to use will depend on what you are trying to show. Line charts are better for showing trends, column charts are better for showing volume and pie charts are better for showing portions of a total.

Excel provides a variety of chart types and several subtypes within each major type. The following explains the uses for some of the chart types:

**Column** – Use to compare values over time or across categories. This is a vertical presentation of a bar chart.

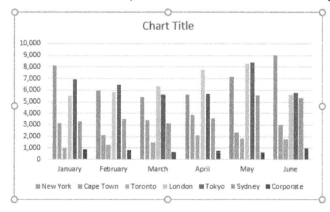

**Line** – Use to compare continuous trends for series of data.

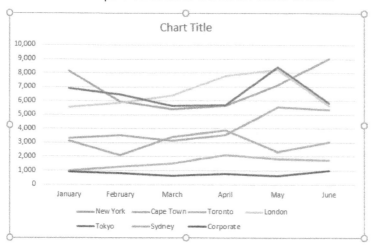

**Pie** – Use to compare the relative size of each portion that together make up the combined total.

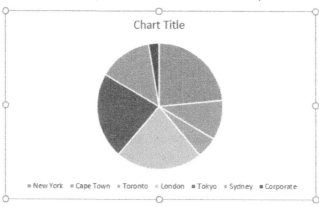

**Bar** – Use to compare values over time or categories. This is a horizontal presentation of a column chart.

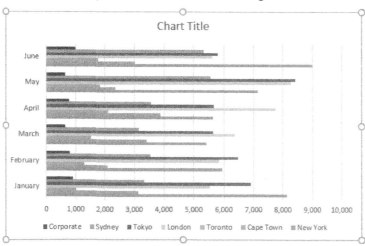

**Area** – Use to compare a continuous change in volume. The example shown here is a stacked area chart in which the total height is the combined total. Like the pie chart, the relative size of each portion can be compared to each other as well as for each point along the horizontal axis. Like the Line chart, it useful for displaying trends.

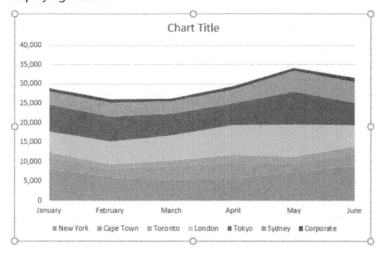

**XY (Scatter)** – Use to determine data patterns where points are clustered close together. In the example below, the points are scattered with no apparent pattern.

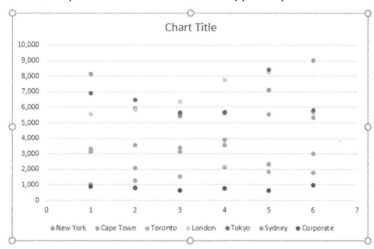

**Stock** – Use to display high-low-close data. To use this display, you must have at least three sets of data for each point on the horizontal axis.

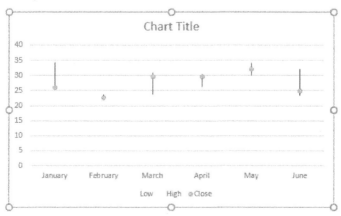

**Surface** – Use to display trends in values with a 3-D presentation and a continuous surface.

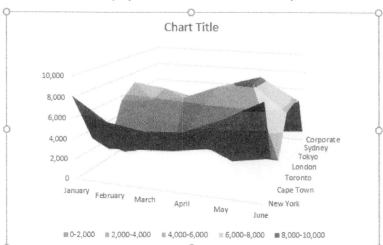

**Radar** – Use to determine patterns or trends with points matched up by lines. It is also called a spider or star chart because of its appearance. This type of chart is most appropriate when the data series are "spiked" with high values in only certain categories (such as months). Examples of spike data are seasonal sales of flu medication, barbeque sauce, and tulip bulbs.

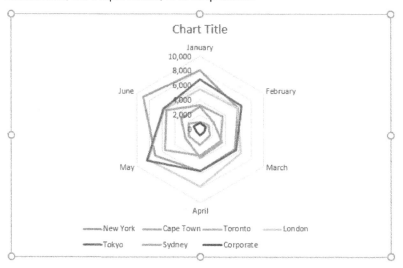

**Treemap** – Like a pie chart, use to compare the relative size of each portion that together make up the combined total, except that each portion shows as a rectangle instead of pie slices. Unlike a pie chart which can only show one set of data values as relative portions of a single total, a treemap is a hierarchical chart in that it can also group the data values as subtotals. In the example below, you can not only compare the January values for each location, but also the compare the (sub)total of each location to each other.

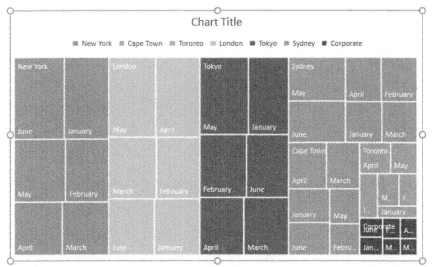

**Sunburst** – Like a treemap chart, use to compare the relative size of each data value and their group subtotals as portions of the combined total. Like a doughnut (similar to a pie) chart, the portions show as slices of the total.

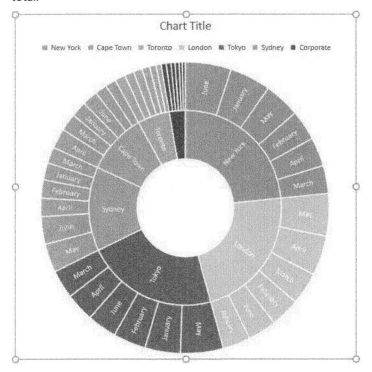

**Histogram** – Use to display frequency (number of times) that each value appears in the data, for example, the number of men and women, or the number of people in different age groups. This type of chart is used primarily for statistical analysis. Only one data series can be selected for this chart.

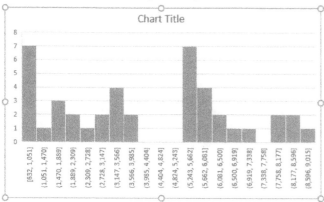

A Pareto chart is a second type of histogram in which the results are sorted in descending order and a line is also drawn using the secondary Y-axis to show the cumulative total percentage. To create a Pareto chart, you can select it directly from the Histogram category in the All Charts tab.

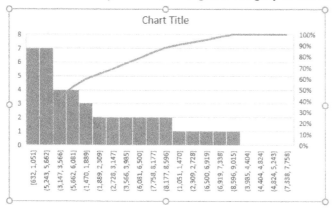

**Box & Whisker** – Use to show more detailed statistical information about the data values, including the mean, range, quartiles, and outliers.

**Waterfall** – Use to graphically show an initial value and a final value, plus the increases and decreases between the two. This is useful for specific uses such as showing financial data that identifies where the major expenses are and how they affect a company's profits.

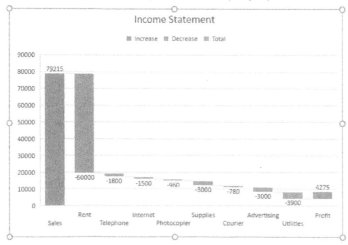

**Combo** – Use to combine two different chart types together for a set of data values, such as a clustered column and a line chart. This is demonstrated in more detail in the Expert courseware.

Most of these chart types have both two-dimensional and three-dimensional choices. Three-dimensional charts can be more interesting to look at, but may be more difficult to read because they tend to look crowded.

To change the chart type, click on the chart to go into chart mode and then use one of the following methods:

- under Chart Tools, on the Design tab, in the Type group, click **Change Chart Type,** or
- right-click in any blank area of the chart and then click **Change Chart Type**.

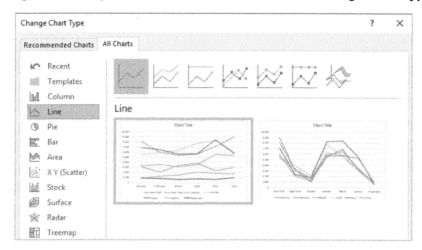

# Learn to change chart types

This exercise demonstrates how to select different chart types.

1   Make sure the *Website Hits - Student* workbook is active on the screen.

2   Click in any blank area of the chart.

3   Under Chart Tools, on the Design tab, in the Type group, click **Change Chart Type**.

The Change Chart Type dialog box appears showing the different chart types from which to choose.

4   In the All Charts tab, click the **Line** option on the left side of the dialog box, then click the **3-D Line** option (the right-most one) on the right side of the dialog box and click **OK**.

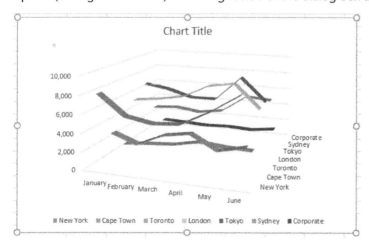

Choose another chart type.

**5**    Under Chart Tools, on the Design tab, in the Type group, click **Change Chart Type**.

**6**    Select a different chart type of your choice and click **OK**.

Change the chart type back to a column chart.

**7**    Under Chart Tools, on the Design tab, in the Type group, click **Change Chart Type**.

**8**    Click the **Clustered Column** option with the calendar months on the horizontal axis (the one on the left) and click **OK**.

**9**    Save the workbook.

# Working with Pie Charts

A pie chart is one of the chart type options that Excel provides. It is commonly used in business applications because it is particularly useful for displaying relative sizes (or percentages) of each piece of the total. For example, if you are writing a report about the importance of segments of your business, you may want to use the pie chart to show the various business segments.

Pie charts are not like the other chart types. For example, column and line charts are excellent choices for visually showing more than one data series—a table with multiple rows and columns of data. Pie charts only allow you to choose one data series, usually the totals for a table, or one row or column of that table.

You may wish to enhance your display further by exploding or moving out a portion of the pie. This draws the viewer's attention to that particular piece of the pie. You can only explode pie slices using the mouse but you cannot use the keyboard to do this. You can explode more than one piece of the pie. However, exploding too many pieces may be distracting to the audience and therefore, lose the point of exploding the pieces.

## Learn to explode a pie chart

This exercise demonstrates how to create a pie chart and explode it.

**1**    Make sure the *Website Hits - Student* workbook is active on the screen.

First, create a new pie chart using only the total values for each office. The pie chart must include the category (X) titles as well as the total data in the chart, so you must highlight two rows that are not next to each other.

**2**    Select cells **A5** to **A11**.

**Note:** For this pie chart, the data series selected will be the total number of website hits for each office.

**3**    Hold down CTRL and select cells **H5** to **H11**.

**4**    On the **Insert** tab, in the Charts group, click **Insert Pie or Doughnut Chart** to display the various pie chart types.

**5**    Point the mouse cursor at the Pie option (left-most item) in the 2-D Pie section of the menu.

Excel now shows a live preview of the pie chart on the screen.

You cannot use the pie chart to show the same data as the other chart types such as the column chart. While other charts are able to show the statistics for each office for each month, a pie chart can only use one data series—in this case, total website hits (cells H5 to H11). If you want to show the hits per month per office, you must use either the treemap or sunburst chart type.

**6** Point the mouse cursor at the Doughnut option to see the live preview of this type of chart.

The doughnut chart is similar to a pie chart, but uses the form of a wheel.

**7** Point the mouse cursor at each of the other pie chart options to see their live preview of the chart.

**8** Click the Pie option in the 2-D section to create the pie chart.

Now explode a piece of the pie.

**9** Click on any pie slice in the chart.

The selection blocks should appear on every pie slice.

**10** Click again on the **New York** pie slice (the one in the upper right).

The selection blocks should now appear only around this piece.

**11** Click and drag the **New York** pie slice away from the rest of the pie. When you have the pie slice in the desired position, release the mouse button.

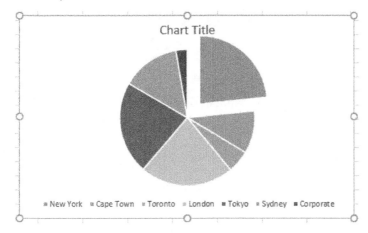

**12** Move the pie chart to the right of the clustered column chart.

**13** Save the workbook.

# Modifying the Chart Design and Location

**Objective 5.1.3, 5.2.2, 5.2.3**

**Add Chart Element** – Used to add, modify, or format chart components such as the chart title, data labels, legend, horizontal or vertical axis. Although the Ribbon option is labeled as **Add Chart Element**, it can also be used to remove the element from the chart.

**Quick Layout** – Used to select from one of several predefined chart layouts for the current chart type.

**Change Colors** – Used to select from one of several predefined color sets for the data points, lines, or bars.

**Chart Styles** – Used to select from one of several predefined chart visual styles.

**Switch Row/Column** – Used to exchange the data rows and columns as the data series for the chart.

**Select Data** – Used to select a different cell range for the chart.

**Change Chart Type** – Used to change the chart to a different chart type.

**Move Chart** – Used to move the chart between a worksheet and a dedicated chart sheet.

As demonstrated in an earlier exercise, you can create a chart on a selected set of data with just a few clicks of the mouse. However, the chart will use a standard set of default settings. You will typically want to modify the chart design to create exactly the look you want. The Design tab contains commands to help with the design of the chart such as which data Excel will display in the chart or selecting a different chart type.

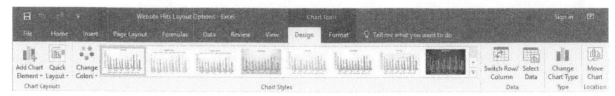

Excel provides a variety of pre-built layouts that you can apply to your chart. You can further modify the chart with your own layout changes.

By default, Excel places the chart in the same worksheet where the source data is located. You can move this chart to its own chart sheet, back to its original worksheet, or to a different worksheet.

# Learn to change chart layout options

This exercise demonstrates how to change layout options for a chart.

1   Make sure the *Website Hits - Student* workbook is active on the screen.

2   Click in a blank area of the clustered column chart to put it into editing mode.

3   Under Chart Tools, on the **Design** tab, in the Chart Layouts group, click **Quick Layout**.

4   Point to some of the layouts in the drop down menu and observe the change in the chart.

5   Click **Layout 1**.

Select different chart styles and see how the chart is affected.

6   Under Chart Tools, on the Design tab, in the Chart Styles group, point to some of the chart styles and observe the change in the chart.

7   Click twice in the Chart Title box in the chart, highlight the default text *Chart Title* and type: Monthly Website Hits as the new title. Excel replaces the default text with your new title.

   Alternatively for step 7, click once on the Chart Title box to select it, type the new title (which will only appear in the Formula Bar) and press ENTER. However, if you click on the chart title box more than once, you will activate the edit mode for the text – as described in step 7 – and the selection box turns into dashed lines. When the title is in edit mode, you must delete the existing text ("Chart Title" in this case) and enter the new title. Although this method involves more steps, it works every time.

Add titles to each of the two chart axes.

8   Under Chart Tools, on the Design tab, in the Chart Layouts group, click **Add Chart Element**, then click **Axis Titles** and **Primary Horizontal**.

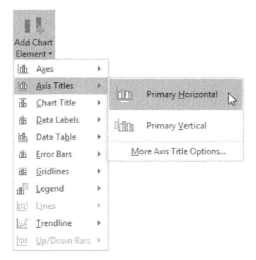

9   Click in the horizontal axis title box in the chart, and replace the default title with: Month as the new axis title.

10  Under Chart Tools, on the Design tab, in the Chart Layouts group, click **Add Chart Element**, then click **Axis Titles** and **Primary Vertical**.

11  Click in the vertical axis title box in the chart and replace the default title with: # of Hits as the new axis title.

12  Under Chart Tools, on the Design tab, in the Chart Layouts group, click **Add Chart Element**, then click **Legend** and **None**.

Now add the legend back to the chart and place it at the bottom. You can choose from five standard locations to place the legend in the chart. You can also manually move it to any location in the chart, or turn it off.

13  Under Chart Tools, on the Design tab, in the Chart Layouts group, click **Add Chart Element**, then click **Legend** and **Bottom**.

Now move the chart into its own chart sheet.

14  Under Chart Tools, on the Design tab, in the Location group, click **Move Chart**.

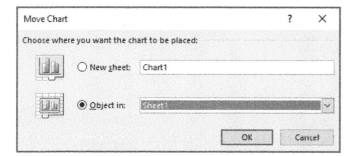

15  In the Move Chart dialog box, click **New sheet** and click **OK**.

16  Click the **Sheet1** worksheet tab.

    The chart is no longer in this worksheet.

17  Click and drag the pie chart to a new position directly underneath the data. The upper left corner of the chart should be in cell A14.

**18** Click the **Chart1** worksheet tab.

By default your chart is created with the major horizontal gridlines. These lines help readers view the top of the bars to the Y-axis markers, especially the bars farthest away from the axis. You can also activate or remove other gridline options.

**19** Under Chart Tools, on the **Design** tab, in the Chart Layouts group, click **Add Chart Element**, then click **Gridlines** and **Primary Major Vertical**.

The addition of vertical lines between the categories now help the readers see each group of data series. You can also add additional sets of horizontal and vertical gridlines.

**20** Under Chart Tools, on the Design tab, in the Chart Layouts group, click **Add Chart Element**, **Gridlines**, then position (but do not click) the mouse cursor over each of the options in the menu.

The Live Preview of the selected option is displayed in the chart. Each of the options acts as a toggle switch – for example, by pointing at the Primary Major Horizontal option, these gridlines turn off.

**21** In the Gridline menu click **Primary Major Vertical** to turn the vertical gridlines off.

If Excel has not clustered the data series the way you want them, you can exchange them.

**22** Under Chart Tools, on the Design tab, in the Data group, click **Switch Row/Column**.

The horizontal axis is now grouped by office with the months clustered together for each office. By changing how you cluster the data, you can see trends that were not obvious using the other grouping method.

**23** Under Chart Tools, on the Design tab, in the Data group, click **Switch Row/Column** again.

The chart should look similar to the following example:

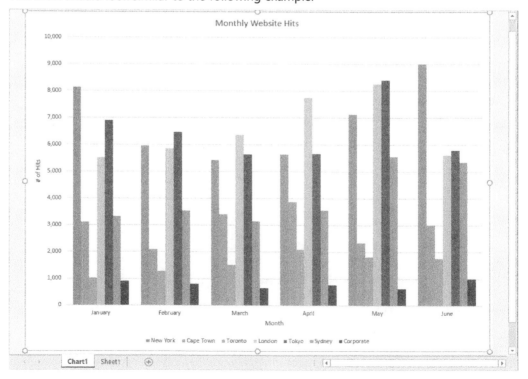

**24** Save the workbook.

## Adding New Data

### Objective 5.1.2

New data series or categories can be added to a worksheet at any time but the chart may not be automatically updated. You can add this new data to the chart to keep it current using any of the following:

- With the chart selected, under Chart Tools, on the Design tab, in the Data group, click **Select Data** to display the Select Data Source dialog box. Change the cell references in **Chart data range** and click **OK**.

- Copy the new data into the clipboard and use **Paste Special** to paste the data into the chart.

- With the chart selected, drag the boundary of the data range selection box on the worksheet to include the new data. This is normally the quickest method.

## Learn to add data to a chart

This exercise demonstrates how to add new data to a chart.

**1** Select the **Sheet1** worksheet in the *Website Hits - Student* workbook.

**2** Scroll up and click the column H header to select the entire column.

**3** On the Home tab, in the Cells group, click **Insert** to add a new column.

**4** Enter the following new data into the worksheet:

| Cell | Value |
|------|-------|
| H4 | July |
| H5 | 10,000 |
| H6 | 4,000 |
| H7 | 2,000 |
| H8 | 10,000 |
| H9 | 8,000 |
| H10 | 6,000 |
| H11 | 1,000 |

Notice that the SUM formulas in column I were automatically changed to include this new column. However, the SUM formula in cell H12 has to be copied from the cell next to it.

**5** Copy the formula in cell **G12** to **H12**.

| ⊿ | A | B | C | D | E | F | G | H | I |
|---|---|---|---|---|---|---|---|---|---|
| 1 | Tolano Adventures | | | | | | | | |
| 2 | Website Hits | | | | | | | | |
| 3 | | | | | | | | | |
| 4 | Office | January | February | March | April | May | June | July | Total |
| 5 | New York | 8,125 | 5,947 | 5,420 | 5,647 | 7,134 | 9,015 | 10,000 | 51,288 |
| 6 | Cape Town | 3,120 | 2,097 | 3,407 | 3,885 | 2,352 | 3,024 | 4,000 | 21,885 |
| 7 | Toronto | 1,017 | 1,281 | 1,512 | 2,107 | 1,825 | 1,761 | 2,000 | 11,503 |
| 8 | London | 5,530 | 5,852 | 6,366 | 7,760 | 8,257 | 5,619 | 10,000 | 49,384 |
| 9 | Tokyo | 6,905 | 6,471 | 5,648 | 5,665 | 8,412 | 5,808 | 8,000 | 46,909 |
| 10 | Sydney | 3,324 | 3,544 | 3,155 | 3,574 | 5,565 | 5,346 | 6,000 | 30,508 |
| 11 | Corporate | 904 | 804 | 641 | 772 | 632 | 998 | 1,000 | 5,751 |
| 12 | Total | 28,925 | 25,996 | 26,149 | 29,410 | 34,177 | 31,571 | 41,000 | |

**6** Click the **Chart1** worksheet tab.

**7** Under Chart Tools, on the **Design** tab, in the Data group, click **Select Data**.

A marquee boundary line appears around the cell range A4 to G11, which is the data currently displayed in the chart. You can change it by simply selecting the entire cell range – including the new column of data – to be used for the chart.

**8**   Select the cell range **A4:H11** in *Sheet1*.

**Note:** You could also have changed the cell reference directly by typing in the new cell range into the Chart data range text box.

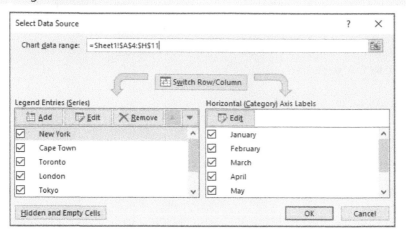

**9**   Click **OK**.

The chart is now updated with this new data.

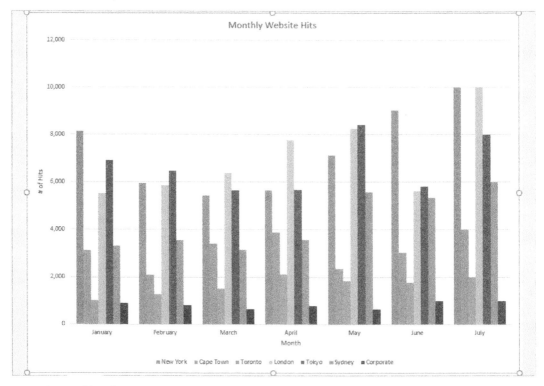

**10**  Save the workbook.

# Using Sparklines

**Objective 2.3.1**

The Sparklines feature allows you to create a miniature chart inside a worksheet cell. This feature allows you to improve the visibility and readability of your worksheet without having to create one or more full-size charts which may take a lot of space. Like a regular chart, the sparkline displays a visual representation of each value in a horizontal or vertical range of cells. Because Excel displays the entire chart in a single worksheet cell, only the data points are shown without any chart components such as a legend, titles, or axis.

There are three types of sparklines:

**Line** – Use this chart type to represent the values. The relative height of each point indicates the size of each value.

**Column** – Use this chart type also to represent the values. The relative height of each column indicates the size of each value.

**Win/Loss** – Use this chart type to indicate whether each value is positive (greater than zero) or negative (less than zero). In this chart, every bar is the same shape and size. However, positive values appear as higher bars and negative values appear as lower bars. Note that this example highlights negative values further by showing them in red.

Sparkline charts have additional capabilities that you will not find in regular charts. Two examples are:

• You can display data in the regular way with a sparkline chart at the same time in the same cells.

- You can activate markers in a sparkline chart such as high, low, first, last, and negative points. Without gridlines and axis markers, these markers help identify important points on the chart.

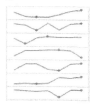

The Sparkline Tools Design tab offers a range of different settings and options to modify and customize sparkline charts.

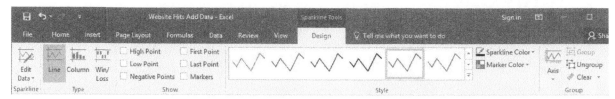

To remove the sparkline chart(s) from your worksheet, use the **Clear** button.
To remove the sparkline from just one cell, use **Clear Selected Sparklines**.
To remove the entire group, use **Clear Selected Sparkline Groups**.

# Learn to insert sparklines

This exercise demonstrates how to insert a sparkline chart into a worksheet.

**1** Make sure the *Website Hits - Student* workbook is active on the screen.

**2** Click the **Sheet1** worksheet tab.

Widen the column so that Excel has more space in which to display the sparkline.

**3** Click in any cell in column **J**. Then, on the Home tab, in the Cells group, click **Format** and then click **Column Width**.

**4** In the Column width text box, change the value to 17 and click **OK**.

Choose different chart layouts and see how the chart is affected.

**5** On the **Insert** tab, in the Sparklines group, click **Line Sparkline**.

**6** Delete any cell references that may be in the Data Range text box, then select the cell range **B5** to **H5**. You may have to move the Create Sparklines dialog box aside to select this cell range.

**7** Click in the **Location Range** text box, delete any cell references that may be in that text box, then select cell **J5** from the worksheet and click **OK**.

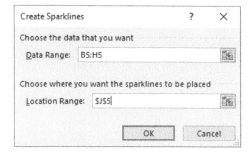

A sparkline chart now appears in cell **J5**. You can copy this to the other cells in column J.

**Hint:** To create a sparkline group at one time using the Create Sparklines dialog box, in step 7, you would select the entire cell range of B5 to H11 as the Data Range and cells J5 to J11 as the Location Range.

8    With cell **J5** selected, click and drag the AutoFill handle in the lower right corner of cell **J5** down to cell **J11**.

After pasting the sparkline chart to the other cells, Excel automatically designates the entire range of cells as a sparkline group. Therefore, a format change to one of those cells automatically applies to the other cells in the group. Whenever you select one or more cells in a sparkline group, a boundary line appears around the group to indicate that those cells belong together.

You can also use the copy and paste method to copy the sparkline chart from one cell to the other cells. When you use this technique, however, Excel does not treat the originating cell as a member of the sparkline group. Because of this, you should always use the AutoFill technique to create a sparkline group in adjacent cells. Otherwise, you will have to manually add the originating cell to the sparkline group.

Have the sparkline charts display markers for the highest and lowest points.

9    Click on any cell in the range **J5** to **J11**, then click the **Design** tab under Sparkline Tools.

10   Under the Sparkline Tools, on the Design tab, in the Show group, click the **High Point** and **Low Point** check boxes to turn them on.

Change the sparkline charts to the other types to see how they would look.

11   Under the Sparkline Tools, on the Design tab, in the Type group, click **Convert to Win/Loss Sparkline** to change the sparkline to a group of columns.

12   Under the Sparkline Tools, on the Design tab, in the Type group, click **Convert to Column Sparkline** to change the sparkline to a group of columns of varying heights.

To remove one or more sparkline charts within the sparkline group, use the Clear Selected Sparkline option. You can also remove the entire sparkline group at one time using the Clear Selected Sparkline Groups option.

13   Under the Sparkline Tools, on the Design tab, in the Group group, click the arrow next to **Clear** and click **Clear Selected Sparkline Groups**.

14   In the Quick Access Toolbar, click **Undo**.

| | A | B | C | D | E | F | G | H | I | J |
|---|---|---|---|---|---|---|---|---|---|---|
| 1 | Tolano Adventures | | | | | | | | | |
| 2 | Website Hits | | | | | | | | | |
| 3 | | | | | | | | | | |
| 4 | Office | January | February | March | April | May | June | July | Total | |
| 5 | New York | 8,125 | 5,947 | 5,420 | 5,647 | 7,134 | 9,015 | 10,000 | 51,288 | |
| 6 | Cape Town | 3,120 | 2,097 | 3,407 | 3,885 | 2,352 | 3,024 | 4,000 | 21,885 | |
| 7 | Toronto | 1,017 | 1,281 | 1,512 | 2,107 | 1,825 | 1,761 | 2,000 | 11,503 | |
| 8 | London | 5,530 | 5,852 | 6,366 | 7,760 | 8,257 | 5,619 | 10,000 | 49,384 | |
| 9 | Tokyo | 6,905 | 6,471 | 5,648 | 5,665 | 8,412 | 5,808 | 8,000 | 46,909 | |
| 10 | Sydney | 3,324 | 3,544 | 3,155 | 3,574 | 5,565 | 5,346 | 6,000 | 30,508 | |
| 11 | Corporate | 904 | 804 | 641 | 772 | 632 | 998 | 1,000 | 5,751 | |
| 12 | Total | 28,925 | 25,996 | 26,149 | 29,410 | 34,177 | 31,571 | 41,000 | | |

15   Save the workbook.

# Printing Charts

You can print charts as part of a worksheet or on their own as individual chart sheet(s). Depending on the circumstances, each method has its own set of advantages.

When you print a chart as part of a worksheet, you are printing a worksheet. In other words, any data or other charts that are also on the worksheet will also be printed at the same time. Therefore, you can change the appearance of the printout by rearranging the worksheet: the chart can be moved around with the data above, below, or next to it. You can also change the size of the chart and the formatting of the data. However, you cannot fit large charts onto one printed page. You must either reduce them in size or manually cut and paste them together on the paper you are using.

If you select only the chart for printing, whether it is on a worksheet or in its own chart sheet, only that chart will be printed. Any data or other charts that may be on the same worksheet will not be included in the printout. The chart will automatically resize itself to the size of the page.

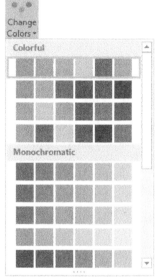

The color charts that Excel creates are interesting to look at on the screen but you may get very different results if you are printing using a black and white printer. The many different chart colors will then convert to various shades of gray which are difficult to distinguish from each other. To ensure that you get the best results, under Chart Tools, on the Design tab, in the Chart Styles group, click **Change Colors** then click one of the Monochromatic (that is, single-color) options to select a color palette that is more favorable to black and white printers.

As an alternative to selecting a monochromatic color palette, you can manually select a different fill pattern of your choosing for each series. These fill patterns allow readers to quickly identify the series (city in this example) within each group.

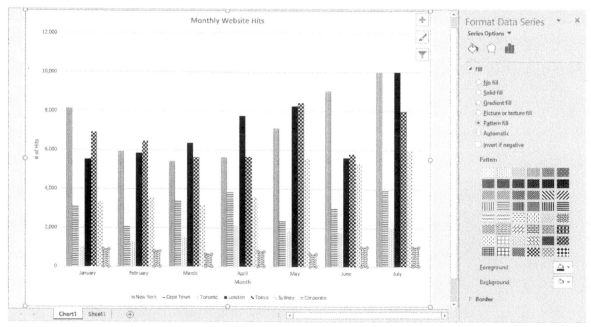

# Learn to preview charts for printing

This exercise demonstrates how to print a chart either as part of a worksheet or as a separate chart sheet.

**1** Make sure the *Website Hits - Student* workbook is active on the screen.

Preview the *Sheet1* worksheet for printing both the data and the chart.

**2** Click any cell outside of the pie chart so that the chart is not selected.

**3** Click **File** and then click **Print**.

**4** Click **Portrait Orientation** and then click **Landscape Orientation** to change the orientation.

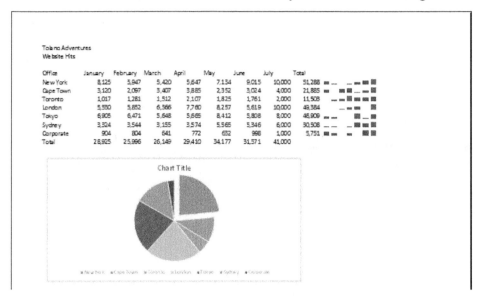

As long as a chart is not in edit mode, Excel prints the worksheet with all of the contents including any chart(s).

Now preview only the pie chart on its own for printing.

**5** Click the ⊙ **Back** button, then click in a blank area inside the pie chart to put it into edit mode.

**6** Click **File** and then click **Print**.

**7** If necessary, click **Portrait Orientation** and then click **Landscape Orientation** to change the orientation.

**8** Click the ⊙ **Back** button, then click in a blank cell outside of the pie chart.

**9** Click the **Chart1** worksheet tab.

**10** Click **File** and then click **Print**.

**11** Click the ⊙ **Back** button, and then save and close the workbook.

# Using the Quick Analysis Tool

**Objective 5.1.4**

As described earlier in this lesson, the first step when creating a chart is to select the range of cells. This same action is used for a number of different tasks including adding subtotals and conditional formatting. Whenever a range of cells is selected, a Quick Analysis icon is displayed next to the bottom right corner cell as shown in this example:

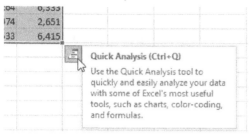

When you click on the icon, a pop-up menu displays with multiple options that are often selected for a cell range:

Used to add conditional formatting to the selected range of cells.

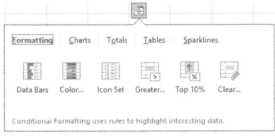

Used to add a chart for the selected range of cells.

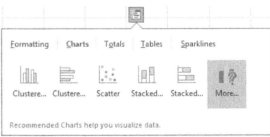

Used to add summary totals below or to the right of the selected range of cells.

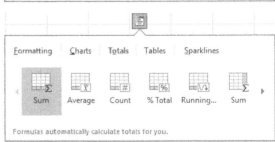

Used to convert the range of cells to a table or to create a PivotTable.

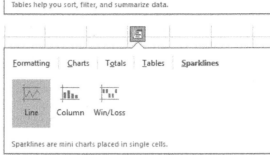

Tables help you sort, filter, and summarize data.

Used to add sparklines to the right of the selected range of cells.

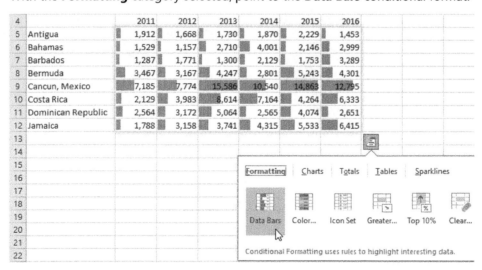

Sparklines are mini charts placed in single cells.

# Learn to use the Quick Analysis tool

This exercise demonstrates the use of the Quick Analysis tool to create conditional formatting, charts, totals, and sparklines for a range of cells.

1   Open the *Caribbean Vacation Bookings* workbook and save it as: Caribbean Vacation Bookings - Student.

2   Select the cell range **B5** to **G12**.

3   Click the **Quick Analysis** icon below the bottom right corner of the selected range.

    When selected, the Quick Analysis menu displays the conditional formatting options by default.

4   With the **Formatting** category selected, point to the **Data Bars** conditional format.

| | 2011 | 2012 | 2013 | 2014 | 2015 | 2016 |
|---|---|---|---|---|---|---|
| Antigua | 1,912 | 1,668 | 1,730 | 1,870 | 2,229 | 1,453 |
| Bahamas | 1,529 | 1,157 | 2,710 | 4,001 | 2,146 | 2,999 |
| Barbados | 1,287 | 1,771 | 1,300 | 2,129 | 1,753 | 3,289 |
| Bermuda | 3,467 | 3,167 | 4,247 | 2,801 | 5,243 | 4,301 |
| Cancun, Mexico | 7,185 | 7,774 | 15,586 | 10,540 | 14,863 | 12,795 |
| Costa Rica | 2,129 | 3,983 | 8,614 | 7,164 | 4,264 | 6,333 |
| Dominican Republic | 2,564 | 3,172 | 5,064 | 2,565 | 4,074 | 2,651 |
| Jamaica | 1,788 | 3,158 | 3,741 | 4,315 | 5,533 | 6,415 |

5   Move the mouse cursor to point to each of the other conditional formatting options.

6   Click the **Greater Than** conditional format.

    The cells in the range containing the largest values are highlighted.

7   In the Greater Than dialog box, change the value to 5000 and click **OK**.

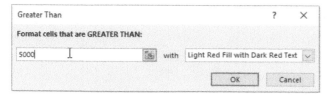

If no longer needed, the conditional formatting can be easily removed.

8  Click the **Quick Analysis** icon again and click **Clear Format** in the Formatting category.

Charts can be created easily as well. However, you should include the row and column containing the headers.

9  Select the cell range **A4** to **G12**, then click the **Quick Analysis** icon and click the **Charts** category.

10  Hover over the first **Clustered Column** on the left, then over the second one, and compare the differences between the two.

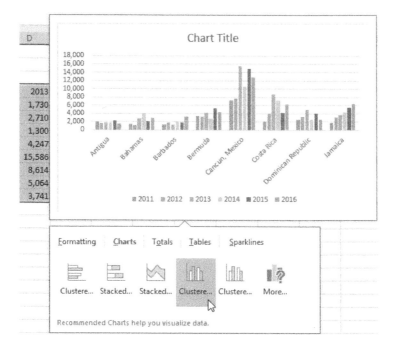

11  Click the **Clustered Column** option on the left, then drag the chart to a new position below the worksheet data. Be sure there is at least one blank row between the data and the chart.

Now use Quick Analysis to create summary calculations for you.

12  Select cell range **A5** to **G12** again and click the **Quick Analysis** icon.

13  Click the **Totals** category, then point to the Sum option on the left, and then point to the Sum option on the right.

---

Notice that the icon indicates where the summary total calculations are placed in the worksheet.

| 4 | | 2011 | 2012 | 2013 | 2014 | 2015 | 2016 | | | |
|---|---|---|---|---|---|---|---|---|---|---|
| 5 | Antigua | 1,912 | 1,668 | 1,730 | 1,870 | 2,229 | 1,453 | **10,862** | | |
| 6 | Bahamas | 1,529 | 1,157 | 2,710 | 4,001 | 2,146 | 2,999 | **14,542** | | |
| 7 | Barbados | 1,287 | 1,771 | 1,300 | 2,129 | 1,753 | 3,289 | **11,529** | | |
| 8 | Bermuda | 3,467 | 3,167 | 4,247 | 2,801 | 5,243 | 4,301 | **23,226** | | |
| 9 | Cancun, Mexico | 7,185 | 7,774 | 15,586 | 10,540 | 14,863 | 12,795 | **68,743** | | |
| 10 | Costa Rica | 2,129 | 3,983 | 8,614 | 7,164 | 4,264 | 6,333 | **32,487** | | |
| 11 | Dominican Republic | 2,564 | 3,172 | 5,064 | 2,565 | 4,074 | 2,651 | **20,090** | | |
| 12 | Jamaica | 1,788 | 3,158 | 3,741 | 4,315 | 5,533 | 6,415 | **24,950** | | |

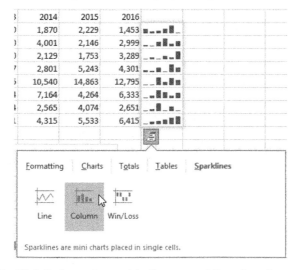

**14** Click the ▶ button to scroll the Quick Analysis menu to the right to see more options, then point to each of the options.

**15** Click in a blank area of the worksheet to close the Quick Analysis menu.

Now insert sparklines. Be sure to select only the cells containing actual data which do not include the headings.

**16** Select the cell range **B5** to **G12**, then click the **Quick Analysis** icon.

**17** Click the **Sparklines** category, and point to each of the sparklines options.

| } | 2014 | 2015 | 2016 | |
|---|---|---|---|---|
| ) | 1,870 | 2,229 | 1,453 | ▪_▪▪▪_ |
| } | 4,001 | 2,146 | 2,999 | _▪▪▪_▪ |
| ) | 2,129 | 1,753 | 3,289 | _▪_▪_▪ |
| 7 | 2,801 | 5,243 | 4,301 | _▪_▪▪ |
| ; | 10,540 | 14,863 | 12,795 | _▪▪▪▪ |
| ł | 7,164 | 4,264 | 6,333 | _▪▪▪_▪ |
| ł | 2,565 | 4,074 | 2,651 | _▪▪_▪_ |
| L | 4,315 | 5,533 | 6,415 | _▪▪▪▪ |

Formatting    Charts    Totals    Tables    **Sparklines**

Line    Column    Win/Loss

Sparklines are mini charts placed in single cells.

**18** Click **Column** to enable these sparklines in column H.

**19** Save and close the workbook.

# Drawing Shapes

**Objective 5.3.1, 5.3.2, 5.3.3**

As a core component of the Microsoft Office Suite, Excel uses the same drawing tools found in Microsoft Word and PowerPoint. In Excel, you can use these drawing tools to highlight significant parts of the worksheet or chart.

However, you should avoid over-using the drawing tools. Excel is a spreadsheet and its primary strength is the ability to perform many calculations quickly. While graphics in a text document or presentation can draw attention to important points, excessive use of graphics in a spreadsheet can have the opposite effect by drawing attention away from key data.

You can create shapes on the Insert tab, in the Illustrations group, under Shapes as shown here.

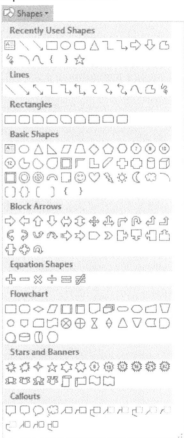

The Shapes menu has 160 different shapes available including text boxes (to display text), rectangles, ovals, and lines as well as a variety of other commonly used shapes. At first, it may seem odd to have a text box when you have the ability to enter text directly into a worksheet cell. However, it is important to understand that a text box shape (as well as any other shape) is independent of worksheet cells. In other words, you cannot reference the contents of a shape with a formula. For example, if cell A1 contained a text box displaying the value "10", then the formula =A1 in cell C1 will display "0". On the other hand, you can format any shape including text boxes to be of any size because it is positioned in a separate layer "in front of" the worksheet cells.

Notice that you only have rectangles and ovals as shapes but not squares and circles. You can use the SHIFT key to draw symmetrical shapes such as using the rectangle to draw a square shape or the oval to draw a circular shape. While holding down the SHIFT key, Excel will force the shape to be a perfect square, circle, or other symmetrical shape.

Note the following points about creating or working with shapes:

- You can create most shapes using the same method. Once activated, the mouse arrow changes to a + symbol. You can then click where you wish the top left corner of the object to begin and drag to the required size.

- Excel organizes groups of shapes by type, some of which are three-dimensional.

- When you use the Text Box feature, Excel changes the mouse cursor to a ↓ symbol. Click in the location where you want the text to begin and start typing.

While Excel's drawing capability provides numerous tools with which to create simple drawings, it is not the same as having a dedicated graphics program. If you need more features and flexibility when manipulating pictures or drawings, it is better to use a dedicated graphics program.

# Moving and Resizing Shapes

**Objective 5.3.3**

After you have drawn the object, you can change its size and appearance. For instance, you will rarely be able to place a shape or object in exactly the right position on the worksheet in your first try. You may also need to adjust the size of your drawing to fit the space available.

To resize an object or shape, you must first select it. The shape or object then displays its eight handles (except lines which only have two handles). By clicking and dragging these handles, you change the shape or object's size and proportion.

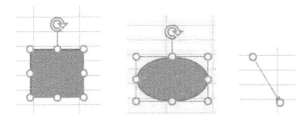

Clicking any of the corner handles enables you to change both the length and width of the two adjoining sides at the same time. Dragging any of the midpoint handles resizes only that one side.

If you want to move a shape to a new position, you do not need to select it first. When you position the mouse cursor over the shape, the cursor changes to ⬩ to indicate that it is ready to move the shape directly underneath it. You can then drag the shape to another location on the worksheet.

To copy a shape object to another location on a worksheet, click the shape to select it, use any of the existing methods to copy it to the internal Clipboard, then use any of the existing methods to paste it

To delete a shape object, click the shape to select it, then press DELETE.

# Formatting Shapes

**Objective 5.3.3**

Excel creates shapes using the settings in the currently selected theme. After you draw the shape on the worksheet, you can customize it using the formatting options in the Ribbon.

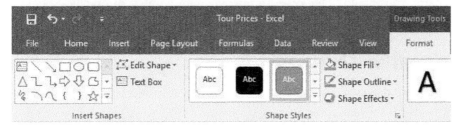

Found under Drawing Tools, on the Format tab, the Shape Styles group includes several formatting tools:

**Theme Fills** – Select from a set of predefined outline and fill color combinations to apply to the shape.

**Shape Fill** – Select colors and patterns to fill the inside of the shape. By default, Excel uses the fill color for the current default theme. You can choose No Fill to make the shape transparent leaving only the shape's border color.

Instead of a solid color fill, you can also choose a picture, gradient (where the shade intensity changes from one end of the object to the other), or texture to fill the inside of the shape.

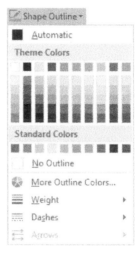

**Shape Outline** – Select colors and patterns for the border(s) around the shape. As with Shape Fill, you can choose No Outline to make the border transparent.

The Weight setting allows you to choose the thickness of the border and the Dashes setting determines whether to use a solid line or a pattern of dots, dashes, or both.

For line and arrow shapes, you can choose from several arrow patterns.

**Shape Effects** – Add a three-dimensional effect to the shape such as a shadow or a reflection (as if a mirror were placed on one edge).

With these various drawing tools and formatting options, your only limits to creating colorful objects on your worksheet are your imagination and time. However, keep in mind that you use spreadsheets primarily for numbers, formulas, and charts. You should, therefore, use the minimum number of graphical objects you need to focus the attention to those parts of your worksheet.

# Learn to work with shapes

This exercise demonstrates how to draw shapes, change their shape, move them around the worksheet, and change their formatting.

1   Open the *Tour Prices* workbook and save it as Tour Prices - Student.

Add a text box to the worksheet.

2   On the **Insert** tab, in the Illustrations group, click **Shapes** and then click **Text Box** (located in the Basic Shapes section, first row, far left). The mouse cursor changes to a ↓ symbol to indicate that you can draw the text box on the worksheet.

**Hint:** You can also use the Text Box command from the Text group on the Insert tab.

**3**   In a blank area of the worksheet to the right of column H, click and hold down the mouse button and drag the mouse to draw a box about 1 inch wide by 1 inch high.

**4**   Inside the text box, type: A Tolano Adventures exclusive!

Excel now displays the Drawing Tools Format tab because you have selected a shape (text box).

You can also add a new shape using the Format tab. However, Excel only displays the Format tab when you have selected a shape that has already been created. Therefore, the first shape can only be created from the Insert tab. After the first shape, you can add more shapes using either the Insert or the Format tabs.

**5**   Under Drawing Tools, on the **Format** tab, in the Insert Shapes group, click **Oval**. The mouse cursor changes to a + symbol.

**6**   Click and hold down the left mouse button above and to the left of cell **H9**. Then, while holding down the mouse button, drag the mouse cursor to a new position below and to the right of cell **H9**.

An oval shape now covers the area in and around cell H9.

**Hint:** If you hold the SHIFT key while dragging the mouse to draw the shape, Excel creates a perfect circle. If you use the SHIFT key with the rectangle tool, Excel draws a square.

**7**   With the oval shape still selected, under Drawing Tools, on the Format tab, in the Shape Styles group, click **Shape Fill**. Click **No Fill**.

After drawing a shape, you will usually need to move it to where you want it placed.

**8**   Point the mouse cursor to the edge of the oval. The mouse cursor changes to a 🔖 symbol. Click and drag the oval shape so that the 8,000 value in cell H9 is in the center of the oval.

**9**   Point the mouse cursor at one of the four corner handles. Click and drag this handle to make the oval smaller or larger. If necessary, move the oval shape again to place the 8,000 value in the center.

**Hint:** You can also use the LEFT, RIGHT, UP and DOWN ARROW keys on the keyboard to move a shape. These keys are often better suited than the mouse for moving shapes very short distances.

**10**   Under Drawing Tools, on the Format tab, in the Insert Shapes group, click **Line Arrow**.

**11**   Point the mouse cursor at the left middle handle of the text box. Notice that four connection handles are displayed around a shape when the mouse cursor is nearby.

**12**   Click and drag the mouse from the handle in the text box to one of the connection handles that will appear around the oval as you move the mouse cursor towards it.

**13**   Under Drawing Tools, on the Format tab, in the Shape Styles group, click **Shape Outline**. Click **Weight** and then click **1½ pt**.

Notice that this change only affected the arrow because it is the currently selected shape.

**Note:** When you select any of the commands in the Drawing Tools Format tab to modify a shape, the changes will only affect the shape that is currently selected.

Not only can you change the thickness of a line, you can also change its color and switch from a solid line to one of several types of dashed lines. These same formatting changes can also be done to the border outline of other shapes such as ovals and rectangles.

14  Under Drawing Tools, on the Format tab, in the Shape Styles group, click **Shape Outline**. Click **Blue, Accent 1, Darker 25%** (fifth column from the left, second from the bottom) in the Theme Colors section.

When you drew the line from the text box to the oval shape, you connected all three objects together by starting and ending on one of the connection handles. This connection stays in place even when you move the shape.

15  Click on the oval shape. The handles should appear around the oval shape but not around any other shape.

16  Ensure the mouse cursor appears as a ⛶ symbol to indicate that it will be used to move a shape then click and drag the oval shape to encompass the Antarctica text in cell **B9**.

17  Under Drawing Tools, on the Format tab, in the Shape Styles group, click **Shape Outline**. Click **Weight** and then click **1½ pt**.

18  If necessary, adjust the size and position of the oval around the text label Antarctica.

Add color around the edges of the text box.

19  Click anywhere in the text box to select it again.

20  Under Drawing Tools, on the Format tab, in the Shape Styles group, click **Shape Effects**. Click **Glow**, and then click the Glow Variation **Green, 11 pt glow, Accent color 6** (right-most column, second from the bottom).

The completed worksheet should look similar to the following:

| Tour Prices Breakdown (Average based on 7-day Trip) | | | | | | |
|---|---|---|---|---|---|---|
| Travel Item | Group | Tour | Flight | Hotel | Misc. | Total Cost |
| Kilimanjaro Climb | RC | 4,000 | | | 1,000 | 5,000 |
| Mt. Shasta Climb | RC | 700 | | | | 700 |
| North Carolina | RC | 500 | | | | 500 |
| Tucson, Mt. Lemmon, Cochise Stronghold | RC | 350 | | | | 350 |
| Antarctica | E | 4,000 | 3,000 | | 1,000 | 8,000 |
| Sydney Whale Watching (*Family of 4) | E | 250 | | | | 250 |
| Vancouver Whale Watching (*Family of 4) | E | 500 | | | 100 | 600 |
| Maui Whale Watching (*Family of 4) | E | 200 | 2,000 | 1,000 | | 3,200 |

A Tolano Adventures exclusive!

21  Save the workbook.

# Inserting Pictures

### Objective 5.3.2

Excel can insert pictures, photographs, and clip art images into worksheets. It will accept pictures in any of the common image formats such as bmp, gif, jpeg, png and tiff.

To insert pictures, clip art, and other types of images from your local computer into the worksheet, on the Insert tab, in the Illustrations group, click **Picture**. The Insert Picture dialog box, then, enables you to search for and select a picture file to insert.

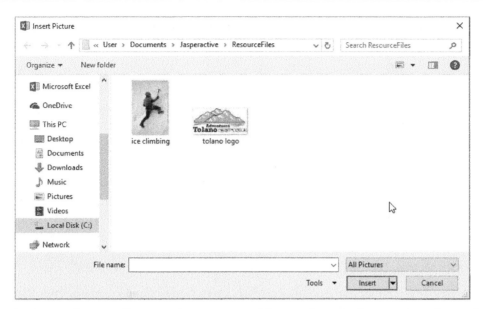

To insert pictures, clip art, and other types of images from the Internet into the worksheet, on the Insert tab, in the Illustrations group, click **Online Pictures**. The Insert Pictures pop-up window then displays enabling you to search for clip art from the Internet.

Pictures can also be inserted into the header or footer to display on every printed page. This is often used for corporate logos.

# Learn to work with pictures

This exercise demonstrates how to insert pictures into a worksheet.

1    Make sure the *Tour Prices - Student* workbook is open on the screen.

Add your first picture to the worksheet.

2    Click on the first blank cell below the text box containing the words "A Tolano Adventures exclusive!" This is where the picture will be placed.

3    On the **Insert** tab, in the Illustrations group, click **Pictures**.

4    In the Insert Picture dialog box, navigate to the student data files folder, where the *Ice Climbing* file is located.

5    Select the *Ice Climbing* file and click **Insert**.

When you insert a picture into a worksheet, Excel displays it with handles around it. These handles can be used to resize the picture.

6    Click and drag the bottom right corner handle up to reduce the size of the logo image to a height of 4 to 5 worksheet rows.

**Note:** When resizing a picture, you should only use one of the four corner handles to ensure the aspect ratio is maintained.

Now search for a picture from the Internet.

7    On the **Insert** tab, in the Illustrations group, click **Online Pictures**.

The Online Pictures pop-up window is displayed.

8   In the **Bing** search text box, type: travel and press ENTER.

9   Scroll through the pictures, then click one of your choosing and click **Insert**.

10  If necessary, make the picture smaller by dragging one (or more) of the corner handles. Click and drag the picture to an empty area of the worksheet directly below the ice climbing picture. Try to keep the pictures from extending past column L so that the entire worksheet can print on one page in landscape mode.

Now add the company logo as a header for the worksheet.

11  On the **Insert** tab, in the Text group, click **Header & Footer**.

The worksheet is now displayed in Page Layout view.

12  Click in the left header section. This will position the picture on the left side of the header.

13  Under Header & Footer Tools, on the Design tab, in the Header & Footer Elements group, click **Picture**.

    The Insert Pictures selection box is displayed.

14  Click **Browse** to search for a picture file from the local computer.

15  In the Insert Picture dialog box, if necessary, navigate to the student data files folder, select the *Tolano Logo* file, and click **Insert**.

    The code &[Picture] now appears in the left header section, indicating that a picture has been inserted here.

16  Click in a blank area of the worksheet to view the results.

You can also format the picture and resize it.

17  Click in the left header section, so that it is visible again showing the &[Picture] code.

18  Under Header & Footer Tools, on the **Design** tab, in the Header & Footer Elements group, click **Format Picture**.

19  In the Format Picture dialog box, verify that the **Lock aspect ratio** check box is turned on, then reduce the **Scale Height** or **Scale Width** to **50%**.

20  Click **OK** and click in a blank area of the worksheet to view the results.

21  Click **File** and **Print**.

22  Jump to page 2 to verify that the logo appears on that page as well.

23  Change the Portrait Orientation to **Landscape Orientation**.

Your worksheet should look similar to the following:

| Tour Prices Breakdown (Average based on 7-day Trip) | | | | | | |
|---|---|---|---|---|---|---|
| Travel Item | Group | Tour | Flight | Hotel | Misc. | Total Cost |
| Kilimanjaro Climb | RC | 4,000 | | | 1,000 | 5,000 |
| Mt. Shasta Climb | RC | 700 | | | | 700 |
| North Carolina | RC | 500 | | | | 500 |
| Tucson, Mt. Lemmon, Cochise Stronghold | RC | 350 | | | | 350 |
| Antarctica | E | 4,000 | 3,000 | | 1,000 | 8,000 |
| Sydney Whale Watching (*Family of 4) | E | 250 | | | | 250 |
| Vancouver Whale Watching (*Family of 4) | E | 500 | | | 100 | 600 |
| Maui Whale Watching (*Family of 4) | E | 200 | 2,000 | 1,000 | | 3,200 |
| Bogota Cycling (*Two People) | Eco | | 1,500 | 1,500 | 200 | 3,200 |
| Perth Cycling (*Two People) | Eco | | 4,000 | 3,500 | 500 | 8,000 |
| Copenhagen Cycling (*Two People) | Eco | | 2,100 | 3,000 | 400 | 5,500 |

A Tolano Adventures exclusive!

**24** Click the **Back** button, and on the **View** tab in the Workbook Views group, click **Normal** to return the worksheet to the normal view.

**25** Save the workbook.

# Using the Image Editor

**Objective 5.3.3**

Excel provides several image-editing tools to allow you to adjust and correct photographs and clip art objects on your worksheet. When you add or select a picture or clip art, Excel displays this Format tab on the Ribbon:

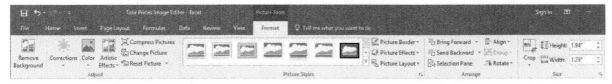

Some image-editing tools on the tab include:

**Remove Background** – Remove the background surrounding the main subject within the photograph. If this tool is selected, Excel displays another tab to help you identify the areas of the photograph to keep or remove.

**Corrections** – Change the brightness and contrast settings, and adjust the sharpness of the edges around the various objects within the picture or clip art.

**Color** – Adjust the color saturation and color tone settings, or change the color of the picture or clip art.

**Artistic Effects** – Modify the photograph using various filters to achieve special effects.

**Picture Border** – By default, pictures and clip art do not have a border. Use this option to set the color, weight, and dashes options for the border around the object. These are the same options as for drawing shapes.

**Picture Effects** – Set various three-dimensional picture effects. These are the same options as for drawing shapes.

**Picture Layout** – Crop or resize the picture or clip art to a shape (such as a circle or square), and possibly add a text box.

**Visual Styles** – Apply a predefined set of borders or a three-dimensional effect to the picture or clip art. Excel also crops it to fit the shape used.

**Crop** – Hide the outer parts of the picture or clip art to achieve a stronger focus on the main subject.

**Shape Height**, **Shape Width** – Manually set the height and width of the picture or clip art.

As with drawing shapes, you should not over-use pictures or other images in your worksheet in order to avoid distracting readers from the main data.

# Learn to edit images

This exercise demonstrates how to edit inserted images.

1   Make sure the *Tour Prices - Student* workbook is open on the screen

Select one of the pictures and try some of the editing options in the Adjust group on the Format tab. These editing options apply to the inside of the picture.

2   Click on the ice climbing picture. Excel displays handles around its edges.

3   Under Picture Tools, on the **Format** tab, in the Adjust group, click **Corrections**.

4   Position the mouse cursor over some of the options available and observe the Live Preview effect on the picture. Click in a blank area away from the Corrections drop-down menu.

5   Under Picture Tools, on the Format tab, in the Adjust group, click **Color**.

6   Position the mouse cursor over some of the options available and observe the Live Preview effect on the picture.

7   Under Picture Tools, on the Format tab, in the Adjust group, click **Artistic Effects**.

8   Position the mouse cursor over some of the options available and observe the Live Preview effect on the picture. Click in a blank area away from the Artistic Effects drop-down menu.

The Picture Styles group on the Format tab offers another set of editing tools that apply to the outside edge of the picture.

9   Under Picture Tools, on the Format tab, in the Picture Styles group, click the **More** button next to the Picture Styles.

10  Position the mouse cursor over some of the options available and observe the Live Preview effect on the picture. Click in a blank area away from the Picture Styles drop-down menu.

11  Under Picture Tools, on the Format tab, in the Picture Styles group, click **Picture Layout**.

12  Position the mouse cursor over some of the options available and observe the Live Preview effect on the picture. Click in a blank area away from the Picture Layout drop-down menu.

Add a border around the picture.

**13** Under Picture Tools, on the Format tab, in the Picture Styles group, click **Picture Border**, then click **Weight**, and click **1 pt**.

**14** Click on a blank worksheet cell to see the border around the picture.

The border can also be removed.

**15** Click the ice climbing picture to select it, then under Picture Tools, on the Format tab, in the Picture Styles group, click **Picture Border**, then click **No Outline**.

Now remove the background for one of the pictures.

**16** Under Picture Tools, on the Format tab, in the Adjust group, click **Remove Background**.

Excel removes the background and keeps the main subject in the picture.

**17** On the Background Removal tab, in the Close group, click **Keep Changes**.

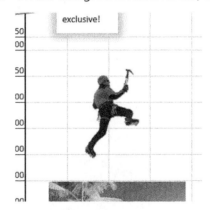

**18** Save and close the workbook.

# Modifying Graphics Objects

## Using the Format Shape Pane

**Objective 5.3.3**

Whenever you select a graphics object or picture, the Ribbon adds a Format tab with a variety of formatting settings. As is often the case, there are more formatting settings than space available in the Ribbon.

The full set of formatting settings is available from the Format Shape pane. This pane can be accessed in a number of ways including:

- Under Drawing Tools, on the Format tab, in the Shape Styles group, click the **Format Shape** dialog box launcher.

* Right-click on the shape and click **Format Shape** or **Size and Properties** from the pop-up menu.

The Format Shape pane is then displayed on the right side of the worksheet:

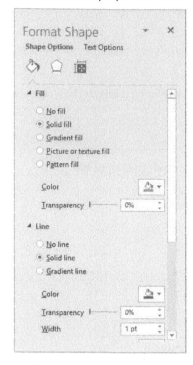
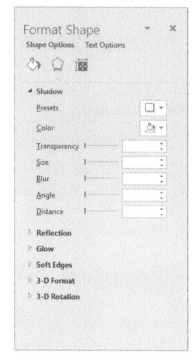
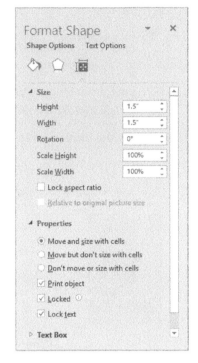

Similarly, the Text Options in the Format Shape pane is used for formatting options for text boxes and WordArt objects. This pane can be accessed by:

* Under Drawing Tools, on the Format tab, in the Word Styles group, click the **Format Text Effects** dialog box launcher.

* Right-click on the shape and click **Format Shape** or **Format Text Effects** from the pop-up menu.

The Format Shape pane is then displayed set to the Text Options:

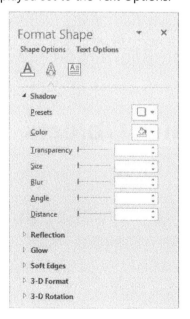

Similarly, the Format Picture pane is used for formatting options for clip art and pictures. This pane can be accessed by:

- Under Picture Tools, on the Format tab, in the Picture Styles group, click the **Format Shape** dialog box launcher.

- Right-click on the shape and click **Format Picture** or **Size and Properties** from the pop-up menu.

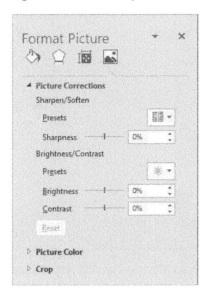

If the Size & Properties group is selected in the Format Shape/Format Picture pane, then the Properties settings are displayed:

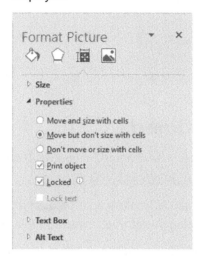

The first three settings (move and size options with cells) determine the behavior of the picture or shape when the cells underneath are moved or resized. For example, suppose you drew a circle that at least partially touches cell N18. If the property setting for the circle is set to Move and size with cells, then the circle will become taller if you increase the height of row 18, or the circle will become wider if you increase the width of column N. Similarly, the circle will move higher if you delete row 16 (or any other row above the circle).

The Print object setting allows this shape or picture to be included for printing if the worksheet is printed. If the worksheet protection is enabled, the Locked setting is used to protect it from being changed.

# Resizing, Reshaping, and Scaling Graphics Objects

Changing the size, shape and position of a graphics object can be done very easily with Excel. Usually the mouse is the fastest method of making these changes.

In some cases, you may not want the unrestrained freedom to make certain kinds of changes such as changing the proportion of the height to the width which we refer to as *aspect ratio*. To maintain this ratio, you can lock it temporarily when you use the mouse to resize an object by using one of these keys at the same time:

CTRL – Lock the center of the object while its size and shape changes.

SHIFT – Lock the aspect ratio of the object while its size changes.

CTRL+SHIFT – Lock both the position and the aspect ratio of the object.

If you are drawing the object for the first time, using these keyboard keys will make the object symmetrical. For example, square instead of rectangular, and circular instead of oval. If the object has already been drawn, using these keyboard keys will maintain the current aspect ratio. For example, an oval will remain an oval except that the object will be proportionately larger or smaller.

In addition, you can reshape many objects. When you select one of these objects, Excel displays an adjustment handle in the form of a small yellow circle. By clicking and dragging this handle, you can modify the shape of one part of the object without changing the shape of the rest of it.

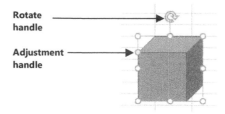

# Rotating Graphics Objects

Rotating a graphics object refers to changing its angle. The object can be rotated clockwise or counter-clockwise. You can rotate most graphics objects including shapes, pictures, and clip art.

However, the rotate option is not offered for lines because they only have two handles. You can change the angle of lines simply by dragging one of the handles to a different position.

Use one of the following methods to rotate a selected object in Excel:

* Click and drag the rotate handle above the object in the direction for the rotation angle.

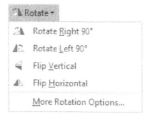

* Under Drawing Tools, on the Format tab, in the Arrange group, click **Rotate** to select one of the pre-defined angles.

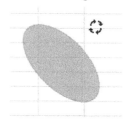

* Under Drawing Tools, on the Format tab, in the Size group, click the dialog box launcher. In the Size category of the Format Shape dialog box, enter the angle in the **Rotation** field.
* Right-click the object and click **Size and Properties**. In the Size category of the Format Shape pane, enter the angle in the **Rotation** field.

# Learn to work with graphic objects

This exercise demonstrates how to resize, reshape and rotate shapes and pictures.

**1**    Create a new blank workbook.

**2**    On the **Insert** tab, in the Illustrations group, click **Shapes**. Then draw a cube (located in Basic Shapes) approximately 1.5" wide by 1.5" high (or 4 cm wide by 4 cm high). You do not need to be precise – you will adjust its size in the next step.

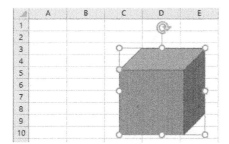

**3**    Under Drawing Tools, on the Format tab, in the Size group, click on the spin buttons for both the **Shape Height** and **Shape Width** boxes until both are 1.5" (or 4 cm). Your new shape is now a perfect cube.

**4**    Click the spin button for the **Shape Width** until the value is 3" (or 8 cm).

**Hint:** You can also type the new values directly into the text boxes. This may be easier than using the mouse to change the length or width of a shape.

The square cube is now rectangular.

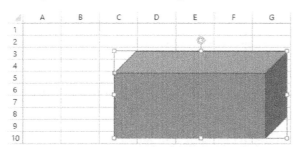

**5**    Click **Undo** in the Quick Access Toolbar.

**6**    With the cube selected, click and drag the bottom right corner handle downward and to the right. Move to the right more than downward so that the cube is no longer square. Release the mouse button.

Now change the size of the cube using the mouse again but lock the aspect ratio so that it stays a cube.

**7**    Click **Undo** in the Quick Access Toolbar.

**8**    Hold down the SHIFT key, and click and drag the bottom right corner handle downward and to the right. Release the mouse button.

Notice that the new shape remains a perfect cube even if you try to move the mouse in different directions. Also, the top left corner (the opposite end of the handle you are moving) does not move as the shape grows. This is the effect of using the SHIFT key while resizing the shape.

Change the size of the cube again but lock the center position of the shape.

**9**    Click **Undo** in the Quick Access Toolbar.

**10** Hold down the CTRL key, and click and drag the bottom right corner handle to the right. Release the mouse button when the left edge of the shape has moved past the left edge of the worksheet.

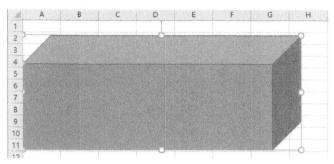

Notice that, while dragging the mouse, the center of the shape does not move. Therefore, the width of the shape grows equally on both the left and right side as you drag the handle to the right. This is the effect of using the CTRL key while resizing the shape.

If the left edge of the shape moves past the left edge of the worksheet, Excel cuts the left edge of the shape back when you release the mouse button. This is the exception to the rule of using the CTRL key to lock the center of the shape in the same position.

Now rotate an object manually using the rotate handle.

**11** Click **Undo** in the Quick Access Toolbar.

**12** Position the cursor over its rotate handle.

Excel replaces the cursor symbol with the rotate symbol (⟳).

**13** Click and drag the rotate handle clockwise (to the right) by 45°.

**Note:** You can force the shape to rotate in 15° increments by holding down the SHIFT key. For this exercise, you do not need to rotate by exactly 45°.

**14** Click **Undo**, and under Drawing Tools, on the Format tab, in the Arrange group, click **Rotate**. Then click **More Rotation Options**.

Excel displays the Format Shape pane showing the many shape formatting options.

**15** Change the Rotation value to 45° by clicking the increment or decrement buttons, then close the Format Shape task pane.

**Hint:** You can enter a number directly into the Rotation text box. You can also enter negative values and angles greater than 360°.

**16** Click **Undo** in the Quick Access Toolbar.

**17** Under Drawing Tools, on the Format tab, in the Arrange group, click **Rotate**. Position the mouse cursor over each of the four menu options and observe the Live Preview effects on the shape.

**18** Click on any blank area of the worksheet to close the menu.

Now change the shape of the cube using the adjustment handle.

**19** Click and drag the adjustment handle ⬡ in different directions to see how the cube changes shape.

**20** Close the workbook without saving it.

# Lesson Summary

Now that you have completed this lesson, you should be able to:

☑ create charts

☑ move a chart to a different location on a worksheet or its own chart sheet

☑ resize a chart to a different size or shape

☑ change the chart type

☑ work with pie charts

☑ change the chart design

☑ add new data to the chart

☑ create, customize, and remove a sparkline chart

☑ print a chart

☑ use the Quick Analysis Tool

☑ draw different types of shapes on a worksheet

☑ move, resize, and format shapes

☑ insert clip art and pictures

☑ use the Image Editor tools

☑ use the Format Shape pane

☑ resize, reshape, and rotate graphics objects

# Review Questions

1.  You might want to use a chart in your worksheet to:

    a.  Hide sensitive information.

    b.  Identify trends or patterns in the data.

    c.  Automate repetitive actions.

    d.  Ensure a consistent look for all pages in the workbook.

2.  Which of the following are chart types supported in Excel?

    a.  Area, block, combo.

    b.  Block, column, bar.

    c.  Column, line, XY (scatter chart).

    d.  Stock, surface, sonar.

3.  Which of the following types of chart is suited for displaying relative sizes (or percentages) of each piece of a total?

    a.  Scatter                   c.  Bar

    b.  Line                      d.  Pie

4.  How many series of data can be shown on a pie chart?

    a.  One                       c.  Three

    b.  Two                       d.  Any number

5.  Which of the following are changes you can make to a chart design?

    a.  Fill or outline color, Reflection, change the chart type.

    b.  Add a chart title or legend, select a different chart layout, exchange the data rows and columns, and change the chart type.

    c.  Shadow effects, height and width, fill or outline color.

6. Which of the following are types of sparkline charts?

   a. Star, Column and Bar.

   b. Column, Star and Win/Loss.

   c. Line, Bar and Column.

   d. Line, Column and Win/Loss.

7. If you have a worksheet that contains both a chart and the data for the chart, you have the ability to select only the chart to print on its own.

   a. True                              b. False

8. Which of the following is the Quick Analysis Tool used for?

   a. Insert a trend line to a chart.

   b. Perform what-if analysis.

   c. Insert charts, sparklines, pivot tables, and conditional formatting

   d. Inspect a chart for errors.

9. To add shapes and illustrations to a worksheet, you use commands on which tab of the Ribbon?

   a. View                          c. Data

   b. Insert                        d. Home

10. Before you can change the shape fill color of a graphic object, you must:

   a. Remove any existing shape effects.

   b. Adjust the size of the object.

   c. Select it.

   d. Adjust the scale of the object.

11. Which of the following are types of formatting options can you apply to a graphic object?

   a. Fill or outline color, reflection, three-dimensional rotation, shadow effects.

   b. Shadow effects, change the chart type, select a different set of worksheet data.

   c. Add a chart title or legend, picture effects, three-dimensional rotation, borders.

12. Which types of formatting can you apply to both pictures and clip art?

   a. Shadow effects, borders, change the chart type.

   b. Borders, reflection, fill or outline color, shadow effects.

   c. Colors, artistic effects, visual styles, picture effects.

Microsoft®

# Excel 2016

Core Certification Guide

# Lesson 7: Organizing Data

## Lesson Objectives

In this lesson, you will look at various methods of organizing data to improve your ability to analyze it. On completion of this lesson, you will be able to:

☐ create, modify, and delete range names

☐ use Go To to jump to a cell or named range

☐ convert a range of cells to a table

☐ modify a table by adding and deleting rows and columns of data

☐ apply and remove formatting on a table

☐ convert a table to a range of cells

☐ sort data

☐ use filtering on data

☐ remove duplicate rows of data

☐ outline and group data using automatic subtotals

☐ outline and group data by manually inserting subtotals

## Working with Named Ranges

### Creating Named Ranges

When developing worksheets, you will find that they quickly become very large and it becomes difficult to keep track of all the cells. One useful feature to help you cope with the vast amount of data is the ability to create a meaningful name for a cell or range of cells. For example, it is much easier to understand the formula =Total_Revenues–Total_Expenses than a cryptic formula such as = C7–C18. With meaningful names, it becomes easier for users to understand the purpose of these cells.

To define a range with a name, select the range and then use one of the following methods:

- on the Formulas tab, in the Defined Names group, click **Define Name**, or
- click in the **Name Box** and type the name, or
- right-click the selected range and then click **Define Name**.

Once you define a name for a cell or a range of cells, you can use that name when creating formulas. Excel also provides tools to convert formulas by replacing the cell references with their new range names.

You can also quickly jump to a named range by using Go To or by selecting the named range from the Name Box list to the left of the formula bar.

In addition to making spreadsheets easier to read by using meaningful names, range names can reduce the number of errors made. For example, the formula =C7–C18 can easily be entered incorrectly. However, if you incorrectly enter any range name in a formula such as =Total_Revenues–Total_Expenses, Excel will not be able to match that range name to any cell and will display an error message.

Range names also reduce errors if you change the cells included in the range. For example, suppose you change the cell range for the range name Expenses from C10:C18 to C10:C19. By changing the cell range once, then every formula in the workbook that uses the Expenses range name will be automatically updated. If you did not use a range name, then you must ensure that the cell range C10:C18 is changed everywhere it is used in the workbook. You will likely miss one or more of them.

Range names can be from 1 to 255 characters in length. They may contain alphabetic or numeric characters (alphanumeric), underscores (_), backslashes (\), periods (.) and question marks (?). You cannot use spaces in range names. The first character must be alphanumeric, an underscore, or a backslash.

# Learn to create range names

This exercise demonstrates how to create range names and set up formulas using those range names.

**1** Open the *Income Statement* workbook and save as: Income Statement - Student.

Now create a range name to use in sales calculations.

**2** Select cells **C5:C6**.

**3** On the **Formulas** tab, in the Defined Names group, click **Define Name**.

The New Name dialog box displays with the cell range entered.

**4** In the Name field, type: Revenues and click **OK**.

From now on, whenever you select these two cells, the range name Revenues displays in the Name Box, which appears to the left of the formula bar.

**5** Select each of the cells in the cell range **C5:C6** and observe what displays in the Name Box.

6 Select the cell range **C5:C6** and observe what displays in the Name Box.

This demonstrates that the range name only appears when the entire range is selected.

7 Select cells **C10:C17**. On the Formulas tab, in the Defined Names group, click **Define Name**.

8 In the **Name** field, type: Expenses and click **OK**.

**Hint:** You can also create a range name by selecting the desired cell(s) and clicking in the Name Box on the formula bar. You can then type the desired name and press ENTER.

Now enter summary formulas using this range name.

9 Select cell **C7**.

**Note:** Range names are not case sensitive – you can enter any mixture of upper and lower case characters.

10 Type: =SUM(Revenues) and press ENTER.

Notice that as you type the first one or two characters of the range name, a quick tip box appears, showing you this name and other functions with similar names. You can use the mouse to double-click the range name in the quick tip box to select it and continue with entering the rest of the formula.

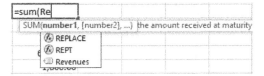

11 Select cell **C18**, type: =SUM(ex to enter the first part of the formula.

12 Double-click on the **Expenses** name in the quick tip box to select it, continue with typing: ) and press ENTER.

13 Select cells **B7:C7**.

14 On the Formulas tab, in the Defined Names group, click **Create from Selection**.

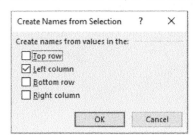

15 Verify that the **Left column** check box is the only one turned on and click **OK**.

16 Select cell **C7**.

Note that the range name in the Name Box is **Total_Revenues**.

**Hint:** Excel does not permit blank spaces in range names. You can use the underscore character as one alternative between the words in a multi-word range name.

Next you will create a range name for the *Total Expenses* cell, but this time, using the Name Manager.

17 Select cell **C18**.

18 On the Formulas tab, in the Defined Names group, click **Name Manager**.

The Name Manager dialog box is now displayed.

**19** In the Name Manager dialog box, click **New** to create a new range name.

**20** Verify that the **Name** is Total_Expenses and that the Refers to field contains the formula =Sheet1!$C$18, then click **OK**.

If the Name Manager dialog box is blocking access to the worksheet behind it, you can minimize it temporarily by clicking the **Collapse** button to the right of the Refers to field. You can then select a range of cells from the worksheet.

The Name Manager dialog box now has this new range name added, similar to the following example:

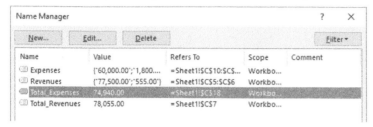

**21** Click **Close** to close the Name Manager dialog box.

Enter the formula to calculate the Net Income, using the range names.

**22** Select cell **C20**, and type: =

**23** On the Formulas tab, in the Defined Names group, click **Use in Formula**.

**24** Click **Total_Revenues**, then press – (minus) to indicate that you are going to perform a subtraction.

**25** On the Formulas tab, in the Defined Names group, click **Use in Formula**. Click **Total_Expenses** and press ENTER.

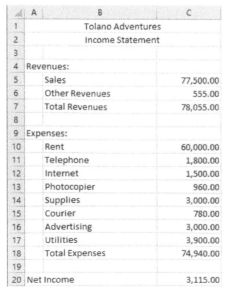

| | A | B | C |
|---|---|---|---|
| 1 | | Tolano Adventures | |
| 2 | | Income Statement | |
| 3 | | | |
| 4 | Revenues: | | |
| 5 | | Sales | 77,500.00 |
| 6 | | Other Revenues | 555.00 |
| 7 | | Total Revenues | 78,055.00 |
| 8 | | | |
| 9 | Expenses: | | |
| 10 | | Rent | 60,000.00 |
| 11 | | Telephone | 1,800.00 |
| 12 | | Internet | 1,500.00 |
| 13 | | Photocopier | 960.00 |
| 14 | | Supplies | 3,000.00 |
| 15 | | Courier | 780.00 |
| 16 | | Advertising | 3,000.00 |
| 17 | | Utilities | 3,900.00 |
| 18 | | Total Expenses | 74,940.00 |
| 19 | | | |
| 20 | Net Income | | 3,115.00 |

**26** Save the workbook.

## Modifying and Deleting Named Ranges

You can use the Name Manager to modify and delete range names or change the cell range references.

Be cautious when deleting named ranges. When you delete a named range, any formula that refers to this name no longer displays the correct value. Deleting a range name may also cause a domino effect with other formulas that indirectly refer to this formula.

# Learn to modify name ranges

This exercise demonstrates how to use the Name Manager to update and delete range names.

1   Ensure the *Income Statement - Student* workbook is open.

A common situation is adding more rows to a named range. As long as you add the rows inside the range, Excel automatically includes the new data as part of the range. If you add the new data outside of the range, you will need to expand the range to include the new row(s).

2   Click the gray header for row 18 to highlight the entire row. Right-click in the highlighted row and click **Insert** in the menu.

3   Select cell **B18**, type: Travel and press TAB.

4   In cell **C18** type: 1400 and press ENTER.

Note that none of the figures in the report changed because the new entry sits outside of the named range Expenses. Now expand the named range to include the new entry.

When you first created the range name, you could have included additional blank cells for future growth. Then, as you add new entries to the list, Excel automatically recalculates the total expenses formula.

5   On the Formulas tab, in the Defined Names group, click **Name Manager**.

6   In the Name Manager dialog box, click the **Expenses** row to select it.

7   In the Refers to text field, change the range to =Sheet1!$C$10:$C$18 as the range.

8   Click **Update** (the checkmark) to the left of the field to update the changes, and click **Close**.

The worksheet should now show the correct calculations for each of the functions:

| | A | B | C |
|---|---|---|---|
| 1 | | Tolano Adventures | |
| 2 | | Income Statement | |
| 3 | | | |
| 4 | Revenues: | | |
| 5 | | Sales | 77,500.00 |
| 6 | | Other Revenues | 555.00 |
| 7 | | Total Revenues | 78,055.00 |
| 8 | | | |
| 9 | Expenses: | | |
| 10 | | Rent | 60,000.00 |
| 11 | | Telephone | 1,800.00 |
| 12 | | Internet | 1,500.00 |
| 13 | | Photocopier | 960.00 |
| 14 | | Supplies | 3,000.00 |
| 15 | | Courier | 780.00 |
| 16 | | Advertising | 3,000.00 |
| 17 | | Utilities | 3,900.00 |
| 18 | | Travel | 1,400.00 |
| 19 | | Total Expenses | 76,340.00 |
| 20 | | | |
| 21 | Net Income | | 1,715.00 |

Try deleting a named range and see how it affects the worksheet.

**9**   On the Formulas tab, in the Defined Names group, click **Name Manager**.

**10**   Click the **Revenues** row and then click **Delete**.

Excel displays a message box asking you to confirm the deletion of this range name.

**11**   Click **OK** for the confirmation message box and then click **Close** to close the Name Manager dialog box.

As shown in the following example, when you remove a named range, Excel displays an error indicator regarding any formulas that depend on that name. Note also that the change has affected the formula in cell **C21** as well, even though it does not use the range name Revenues directly.

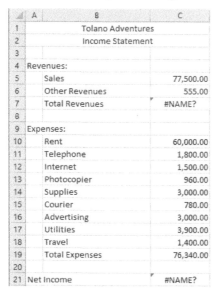

**12**   In the Quick Access Toolbar, click **Undo**.

**13**   Save the workbook.

# Go To a Cell or Named Range

**Objective 1.2.2**

Moving from cell to cell in a worksheet is very simple because the process is the same as with other Windows programs. You can select a cell that appears on the screen simply by clicking on it. If you need to scroll to sections of the worksheet that are currently off the screen, you can use the scroll buttons.

With Excel, you can use a quicker method of jumping to a specific cell (as long as you know exactly what the cell address is) by using the Go To feature. With very large worksheets, the Go To feature helps you to navigate around them more easily.

To display the Go To dialog box, use one of the following methods:

- press F5, or

- press CTRL+G.

Alternatively, you can also use the Name Box located to the left of the formula bar to select a named range of cells or to jump to a specific worksheet cell.

# Learn to use the Go To feature

This exercise demonstrates how to jump to a cell or named range using the Go To dialog box and the Name Box.

1   Ensure the *Income Statement - Student* workbook is open.

2   Click on cell **A3** to jump to that cell using the mouse.

Now select a cell range using the Go To dialog box.

3   Press F5.

4   In the Go To dialog box, click **Expenses** and click **OK**.

Use the Name Box to jump to another named range.

5   Click the drop-down button in the **Name Box**, and click **Revenues**.

The cell range C5 to C6 is now selected. Use the Go To dialog box to jump to another cell in the worksheet.

6   Press CTRL+G, type: H14 in the Reference text box (be sure that the H14 is the only address in that text box) and click **OK**.

7   Click in the **Name Box**, type: F3 and press ENTER.

8   Save and close the workbook.

# Using Tables
## Creating a Table

**Objective 3.1.1, 3.2.3**

Many worksheets consist of a rectangular block of data in which the rows of data have a common structure and format. Excel offers you the ability to define this block as a table. As a table, you can use a variety of tools such as selecting summary formulas, formatting, sorting, and filtering. These same features are available even without using tables but you have to manually select the range of cells (with summary formulas and sorting, Excel will guess which cells you want but you still have to verify the range is correct) before using the features. However, by defining a range of cells as a table, you indicate to Excel that this group belongs together as a single unit. These same tools are then easier to apply because Excel now knows which cells to include.

A table is not the same as a named range of data but you can define a range name for a table if you wish.

To create a table, the data must be contiguous. That is, there must not be any blank rows or columns in the range of cells. Also, the data must be arranged in row order, with a header at the top of each column and the data listed below.

To convert a range of cells containing data to a table, use one of the following methods:

- on the Insert tab, in the Tables group, click **Table**, or

- on the Home tab, in the Styles group, click **Format as Table**, then click a table style, or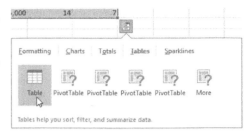

- after selecting the cell range, click the **Quick Analysis** icon, then click the **Tables** category and click **Table**, or

- press CTRL+T.

Once you create the table, Excel activates an AutoFilter icon next to each column title and applies the current active theme. The Table Tools Design tab is also added to the Ribbon:

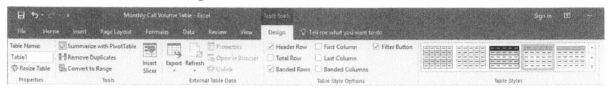

One of the table features is the ability to insert an automatic Total Row at the bottom of the table.

# Learn to create tables

This exercise demonstrates how to create a table, assign a name of your choice to the table, and add a total row at the bottom.

**1** Open the *Monthly Call Volume* workbook and save it as: Monthly Call Volume - Student.

Convert the range of cells to a table.

**Hint:** When creating a table, leave at least one empty row and column on all sides of the table to separate it from any other data on the worksheet.

**2** Click on any cell in the range **A4:E15**.

**3** On the **Insert** tab, in the Tables group, click **Table**.

**4** Confirm that **My table has headers** is turned on and then click **OK**.

The data is now converted into a table. Change the table name to something that is more meaningful to you.

**5** Under Table Tools, on the Design tab, in the Properties group, click in the **Table Name** field and replace the default table name with: CallVolume (do not include a space between the words).

You will next turn on the automatic Total row.

**Note:** When you activate the Total row, Excel automatically moves any data below the table down by one row.

**6** Under Table Tools, on the Design tab, in the Table Style Options group, click **Total Row** to turn it on.

Enter some common statistical formulas using the data in the table.

**7** Select cell **B16**, click the drop-down arrow that appears next to it, and click **Average**.

**8** Repeat step 7 for the **Count**, **Max**, and **Min** options for cell B16.

**9** Repeat step 7 for the **Sum** option for cell B16.

**10** Select each of the cells **C16:D16** and select the **Sum** calculation.

**Note:** You cannot copy the contents of a column total to other cells in a table.

If you also want to display row totals (in a new column to the right of the table), you will have to insert them manually. Tables do not have the ability to create row totals automatically. Row totals show the sum total (or other statistical summary calculations of your choosing) for each row of data.

**11** Click on cell **F4** and enter: Total.

**12** With cell **F5** as the active cell, on the Home tab, in the Editing group, click **AutoSum** and press ENTER.

Even though you only entered the row total for the first row, Excel has automatically inserted them for the rest of the rows, except the Total row. This demonstrates one of the advantages of identifying this range of cells as a table.

**13** Click on cell **F5**.

You can see that the formula used for this sum total is specifically used for tables.

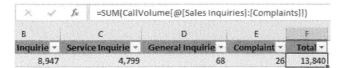

| B | C | D | E | F |
|---|---|---|---|---|
| Inquirie ▾ | Service Inquirie ▾ | General Inquirie ▾ | Complaint ▾ | Total ▾ |
| 8,947 | 4,799 | 68 | 26 | 13,840 |

Now insert the Total Row calculation for this new column.

**14** Select cell **F16**, click its drop-down arrow, and select **Sum**.

|  | A | B | C | D | E | F |
|---|---|---|---|---|---|---|
| 1 |  | **Tolano Adventures** |  |  |  |  |
| 2 |  | Monthly Call Volume |  |  |  |  |
| 3 |  |  |  |  |  |  |
| 4 | Montl ▾ | Sales Inquirie ▾ | Service Inquirie ▾ | General Inquirie ▾ | Complaint ▾ | Total ▾ |
| 5 | Jan-16 | 8,947 | 4,799 | 68 | 26 | 13,840 |
| 6 | Feb-16 | 3,643 | 5,658 | 36 | 14 | 9,351 |
| 7 | Mar-16 | 5,861 | 9,739 | 0 | 7 | 15,607 |
| 8 | Apr-16 | 3,741 | 4,429 | 18 | 25 | 8,213 |
| 9 | May-16 | 4,537 | 5,420 | 59 | 19 | 10,035 |
| 10 | Jun-16 | 3,146 | 1,417 | 77 | 12 | 4,652 |
| 11 | Jul-16 | 2,533 | 7,811 | 19 | 6 | 10,369 |
| 12 | Aug-16 | 7,209 | 2,188 | 71 | 15 | 9,483 |
| 13 | Sep-16 | 1,082 | 8,718 | 56 | 24 | 9,880 |
| 14 | Oct-16 | 2,748 | 8,002 | 72 | 14 | 10,836 |
| 15 | Nov-16 | 5,617 | 5,000 | 14 | 7 | 10,638 |
| 16 | Total | 49,064 | 63,181 | 490 | 169 | 112,904 |

**15** Save the workbook.

## Modifying Table Data

**Objective 3.1.3**

After the table is created, you can add or delete rows and columns of data.

To add a new column of data at the far right of a table, simply enter this data into the first blank column. Excel will automatically extend the table to include this new column. Similarly, Excel will extend the table to include a new row of data that you enter directly below a table, as long as the Total Row feature is not activated. If the Total Row is activated, you must use one of the following methods:

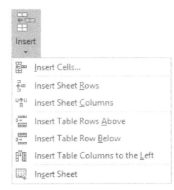

- Manually insert a new blank data row by clicking on the bottom right cell containing data (immediately above the Total Row), and then clicking the TAB key.

- Manually insert a new blank data row by clicking any cell in the bottom data row, then on the Home tab, in the Cells group, click the **Insert** arrow, and click **Insert Table Row Below**.

- Add the new row of data below the Total Row, and then manually extend the table to include the new row.

The Insert button in the Home tab can be used to insert a new row or column anywhere in the table, not just as the last row of data. Be aware that the Insert drop-down menu may show different Insert Table options, including various combinations of Insert Table Rows Above, Rows Below, Columns to the Left and Columns to the Right, depending on which cell in the table is currently selected as the active cell.

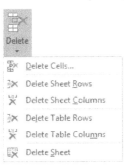

Similarly, on the Home tab, in the Cells group, you can use the **Delete** button to delete rows or columns of data from the table.

# Learn to modify table data

This exercise demonstrates how to insert rows and columns of data into different parts of a table.

**1** Make sure the *Monthly Call Volume – Student* workbook is open.

Now add a new row at the bottom of the table.

**2** Select cell **F15** and press TAB.

Notice that Excel automatically shifts the Total row down by one row and that the formula in cell **F15** is copied down to this new row.

**3** In cell **A16**, type: December 2016 as the new value and press TAB.

**4** Enter the following values into the remaining cells of the row:

| | |
|---|---|
| B16 | 8969 |
| C16 | 7375 |
| D16 | 7 |
| E16 | 1 |

Notice also that the statistical formulas in row 17 (these were all set to display the Sum but you may have selected Average or other formulas instead) automatically updated even though the new data were added at the bottom of the table.

Now add a new column between the Complaints and Total columns.

5  Select cell **F8**, then on the Home tab, in the Cells group, click the **Insert** arrow, and click **Insert Table Columns to the Left**.

6  Click cell **F4** and enter: Other.

7  Enter the following values into the remaining cells of the column:

| | | | |
|---|---|---|---|
| F5 | 500 | F11 | 200 |
| F6 | 300 | F12 | 480 |
| F7 | 250 | F13 | 100 |
| F8 | 450 | F14 | 200 |
| F9 | 400 | F15 | 150 |
| F10 | 220 | F16 | 300 |

8  Select cell **F17**, click the drop-down arrow that appears next to it, and click **Sum**.

By adding a column to the table, you must ensure that the Total column at the far right includes this new column.

9  Click on cell **G5**, and note the formula in the formula bar.

10  Press F2, delete the table cell reference [Complaints], replace it with: [Other], and press ENTER.

If no longer needed, a column (or row) can be easily removed from a table.

11  Click on any cell in the range D4 to D17, then on the Home tab, in the Cells group, click the **Delete** arrow, and click **Delete Table Columns**.

| | A | B | C | D | E | F |
|---|---|---|---|---|---|---|
| 1 | | | **Tolano Adventures** | | | |
| 2 | | | Monthly Call Volume | | | |
| 3 | | | | | | |
| 4 | Month | Sales Inquirie | Service Inquirie | Complaints | Other | Total |
| 5 | Jan-16 | 8,947 | 4,799 | 26 | 500 | 14,272 |
| 6 | Feb-16 | 3,643 | 5,658 | 14 | 300 | 9,615 |
| 7 | Mar-16 | 5,861 | 9,739 | 7 | 250 | 15,857 |
| 8 | Apr-16 | 3,741 | 4,429 | 25 | 450 | 8,645 |
| 9 | May-16 | 4,537 | 5,420 | 19 | 400 | 10,376 |
| 10 | Jun-16 | 3,146 | 1,417 | 12 | 220 | 4,795 |
| 11 | Jul-16 | 2,533 | 7,811 | 6 | 200 | 10,550 |
| 12 | Aug-16 | 7,209 | 2,188 | 15 | 480 | 9,892 |
| 13 | Sep-16 | 1,082 | 8,718 | 24 | 100 | 9,924 |
| 14 | Oct-16 | 2,748 | 8,002 | 14 | 200 | 10,964 |
| 15 | Nov-16 | 5,617 | 5,000 | 7 | 150 | 10,774 |
| 16 | Dec-16 | 8,969 | 7,375 | 1 | 300 | 16,645 |
| 17 | Total | 58,033 | 70,556 | 170 | 3,550 | 132,309 |

Add another row of data to the table using a different method.

12  Enter the following values:

| | |
|---|---|
| A18 | January 2017 |
| B18 | 7000 |
| C18 | 4000 |
| D18 | 20 |
| E18 | 200 |

**13** Ensure that cell F17 is **not** the active cell, then position the cursor at the bottom right corner of cell **F17** so that the cursor changes to a double-headed arrow ⬉.

**14** Click and drag the resize handle down to row 18.

**Hint:** If the Total Row was not activated for this table, the new row would have been automatically added to the table.

Because you had added the new data below the Total Row, Excel did not know if you intended to keep that data separate from the table. Therefore, you had to manually expand the table to include the January row.

**15** Select cell **B17**, then on the Home tab, in the Cells group, click the **Delete** arrow, and click **Delete Table Rows**.

**16** Save the workbook.

# Formatting Table Data

### Objective 3.2.1, 3.2.2

By default, the theme selected for the workbook is applied to all tables in that workbook. You can override it for specific tables by selecting a different table style under Table Tools, on the Design tab, in the Table Styles group.

The table style colors option can be removed, and re-applied later if needed again. If none of these predefined table styles are suitable, you can also create a customized one.

The Table Tools Design tab also allows you to activate or de-activate other table formatting options including:

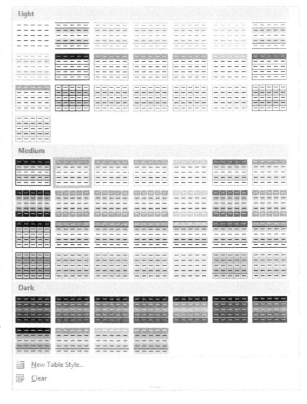

- Highlighting the first or last column – or both – with the bold font option. By default, both options are turned off.

- "Banding" rows by using different color shades for alternating rows. This feature often improves the readability of tables that are very wide because data in the same row have the same color shade. By default, the Banded Rows option is turned on, but Banded Columns is turned off.

- Turn the AutoFilter icon off.

# Learn to format table data

This exercise demonstrates how to change and remove the table style, and use different table formatting options.

**1** Make sure the *Monthly Call Volume – Student* workbook is open.

**2** If necessary, click on any cell within the table.

Highlight the left-most and right-most columns so that they stand out.

**3** Under Table Tools, on the **Design** tab, in the Table Style Options group, click the **First Column** and **Last Column** check boxes to turn them on.

Notice that the data in these two columns are now bold.

**4** Under Table Tools, on the Design tab, in the Table Style Options group, click the **Banded Columns** check box to turn it on.

Every second column in the table is now white while the others are shaded. This will become more obvious when you turn row banding off.

**5** Under Table Tools, on the Design tab, in the Table Style Options group, click the **Banded Rows** check box to turn it off.

You can also choose from an extensive menu of different built-in table styles.

**6** Under Table Tools, on the Design tab, in the Table Styles group, click the **More** button to display all of the table styles.

**7** Point the cursor to different table styles and observe the live preview effect on the table.

You can also force all table coloring to be turned off, regardless of your banding options.

**8** With the Table Styles menu still displayed, click **Clear**.

| Month | Sales Inquirie | Service Inquirie | Complaints | Other | Total |
|---|---|---|---|---|---|
| | | Tolano Adventures | | | |
| | | Monthly Call Volume | | | |
| Jan-16 | 8,947 | 4,799 | 26 | 500 | 14,272 |
| Feb-16 | 3,643 | 5,658 | 14 | 300 | 9,615 |
| Mar-16 | 5,861 | 9,739 | 7 | 250 | 15,857 |
| Apr-16 | 3,741 | 4,429 | 25 | 450 | 8,645 |
| May-16 | 4,537 | 5,420 | 19 | 400 | 10,376 |
| Jun-16 | 3,146 | 1,417 | 12 | 220 | 4,795 |
| Jul-16 | 2,533 | 7,811 | 6 | 200 | 10,550 |
| Aug-16 | 7,209 | 2,188 | 15 | 480 | 9,892 |
| Sep-16 | 1,082 | 8,718 | 24 | 100 | 9,924 |
| Oct-16 | 2,748 | 8,002 | 14 | 200 | 10,964 |
| Nov-16 | 5,617 | 5,000 | 7 | 150 | 10,774 |
| Dec-16 | 8,969 | 7,375 | 1 | 300 | 16,645 |
| Total | 58,033 | 70,556 | 170 | 3,550 | 132,309 |

Notice that the bolding in the first and last columns, and the Total row in the table are also removed, even though the check boxes in the Table Style Options group are still activated.

**9** Click the **Banded Columns** and **Banded Rows** check boxes on and off to see if your table changes in any way.

In Excel, clearing the table style is the same as selecting the None style.

10   Under Table Tools, on the Design tab, in the Table Styles group, click the **More** button. Point the cursor at the None table style (Light section, first row, far left).

Now reactivate one of the table styles.

11   With the Table Styles menu still displayed, click on the **Table Style Medium 21** option (Medium section, third row, far right).

12   If necessary, turn the **First Column** and **Last Column** check boxes on.

By re-activating a table style that is not None, your table options are also now working again.

13   If necessary, turn the **Banded Rows** check box on and the **Banded Columns** check box off.

| | A | B | C | D | E | F |
|---|---|---|---|---|---|---|
| 1 | | | Tolano Adventures | | | |
| 2 | | | Monthly Call Volume | | | |
| 3 | | | | | | |
| 4 | Month | Sales Inquirie | Service Inquirie | Complaints | Other | Total |
| 5 | Jan-16 | 8,947 | 4,799 | 26 | 500 | 14,272 |
| 6 | Feb-16 | 3,643 | 5,658 | 14 | 300 | 9,615 |
| 7 | Mar-16 | 5,861 | 9,739 | 7 | 250 | 15,857 |
| 8 | Apr-16 | 3,741 | 4,429 | 25 | 450 | 8,645 |
| 9 | May-16 | 4,537 | 5,420 | 19 | 400 | 10,376 |
| 10 | Jun-16 | 3,146 | 1,417 | 12 | 220 | 4,795 |
| 11 | Jul-16 | 2,533 | 7,811 | 6 | 200 | 10,550 |
| 12 | Aug-16 | 7,209 | 2,188 | 15 | 480 | 9,892 |
| 13 | Sep-16 | 1,082 | 8,718 | 24 | 100 | 9,924 |
| 14 | Oct-16 | 2,748 | 8,002 | 14 | 200 | 10,964 |
| 15 | Nov-16 | 5,617 | 5,000 | 7 | 150 | 10,774 |
| 16 | Dec-16 | 8,969 | 7,375 | 1 | 300 | 16,645 |
| 17 | Total | 58,033 | 70,556 | 170 | 3,550 | 132,309 |

The AutoFilter icon can also be temporarily deactivated.

14   Under Table Tools, on the Design tab, in the Table Style Options group, click the **Filter Button** check box to turn it off.

15   Click on any of the Header Row cells (A4 to F4) to try to access the AutoFilter icon.

16   Under Table Tools, on the Design tab, in the Table Styles group, click the **Filter Button** check box to turn it on again.

17   Save the workbook.

## Converting a Table to a Cell Range

**Objective 3.1.2**

If you no longer wish to keep the data in a table, you can convert it back to a regular set of rows and columns of data without the table definition. Under Table Tools, on the Design tab, in the Tools group, using the Convert to Range tool to convert the data.

## Learn to convert a table

This exercise demonstrates how to convert a table to a regular range of cells.

1   Make sure the *Monthly Call Volume – Student* workbook is selected.

2   Ensure that the active cell is anywhere within the table, then under Table Tools, on the Design tab, in the Tools group, click **Convert to Range**.

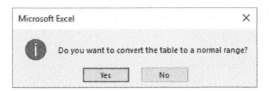

**3**  Click **Yes**.

The worksheet does not appear any different, except that the Table Tools Design tab no longer appears and the column titles no longer display the filter buttons.

**4**  Click the drop-down button on the right side of the Name Box to display the list of any range names in the worksheet.

This indicates that the Convert to Range tool simply converts the data to a set of rows and columns with data. If you want to create range names, you must add them manually.

**5**  Click on any cell in the worksheet to close the Name Box list.

**6**  Save and close the workbook.

# Sorting Data

Worksheets with a large amount of data are often difficult to understand. Excel provides a sorting tool that enables you to change the sequence of the data based on the values in selected columns. After sorting, the data becomes more readable. You can sort and re-sort the data as many times as required, using different columns each time. You can sort the data by columns or rows, but the most common method is sorting by columns (with column headers and the data extending downwards).

## Sorting by Single-Level Data

### Objective 3.3.3

If your data is organized into a table, you can use the sort options built into the AutoFilter button that appears at the top of each column. However, this menu is limited to sorting by one column.

Regardless of whether your data is in a table or not, the Ribbon has two ready-to-use buttons to enable sorting:

- on the Home tab, in the Editing group, click **Sort & Filter** and then click **Sort A to Z** to sort in ascending sequence or **Sort Z to A** to sort in descending sequence, or

- on the Data tab, in the Sort & Filter group, click **Sort A to Z** or **Sort Z to A**.

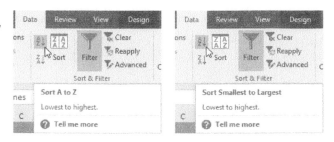

Depending on what type of data you are sorting, the Ribbon menu will display a different command description. If the data is text, the Ribbon menu will display Sort A to Z and Sort Z to A. If the data contains numbers, the Ribbon menu will display Sort Smallest to Largest and Sort Largest to Smallest. If the data contains date values, the Ribbon menu will display Sort Oldest to Newest and Sort Newest to Oldest.

## Sorting by Multi-Level Data

**Objective 3.3.2**

In many cases, you will need to sort by more than one column to handle situations with multiple rows with the same value. For example, you may have a customer list with several people having the same last name. In this situation, you will want to sort the list using two columns – one containing the customer's last name and the other containing their first name.

The example below shows a range of data sorted using three different columns as sort keys. The primary sort key is airline name in ascending order, as indicated by the green marker: A at the top, down to Z at the bottom. The destination name is the secondary sort key, as designated by the first *Then by* selection: for rows with the same airline. These rows are sorted by destination name as indicated by the red box. The third level sort key in this example is the departure time: for rows where the same airline is flying to the same destination on the same day. These rows are sorted by the departure time as designated in the second *Then by* selection. This group is identified by the blue box.

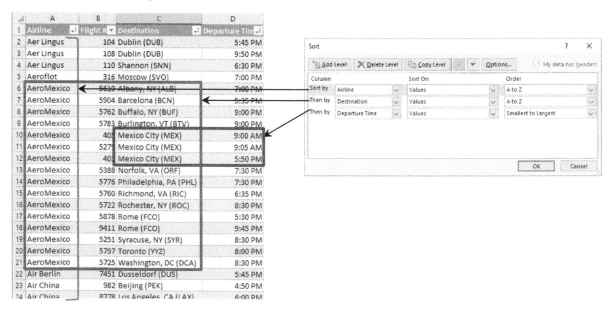

The settings in the Sort dialog box determine how the data is to be sorted:

**Add Level, Delete Level, Copy Level** – These buttons allow you to add, delete or copy columns (or rows) in this dialog box to be used as sort keys. Note that the topmost sort key is the highest (primary) sorting level, followed by the remaining levels in descending order.

**Move up/Move down** – These buttons allow you to change the selected sort level higher or lower in the sorting sequence.

**Options** – This button displays a dialog box that allows you to sort by columns or rows, and choose whether to treat the data as case-sensitive or not. If you turn the case-sensitive option on, then upper case letters are treated as different characters than lower case characters. For example, the letter "A" is not the same as the letter "a".

**My data has headers** – This option tells Excel to treat the first row (or column) of cells as labels or titles for the data below (or to the right). Use this option to prevent sorting the header data together with the other data—they will remain in their place as headers. If the range of cells being sorted does not contain column or row headers, then turn off this setting.

**Column/Row** – This identifies the column or row to be used for sorting. The sequence of these columns or rows specifies the sorting level. By default, the data is sorted by column with the headers in the top row.

**Sort On** – The sort options include *Values* (cell data), *Cell Color*, *Font Color*, or *Cell Icon*. These options identify what to use in the cells for sorting. In most cases you will want to sort using the cell values, which is the default.

**Order** – This option indicates whether to sort the data in ascending (*A to Z, Smallest to Largest, Oldest to Newest*) or descending (*Z to A, Largest to Smallest, Newest to Oldest*) order.

**Sort by** – This is the primary sort key: the first column or row Excel will use to sort the data.

**Then by** – These are optional columns or rows for sorting if multiple rows have the same primary sort key. You can select up to 64 columns or rows as sort levels.

**Note:** The following exercise demonstrates how to sort data in an Excel table. However, you can sort data in any range of cells even if they are not constructed as a table. The sort commands are available on the Home tab in the Editing group using the Sort & Filter button, and on the Data tab in the Sort & Filter group using the Sort button.

# Learn to sort data

This exercise demonstrates how to sort a table of data using one column as a sort key. You will then sort the data again using multiple columns.

1   Open the *Flights Sort* workbook and save as: Flights Sort - Student.

First, sort the data using one of the columns.

2   Click the **AutoFilter** icon for *Airline*, then click **Sort A to Z**.

The data in the table is now sorted by airline name. You can also change the sort sequence to something different, such as by what time each flight leaves.

3   Click the **AutoFilter** icon for *Departure Time*, then click **Sort Smallest to Largest**.

You can see that all of the rows have been completely re-sorted using only the Departure Time column. In other words, both of these steps used single-level sorting. Also notice that for text data, the sort commands are Sort A to Z (ascending sequence) and Sort Z to A (descending sequence). For numeric data (time of day values are treated internally in Excel as numbers), the sort commands are Sort Smallest to Largest and Sort Largest to Smallest.

But the data in the table also shows that most airlines (such as Delta Air Lines) fly to multiple destinations from this airport on the same day. You can sort the data using two different columns at the same time.

4    Ensure that the active cell is anywhere inside the table, then on the Home tab, in the Editing group, click **Sort & Filter** and then click **Custom Sort**.

**Hint:** You can also open the Sort dialog box from the Data tab.

Excel displays the Sort dialog box. Notice that it is currently set to the sorting criteria that had you enabled at step 3 above.

5    Click the arrow next to the **Sort by** field and click **Airline**.

The Airline column is now the primary sort key. Use the Destination column as the secondary sort key, in descending sequence.

6    Click **Add Level** to add another sort key.

7    Click the arrow for **Then by** and then click **Destination**.

8    Click the arrow for **Order** and then click **Z to A**, then click **OK**.

Notice the direction of the arrows in the AutoFilter icon for the Airline and Destination columns.

**Note:** Once sorted, the data cannot be put back to its original sequence except by using the Undo button. But if you saved and closed the workbook in the interim, the Undo option will no longer be available to restore the data back to the original sequence.

9    Click the **AutoFilter** icon for *Departure Time*, then click **Sort Smallest to Largest**.

10   Save and close the workbook.

# Filtering Information

**Objective 3.3.1**

Worksheets are often used to store large amounts of data. Finding information in large worksheets is often difficult because of the sheer volume. Sorting the rows is one way of making it easier to find information. However, you still have to look through many of the rows in the worksheet to find what you are looking for. Another way to locate information quickly is to use a filter to hide the rows you are not interested in viewing. Filtering does not change the content of your worksheet or the sequence of the rows (like the way sorting does), only what you see of your worksheet.

The quickest and easiest way to filter data in Excel is to use the AutoFilter icons on the right side of each of the column titles. If the data is formatted as a table, the AutoFilter icons will be activated by default. If the data is not formatted as a table, you can activate them for any range of data.

| | A | B | C | D |
|---|---|---|---|---|
| 1 | Airline | Flight # | Destination | Departure Time |
| 406 | Lufthansa | 8626 | Pittsburgh, PA (PIT) | 2:55 PM |
| 423 | Lufthansa | 8550 | Fort Lauderdale, FL (FLL) | 3:13 PM |
| 434 | Lufthansa | 8574 | San Juan (SJU) | 3:29 PM |
| 511 | Lufthansa | 401 | Frankfurt (FRA) | 4:00 PM |
| 546 | Lufthansa | 8632 | Buffalo, NY (BUF) | 4:20 PM |
| 564 | Lufthansa | 8620 | Raleigh-Durham, NC (RDU) | 4:39 PM |
| 640 | Lufthansa | 8638 | Syracuse, NY (SYR) | 5:10 PM |
| 671 | Lufthansa | 411 | Munich (MUC) | 5:30 PM |
| 736 | Lufthansa | 8552 | Fort Lauderdale, FL (FLL) | 6:05 PM |
| 741 | Lufthansa | 8654 | Rochester, NY (ROC) | 6:11 PM |
| 801 | Lufthansa | 8634 | Buffalo, NY (BUF) | 6:35 PM |
| 886 | Lufthansa | 8556 | Tampa, FL (TPA) | 7:20 PM |
| 965 | Lufthansa | 8568 | Austin, TX (AUS) | 8:10 PM |
| 1036 | Lufthansa | 8564 | New Orleans, LA (MSY) | 9:29 PM |
| 1043 | Lufthansa | 405 | Frankfurt (FRA) | 9:40 PM |
| 1063 | Lufthansa | 8624 | Raleigh-Durham, NC (RDU) | 9:50 PM |
| 1095 | Lufthansa | 8640 | Syracuse, NY (SYR) | 10:40 PM |
| 1097 | Lufthansa | 8656 | Rochester, NY (ROC) | 10:45 PM |
| 1103 | Lufthansa | 8636 | Buffalo, NY (BUF) | 10:50 PM |
| 1116 | Lufthansa | 8578 | San Juan (SJU) | 11:55 PM |

In its simplest form, the AutoFilter finds and displays the rows where the value in the selected column meets the criteria that you specify. All other rows are hidden from view until you change the filter criteria or you turn the AutoFilter off.

In addition, Excel provides powerful selection criteria that are specific to columns containing text, numbers or dates, such as the following:

**Numbers** – Evaluate numeric data in the selected column using any of the following:

- A comparison operator such as equals, greater than, and less than.
- The top 10 values. Despite the name displayed in the menu, the filter criteria can also be configured differently to select the top or bottom-most rows. You can also select any number of rows, not just 10. And finally, you can select the number of rows or percentage of rows. For example, 10% of 20 rows will result in only two rows being displayed.
- All rows above or below the average of all values in the column.
- A custom filter that allows you to select more complex criteria.

Equals...
Does Not Equal...
Greater Than...
Greater Than Or Equal To...
Less Than...
Less Than Or Equal To...
Between...
Top 10...
Above Average
Below Average
Custom Filter...

**Dates** – Evaluate date-type data using a wide variety of criteria that are specific for dates, as shown in the filter menu list:

**Text** – Evaluate text data in the selected column using any of the following:

- A comparison operator such as equals, greater than, and less than.

- Begins or ends with a snippet of text.

- Contains or does not contain a snippet of text.

- A custom filter that allows you to select more complex criteria.

If you select any of the comparison operators displayed in these filter menus, you will launch the Custom AutoFilter window, which allows you to specify exactly how you want to filter the data. The filter menus for each of the data types that you see listed above are only the most commonly used ones. The Custom AutoFilter window allows you to select additional comparison operators, such as "does not equal" for date data, and "greater than" for text data.

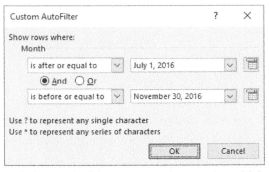

Furthermore, the AutoFilter feature in Excel has the flexibility to help you build more complex queries which you can use to narrow the results and hide rows that you do not want. For example, you can select criteria that examine two or more columns. You can then specify that these filtering criteria on multiple columns work together (using an "and" relationship) or as alternatives (an "or" relationship). In a table, the AutoFilter icon displays an indicator that a filter has been enabled for that column. When multiple filter criteria have been set up in a table, the AutoFilter icons will indicate this as shown in the following.

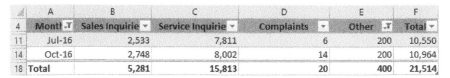

| | A | B | C | D | E | F |
|---|---|---|---|---|---|---|
| 4 | Month | Sales Inquirie | Service Inquirie | Complaints | Other | Total |
| 11 | Jul-16 | 2,533 | 7,811 | 6 | 200 | 10,550 |
| 14 | Oct-16 | 2,748 | 8,002 | 14 | 200 | 10,964 |
| 18 | Total | 5,281 | 15,813 | 20 | 400 | 21,514 |

These more advanced filtering topics are covered in more depth in the Expert level courseware.

This exercise demonstrates how to filter data in an Excel table. However, you can activate the AutoFilter feature and use its filtering capability in any range of cells even if they are not constructed as a table. To activate AutoFilter for a range of cells, on the Home tab in the Editing group, click Sort & Filter and click the Filter button, or on the Data tab in the Sort & Filter group click the Filter button.

# Learn to filter information

This exercise demonstrates how to use AutoFilters on a table of data.

**1**    Open the *Monthly Call Volume Filter* workbook and save it as: `Monthly Call Volume Filter - Student`.

**2**    Click the **AutoFilter** icon for the Month header.

**3**    Click the **+** for 2016 to open that tree and see all data rows in the table for this year value.

The AutoFilter menu displays a list of every unique value in this column. You set the filter by turning the check box on or off for the value(s) you want.

Because Excel recognizes that this column contains date values, it allows you to set your filter at three levels: year, month, and day of month.

**4**    Scroll up and click the **Select All** check box to turn it off, then click the **March** and **June** check boxes to turn them on. Click **OK**.

The table now shows only those two rows. Notice the row numbers of the records that remain displayed from the database. Excel hides the rows that do not meet the criteria and displays only records that have a matching value in the filtered field. Excel also changes the AutoFilter icon to indicate that it is using a field to limit the records displayed.

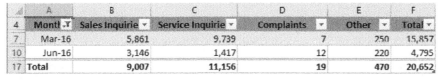

| | A | B | C | D | E | F |
|---|---|---|---|---|---|---|
| 4 | Month | Sales Inquirie | Service Inquirie | Complaints | Other | Total |
| 7 | Mar-16 | 5,861 | 9,739 | 7 | 250 | 15,857 |
| 10 | Jun-16 | 3,146 | 1,417 | 12 | 220 | 4,795 |
| 17 | Total | 9,007 | 11,156 | 19 | 470 | 20,652 |

The conditions you select are called *filter criteria*. Up to this point in this exercise, you used the most common condition – filtering based on whether the value is <u>**equal**</u> to the criteria or not. You can also set up other types of criteria, such as greater than or less than. Now set up a more complex filter criteria called "Between", which is a combination of greater than or equal to, and less than or equal to.

**5**    Click the **AutoFilter** icon for the *Month* header again.

6   Point to **Date Filters** then click **Between** in the menu to open the Custom AutoFilter dialog box.

7   Type or use the Date Picker buttons next to each of the two blank entry fields to specify the date range July 1, 2016 to November 30, 2016.

8   Click **OK**.

Depending on whether the data contains text, date, or numeric values, you will have access to different types of filtering criteria. Some filtering criteria apply to all data types, such as "equal" and "does not equal". Other criteria apply only to specific data types, such as "begins with" can only be used on text data, and "top 10" can only be used on numeric data.

You can also specify multiple filtering criteria to work together at the same time.

9   Click the **AutoFilter** icon for the Other header.

10  Click the **Select All** check box to turn it off, then click the **200** check box to turn it on. Click **OK**.

The results should look similar to the following:

| | A | B | C | D | E | F |
|---|---|---|---|---|---|---|
| 4 | Month | Sales Inquirie | Service Inquirie | Complaints | Other | Total |
| 11 | Jul-16 | 2,533 | 7,811 | 6 | 200 | 10,550 |
| 14 | Oct-16 | 2,748 | 8,002 | 14 | 200 | 10,964 |
| 18 | Total | 5,281 | 15,813 | 20 | 400 | 21,514 |

Now turn off the filter on the Other column.

11  Click the **AutoFilter** icon for the Other header, then click **Clear Filter From "Other"**.

The table has reverted back to displaying all of the months from July to November, which indicates that you had two filters working together at the same time. Turn off the filter on the Month column as well.

12  Click the **AutoFilter** icon for the Month header, then click **Clear Filter From "Month"**.

The full table is displayed again.

13  Click the **AutoFilter** icon for the Other header, click the **Select All** check box to turn it off, then click the **200** check box to turn it on again. Click **OK**.

Three rows of data now appear because the filter on the Other column now applies to the full table instead of just the five months.

14  Save and close the workbook.

# Removing Duplicate Rows

**Objective 3.3.4**

Excel has the ability to find and remove duplicate data rows from a cell range. This is often a useful feature for worksheets with a lot of data especially when the data came from multiple sources or the data entry system does not have an ability to prevent duplicates from occurring.

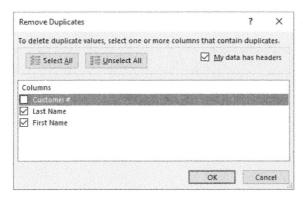

You can select all columns or only selected columns to be used for comparing the data. For example, you can scan a data table containing customer numbers, names, and addresses to find any rows where the same customer is listed two or more times. Alternatively, you can select just the last name and first name columns to find and remove duplicate rows.

On the other hand, Excel will only look for identical data when comparing rows. For example, Excel will consider two rows as different if the address in one row contains "1234 Miller Road" and the other row contains "1234 Miller Rd.". Every blank space, comma, number, and other character in each cell is used to find exact matches.

# Learn to remove duplicate rows

This exercise demonstrates how to use the remove duplicates feature.

**1**   Open the *Customer List* workbook and save it as: Customer List - Student.

Do you think this list has any duplicate data in it?

**2**   Scan through the data on your own to see if all rows are unique.

**Note:** This exercise demonstrates how to remove duplicates in an Excel table. However, you can use this feature in any range of cells even if they are not constructed as a table. To remove duplicates for a range of cells, on the Data tab in the Data Tools group, click the Remove Duplicates button.

Now use the Remove Duplicates command in Excel.

**3**   Select any cell in the table.

**4**   Under Table Tools, on the **Design** tab, in the Tools group, click **Remove Duplicates**.

Alternatively, you can also access this dialog box on the Data tab, in the Data Tools group, click **Remove Duplicates**.

**5**   Click **OK**.

A message box is displayed with the message: "No duplicate values found."

That should be enough to confirm that there are no duplicate rows in the data. Or maybe we did not use the command correctly.

**6**   Click **OK** to close the message box.

**7**   On the Data tab, in the Data Tools group, click **Remove Duplicates**.

This time only use the columns that really matter. Turn off the check box for all other columns.

8    Click the **Customer #** check box to turn it off and click **OK**.

A message box is displayed with the message: "3 duplicate values found and removed; 25 unique values remain."

9    Click **OK** to close the message box.

By comparing the results from the original table, customers 16, 26 and 27 were found to be duplicates.

10   Save and close the workbook.

# Outlining

## Using Automatic Subtotals

**Objective 2.3.3**

Many worksheets become very large due to the sheer amount of information needed for analysis. Inevitably, summary totals are added for each major group of data as well as grand totals. The end result can be a worksheet that is difficult to see from one end to another.

To help organize the data, Excel provides an automatic outlining tool that enables you to insert subtotals whenever the selected field changes in value. You can make a very big worksheet easier to understand by setting it up so that you see only the subtotals for each group of data. An important step is organizing the data so that the subtotals are displayed for the data groups you want.

With the Outline feature turned on, you can quickly open up all or selected groups of data and collapse them again. Before creating the subtotals, you must sort the data by column to group these related rows together. Otherwise, the results will not make much sense.

You can also create multiple subtotals for a single column or several layers of columns. For example, you can calculate the sum, average, and variance subtotals for as many numeric columns as you require. You must add each different type of subtotal as a separate row to identify the type of subtotal.

You can create a more complex type of multiple subtotals by nesting them. For example, suppose you have a sales report listing every sales transaction for a year. As long as you have a separate column for the month value, you can create subtotals based on the month. You can then create another layer of subtotals based on the date of each sale which is in a different column. Assuming that you will have multiple sales each day, you can nest your subtotals by day of each month and by month of the year. The outline feature then allows you to quickly open or collapse your worksheet at the year, month, or day level.

The key difference in creating multiple subtotals is how you use **Replace current subtotals**. When creating the first (or only) subtotal for a worksheet, ensure this check box is turned on. When creating subsequent subtotals, ensure this check box is turned off.

# Learn to insert automatic subtotals

This exercise demonstrates how to create automatic subtotals for one and two numeric columns.

1 Open the *Sales* workbook and save as: Sales Subtotal - Student.

2 Scroll down the worksheet to see how many rows of data are present.

Create an automatic subtotal based on the *Payment Type* but first sort the worksheet by this column.

3 Select any cell in column E.

4 On the Data tab, in the Sort & Filter group, click **Sort A to Z**.

Now create the subtotals on the *Amount Paid* column.

5 On the Data tab, in the Outline group, click **Subtotal**.

6 Click the drop-down button for **At each change in** and select **Payment Type**.

7 In the Use function list box, click the drop-down and select **Sum**.

8 In the Add subtotal to list, click the **Amount Paid** check box to turn it on, and turn off all other check boxes in this list.

9 If necessary, click **Replace current subtotals** and **Summary below data** to turn them on, and clear **Page break between groups** if necessary.

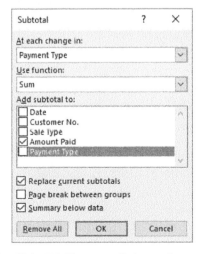

10 Click **OK**. Then scroll down the worksheet to see how the data now appears.

Notice that the worksheet now has three outline levels at the left side. Each of these numbers corresponds to a different level of detail: clicking ⬚ compresses the data rows so that only the grand total is displayed. Clicking ⬚ also compresses the data rows but displays the subtotal rows and grand total. Clicking ⬚ shows all data rows for that level as well as the subtotals and the grand total.

Now practice with the outline features.

**11** Click ⬚ at the top of the outline section and then scroll up to the top of the worksheet.

The ⊞ and ⊟ buttons work the same way as in File Explorer: clicking the ⊞ opens the level and shows the data in the next level. Clicking the ⊟ collapses the details.

**Note:** You can only use the outline buttons with the mouse.

**12** Click ⬚ to display all rows again.

**13** Scroll down (or up) and click the ⊟ to the left of the *Mastercard Total* and then scroll up the worksheet for a few more rows.

Notice that the details for Mastercard have been hidden, while they are still displayed for all other payment types. Now hide the details for all payment types.

**14** Click ⬚ at the top of the outline section and then scroll up to the top of the worksheet.

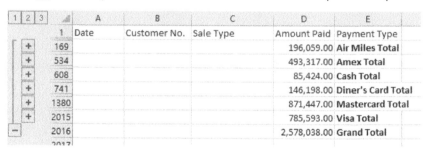

**15** Click ⬚ to display all rows again.

Now remove all of the subtotals from the worksheet.

**16** Click on any cell in the data area to ensure that it is selected, then on the Data tab, in the Outline group, click **Subtotal**.

**17** Click the **Remove All** button to clear the subtotals.

**Note:** When you remove some subtotals, you remove all subtotal functions. You cannot remove some subtotals and keep the rest.

You can also calculate two different types of subtotals for the same (or different) column(s) in the worksheet at the same time.

**18** On the Data tab, in the Outline group, click **Subtotal**.

**19**  Verify the Subtotal dialog box has the following settings and click **OK**:

| | |
|---|---|
| At each change in | Payment Type |
| Use function | Sum |
| Add subtotal to | Amount Paid |
| Replace current subtotals | On |
| Summary below data | On |

**20**  On the Data tab, in the Outline group, click **Subtotal** again.

**21**  In the Subtotal dialog box, configure the following settings and click **OK**:

| | |
|---|---|
| At each change in | Payment Type |
| Use function | Count |
| Add subtotal to | Amount Paid |
| Replace current subtotals | Off |
| Summary below data | On |

Note that when you are adding another subtotal to an existing one, you have to clear Replace current subtotals.

**22**  Scroll down the data and see how the subtotal values now appear.

**23**  Save and close the workbook.

# Manually Grouping and Ungrouping Data

**Objective 2.3.2**

Creating an outline of an Excel worksheet using automatic subtotals is a very useful feature but only if the data are structured consistently, as demonstrated in the previous topic. However, not all worksheets have data designed in such a way that there is a clear break from one group of rows or columns to the next group.

On some worksheets, you need to insert summary functions manually where they are required. To create an outline of a worksheet using this manual grouping method, you must adhere to the following guidelines:

- The worksheet must already contain summation formulas including SUM, SUBTOTAL, or simple addition (+) operators in the rows and/or columns where they need to be.

- The summary formulas must all flow in the same direction. For example, all =SUM formulas must add together cells above or to its left in a single worksheet. If one or more add together other cells to the right or below as well, Excel cannot create an outline.

- Although Excel assumes the summary formulas will refer to the data above or to the left of the cell in which you place the formula, you can override these assumptions by changing the settings. On the Data tab, in the Outline group, click the Dialog box launcher to display the Settings dialog box.

By default, Excel assumes that the subtotals will appear to the right and/or below the group data. Uncheck the boxes if the data flow in one of the opposite directions.

- You can have only one outline for each worksheet.

If you are unable to meet any one of these conditions, Excel may not complete the task and you will have to create the outline manually.

As indicated, the automatic outlining tool can be applied to rows and/or columns of data.

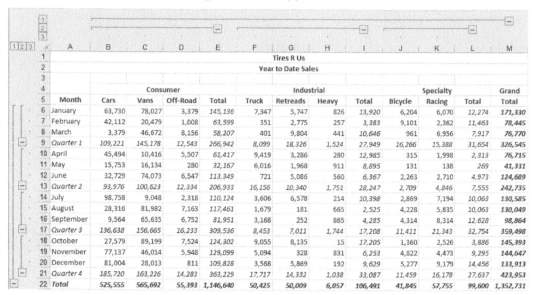

| Month | Cars | Vans | Off-Road | Total | Truck | Retreads | Heavy | Total | Bicycle | Racing | Total | Grand Total |
|---|---|---|---|---|---|---|---|---|---|---|---|---|
| | | Consumer | | | | Industrial | | | | Specialty | | Grand |
| January | 63,730 | 78,027 | 3,379 | 145,136 | 7,347 | 5,747 | 826 | 13,920 | 6,204 | 6,070 | 12,274 | 171,330 |
| February | 42,112 | 20,479 | 1,008 | 63,599 | 351 | 2,775 | 257 | 3,383 | 9,101 | 2,362 | 11,463 | 78,445 |
| March | 3,379 | 46,672 | 8,156 | 58,207 | 401 | 9,804 | 441 | 10,646 | 961 | 6,956 | 7,917 | 76,770 |
| Quarter 1 | 109,221 | 145,178 | 12,543 | 266,942 | 8,099 | 18,326 | 1,524 | 27,949 | 16,266 | 15,388 | 31,654 | 326,545 |
| April | 45,494 | 10,416 | 5,507 | 61,417 | 9,419 | 3,286 | 280 | 12,985 | 315 | 1,998 | 2,313 | 76,715 |
| May | 15,753 | 16,134 | 280 | 32,167 | 6,016 | 1,968 | 911 | 8,895 | 131 | 138 | 269 | 41,331 |
| June | 32,729 | 74,073 | 6,547 | 113,349 | 721 | 5,086 | 560 | 6,367 | 2,263 | 2,710 | 4,973 | 124,689 |
| Quarter 2 | 93,976 | 100,623 | 12,334 | 206,933 | 16,156 | 10,340 | 1,751 | 28,247 | 2,709 | 4,846 | 7,555 | 242,735 |
| July | 98,758 | 9,048 | 2,318 | 110,124 | 3,606 | 6,578 | 214 | 10,398 | 2,869 | 7,194 | 10,063 | 130,585 |
| August | 28,316 | 81,982 | 7,163 | 117,461 | 1,679 | 181 | 665 | 2,525 | 4,228 | 5,835 | 10,063 | 130,049 |
| September | 9,564 | 65,635 | 6,752 | 81,951 | 3,168 | 252 | 865 | 4,285 | 4,314 | 8,314 | 12,628 | 98,864 |
| Quarter 3 | 136,638 | 156,665 | 16,233 | 309,536 | 8,453 | 7,011 | 1,744 | 17,208 | 11,411 | 21,343 | 32,754 | 359,498 |
| October | 27,579 | 89,199 | 7,524 | 124,302 | 9,055 | 8,135 | 15 | 17,205 | 1,360 | 2,526 | 3,886 | 145,393 |
| November | 77,137 | 46,014 | 5,948 | 129,099 | 5,094 | 328 | 831 | 6,253 | 4,822 | 4,473 | 9,295 | 144,647 |
| December | 81,004 | 28,013 | 811 | 109,828 | 3,568 | 5,869 | 192 | 9,629 | 5,277 | 9,179 | 14,456 | 133,913 |
| Quarter 4 | 185,720 | 163,226 | 14,283 | 363,229 | 17,717 | 14,332 | 1,038 | 33,087 | 11,459 | 16,178 | 27,637 | 423,953 |
| Total | 525,555 | 565,692 | 55,393 | 1,146,640 | 50,425 | 50,009 | 6,057 | 106,491 | 41,845 | 57,755 | 99,600 | 1,352,731 |

Excel could not create an automatic outline for this worksheet because there are no repeating values to insert the subtotals. Instead, you have to manually insert the subtotals by row after every 3 months (or Quarter), and by column within each product group.

# Learn to manually group data

This exercise demonstrates how to insert manual subtotals, and then create an outline afterwards.

1   Open the *Sales* workbook again and save it as: Sales Grouping - Student.

Begin by creating a group for the month of January.

2   Scroll down and select row **180**. On the Home tab, in the Cells group, click **Insert**.

3   Enter the following:

| Cell | Value or Formula |
|---|---|
| A180 | Subtotal - January |
| D180 | =SUBTOTAL(9,D2:D179) |

4   Make note of the first row of the February sale.

5   Select rows **2** to **179**. You can select this group of rows by starting at the bottom with row 179 and select the rest of the rows in an upward direction, or scroll to the top of the worksheet, start with row 2, and select downwards.

**Note:** Do not include the row containing the subtotal formula.

6   On the **Data** tab, in the Outline group, click **Group**.

The group outline bar is now displayed for the January rows.

Repeat these steps for the month of February.

**7** Scroll down and select row **339**. Then, on the **Home** tab, in the Cells group, click **Insert**.

**8** Enter the following:

| Cell | Value or Formula |
|------|------------------|
| A339 | Subtotal - February |
| D339 | =SUBTOTAL(9,D181:D338) |

How did you know the range for this SUBTOTAL would start at 181? Because you made note of that in step 4.

**9** Select rows **181** to **338** and then, on the **Data** tab, in the Outline group, click **Group**.

**10** Click ☐ at the left of the headers for rows 339 and 180 to collapse both groups created so far.

You still have another 10 months' worth of data to group, and the process is beginning to appear tedious and error prone because the SUBTOTAL function must reference the correct cell range. For the remaining 10 months, you can use the same steps but in a different sequence to help streamline the process.

**11** Scroll down and insert a new blank row at row 500. You can also use the keyboard shortcut CTRL++ to insert a blank row.

**12** Select rows 340 to 499 and then, on the **Data** tab, in the Outline group, click **Group**.

When selecting the rows to be grouped together, be sure to <u>not</u> include the blank row in the group.

**13** Check that the ☐ appears at the blank row

If you have accidentally left out one or more rows of data, select these missing rows as shown in the following screen example. Then, on the Data tab, in the Outline group, click **Group**. Excel automatically adds these cells to the group.

| | A | B | C | D | E |
|---|---|---|---|---|---|
| 496 | 31-Mar-16 | 363 | Hotel | 188.00 | Amex |
| 497 | 31-Mar-16 | 363 | Flight+Hotel | 2,004.00 | Amex |
| 498 | 31-Mar-16 | 360 | Car rental | 169.00 | Air Miles |
| 499 | 31-Mar-16 | 309 | Nature tour | 211.00 | Visa |

**14** Click ☐ at the left of the row header to collapse this group. Alternatively, click ☐1 (to the left of the column label row).

**15** Enter the headings for the new group:

| Cell | Value or Formula |
|------|------------------|
| A500 | Subtotal - March |
| D500 | =SUBTOTAL(9,D340:D499) |

How did you know the range for this SUBTOTAL? You have collapsed all of the groups created so far, so just look at the row numbers at the left side of the worksheet. The range for March starts at row 340 because that is the next row after the February subtotal. It ends at row 499 because that is the last row just above the March subtotal.

| | A | B | C | D | E |
|---|---|---|---|---|---|
| 1 | Date | Customer No. | Sale Type | Amount Paid | Payment Type |
| 180 | Subtotal - January | | | 228,549.00 | |
| 339 | Subtotal - February | | | 204,455.00 | |
| 500 | Subtotal - March | | | 202,562.00 | |
| 501 | 1-Apr-16 | 378 | Hotel | 792.00 | Visa |
| 502 | 1-Apr-16 | 347 | Flight+Hotel | 1,514.00 | Cash |
| 503 | 1-Apr-16 | 324 | Hotel+Car rental | 892.00 | Amex |

Now switch to a different workbook in which the grouping and subtotals have already been entered for the months of April to December.

**16** Save and close the workbook.

**17** Open the *Sales Grouping 2* workbook and save it as: Sales Grouping 2 - Student.

**18** Enter the following:

| Cell | Value or Formula |
|------|------------------|
| A2022 | Grand Total |
| D2022 | =SUBTOTAL(9,D2:D2021) |

Set Excel to automatically create the outline for the worksheet.

**19** Select a cell inside the data range, such as **C180**.

**20** On the Data tab, in the Outline group, click the arrow for **Group,** and then click **Auto Outline**.

**Hint:** Alternatively, on the Data tab, in the Outline group, click the Dialog box launcher to display the Settings dialog box.

A message box appears with the question, "Modify existing outline?" This message is displayed because you had already created groups in this worksheet. You could have inserted the SUBTOTAL formulas into the worksheet without the grouping. The automatic outlining tool would then have created all of the monthly groups for you. However, for this exercise, you used the monthly groupings to help you enter the correct ranges for each SUBTOTAL.

**21** Click **OK**.

Your data with the manually inserted groupings and subtotals is now converted to an outlined group.

Collapse and expand the worksheet using the outline buttons to confirm that it is working properly as an outlined group.

**22** Click the ⊡, ⊡, ⊡, and ⊟ buttons to view different outline levels of the data.

The worksheet should look something like the following when the ⊡ button is clicked.

| | A | B | C | D | E |
|---|---|---|---|---|---|
| 1 | Date | Customer No. | Sale Type | Amount Paid | Payment Type |
| 180 | Subtotal - January | | | 228,549.00 | |
| 339 | Subtotal - February | | | 204,455.00 | |
| 500 | Subtotal - March | | | 202,562.00 | |
| 657 | Subtotal - April | | | 184,566.00 | |
| 843 | Subtotal - May | | | 228,305.00 | |
| 1019 | Subtotal - June | | | 219,241.00 | |
| 1208 | Subtotal - July | | | 261,207.00 | |
| 1384 | Subtotal - August | | | 252,730.00 | |
| 1532 | Subtotal - September | | | 181,586.00 | |
| 1696 | Subtotal - October | | | 202,040.00 | |
| 1864 | Subtotal - November | | | 211,073.00 | |
| 2021 | Subtotal - December | | | 201,724.00 | |
| 2022 | Grand Total | | | 2,578,038.00 | |

**Note:** When you use the automatic outlining feature, you will not be able to undo it using the Undo button on the Quick Access Toolbar.

**23** Save the workbook.

**24** On the Data tab, in the Outline group, click the arrow for **Ungroup**, and click **Clear Outline**.

All of the groupings have now been removed. The workbook has already been saved with the groupings so discard this version that has the groupings removed.

25  Close the workbook and discard the changes.

# Lesson Summary

Now that you have completed this lesson, you should be able to:

☑  create, modify, and delete range names

☑  use Go To to jump to a cell or named range

☑  convert a range of cells to a table

☑  modify a table by adding and deleting rows and columns of data

☑  apply and remove formatting on a table

☑  convert a table to a range of cells

☑  sort data

☑  use filtering on data

☑  remove duplicate rows of data

☑  outline and group data using automatic subtotals

☑  outline and group data by manually inserting subtotals

# Review Questions

1.  What does the following figure indicate?

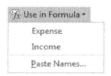

a.  There are two named ranges in the worksheet.

b.  There are two worksheets in the workbook.

c.  There are two functions available to paste into the current worksheet cell.

d.  There are two data series in the chart in the current worksheet.

2.  A range name cannot contain a(n):

a.  backslash

b.  underscore

c.  blank score

d.  A range name cannot contain any of the options listed here.

3.  Which dialog box can be used to add, modify or delete named ranges in a worksheet?

a.  Range Manager dialog box

b.  Sheet Setup dialog box

c.  Name Manager dialog box

d.  Titles dialog box

4.  When converting a range of data to a table, why do you need to tell Excel whether or not the data has headers?

a.  To ensure that the first row of data is treated as the column headers and not included with the data.

b.  When converting a range of data to a table, why do you need to tell Excel whether or not the data has headers?

c.  To ensure that headers will print on each page of a report.

d.  To ensure that the headers are automatically interpreted as print titles.

5.   To create a table, the following conditions must be met:

   a.   All of the data must be of the same type, such as text, numbers, or dates but not a mixture.

   b.   The data can be arranged in row or column order.

   c.   The data in the range of cells must be contiguous, and be arranged in row (not column) order.

   d.    Any range names must be removed first before creating the table.

6.   Banding a table means to:

   a.   Apply a light and dark shade of a color to alternating rows or columns of a table.

   b.   Apply a "band-aid" fix to the table data.

   c.   Discard the contents of a table.

   d.   Create a musical performing group to headline the latest chart hits.

7.   Multiple levels of sorting are useful whenever the column you are using for sorting has multiple rows with the same value.

   a.   True                              b.   False

8.   What is the difference between sorting and filtering?

   a.   Sorting changes both the sequence of the data and hides rows or columns of data temporarily, whereas filtering only hides rows or columns of data temporarily.

   b.   Sorting changes the sequence of the data but displays all of it, whereas filtering both changes the sequence of the data and hides rows or columns of data temporarily.

   c.   Sorting changes the sequence of the data but displays all of it, whereas filtering does not change the sequence of the data, but does hide rows or columns of data temporarily.

   d.   Sorting changes both the sequence of the data and hides rows or columns of data temporarily, whereas filtering only hides rows or columns of data temporarily.

9.   Which of the following comparison operators can be used for filtering text, numbers, and dates:

   a.   Next month                    e.   Top 10

   b.   Equals and Does not equal     f.   Between

   c.   Above average                 g.   Begins with

   d.   Contains

10.  The Remove Duplicates feature will reliably delete all rows that contain duplicate data even though the data may have minor variations such as extra blanks, commas, or different spellings.

   a.   True                              b.   False

11.  Once you have added a set of subtotals (for example, SUM) for a column of numeric data in a range of cells, you can also add more subtotals for the same column such as AVERAGE and MAX.

   a.   True                              b.   False

Microsoft®

# Excel 2016

## Core Certification Guide

# Lesson 8: Using Data Tools

## Lesson Objectives

In this lesson, you will learn about a variety of Excel data tools including importing and exporting data between other applications, searching worksheets for a value, using hyperlinks, and making workbooks more accessible. Upon completion of this lesson, you should be able to:

- ☐ customize the Quick Access Toolbar
- ☐ find data in the worksheet
- ☐ replace data in the worksheet with different data
- ☐ create, modify, and delete hyperlinks
- ☐ import and export data between other programs
- ☐ change workbook document properties
- ☐ use the document inspector tool
- ☐ use the accessibility checker tool

## Customizing Excel

### Customizing the Quick Access Toolbar

**Objective 1.4.3**

The Quick Access Toolbar (QAT) is located at the left of the title bar above the Ribbon and by default, contains the Excel control icons Save, Undo, and Redo command buttons.

You will recall that the Ribbon has multiple tabs to organize the many Excel commands and features into logical groups. You will typically jump from one tab to another to access the different Excel commands needed while using and updating your worksheet. However, the QAT does not have any tabs, giving you very fast access to the buttons in it at all times. It is also easy to access in its location above the Ribbon.

If you use certain Excel commands and features very frequently, you can make them more accessible by adding them to the QAT, saving you the effort of having to switch to a different tab to find it in the Ribbon. The combination of being in a convenient location and the ease of customization makes the QAT an ideal location to place your most frequently used commands.

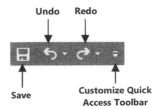

To customize the QAT, use one of the following methods:

- click **Customize Quick Access Toolbar** and click a button from the displayed list or click **More Commands**, or

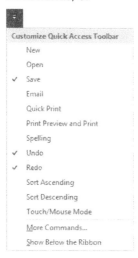

- click **File**, click **Options**, and then click **Quick Access Toolbar**, or

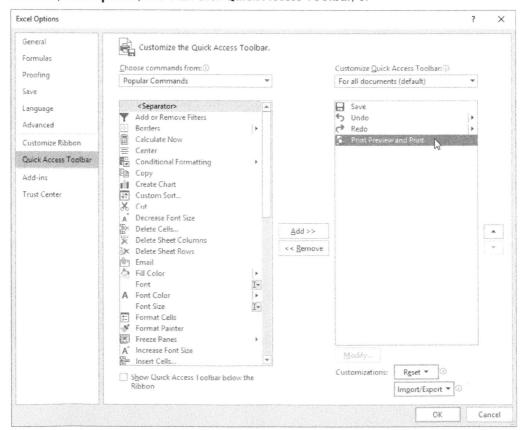

- right-click anywhere on the Ribbon, then click **Customize Quick Access Toolbar** to display the Excel Options Quick Access Toolbar window.

Add to Quick Access Toolbar

Customize Quick Access Toolbar...

Show Quick Access Toolbar Below the Ribbon

Customize the Ribbon...

Collapse the Ribbon

You can even add commands and features to the QAT that are not currently accessible from the Ribbon. As long as the feature is available in the Customer Quick Access Toolbar screen, you can add it to the QAT.

You can also move the Quick Access Toolbar to a different position directly below the Ribbon using one of the following methods:

- click **Customize Quick Access Toolbar** and then click **Show Below the Ribbon**, or
- right-click the Ribbon and then click **Show Quick Access Toolbar Below the Ribbon**.

# Learn to customize toolbars

In this exercise, you will customize the Quick Access Toolbar by adding and removing command buttons.

**1** Create a new blank workbook.

**2** Click **Customize Quick Access Toolbar** at the far right of the Quick Access Toolbar.

**3** Click **Quick Print** from the menu.

**4** Click **Customize Quick Access Toolbar** then click **Print Preview and Print**.

The Quick Access Toolbar should now appear similar to the following:

Remove these two command buttons using different methods for each.

**5** Click the **Customize Quick Access Toolbar** then click **Quick Print**.

**6** Click **File**, click **Options**, and then click **Quick Access Toolbar**.

**7** In the list displayed on the right, click **Print Preview and Print**, click **Remove**, and then click **OK**.

**8** Close the workbook and discard any changes that may have been made.

# Finding and Replacing Data

## Finding Data

### Objective 1.2.1

You can search a worksheet for every occurrence of a value (text label or number), function name, or cell reference. In the event you need to find every cell that contains this search item, the Find tool is invaluable. By default, the Find tool will search for the value in the Find what text box in every cell in the current worksheet. The search value can be as long or short as you need. Any cell that contains this value – even if it is only part of a longer value – will be selected.

To activate the Find tool, use one of the following methods:

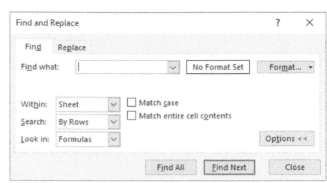

- on the **Home** tab, in the Editing group, click **Find & Select** and then click **Find**, or
- press CTRL+F.

You will have to click the **Options** button to display all of the options shown in the diagram.

**Find what** – The value to search for.

**Within** – Search only within the current worksheet or the entire workbook.

**Search** – Indicate which direction to search:
- By Rows: Search from left to right across each row in the worksheet/workbook starting from the top row.
- By Columns: Search down each column starting from the left-most column.

**Look in** – Specify whether to look only at the value, the underlying formula, or any comment in each cell. The Formulas option is generally more flexible even if the cell contains just a value.

**Match case** – Specify whether or not to match the upper and lower case of alphabetic characters in the cell.

**Match entire cell contents** – Specify whether the cell must only contain the *Find what* value, or the cell may contain other text characters as well. This setting only applies when you are searching for text data.

# Replacing Data

### Objective 2.1.1

You can also replace the search item with a new value, on an individual basis by using Replace, or for all cells at one time that contain the search item by using Replace All. The Replace function simplifies and speeds up the task of replacing one word or value with another. This automated process virtually eliminates any typing errors you would have made if you had to do it manually.

To activate the Replace tool, use one of the following methods:

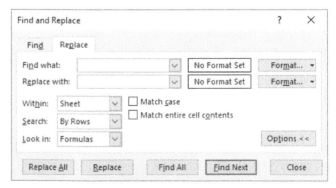

- on the **Home** tab, in the Editing group, click **Find & Select**, and click **Replace**, or
- press CTRL+H, or
- if the Find dialog box is displayed, click the **Replace** tab.

You may want to use Replace to control and verify that each replacement should be made. An alternative is to use the Find tab before using the replace function to search through the worksheet and verify that your search value and options have been set correctly. Once you are certain that your search value and options are correct, you can proceed with using Replace All. If you replaced a cell value by mistake, you can use the Undo command.

# Learn to find and replace data

This exercise demonstrates how to find all cells that contain a specific data value and then replace that data value with a new value.

**1**   Open the *World Capitals* workbook.

First try looking for a word.

**2**   On the Home tab, in the Editing group, click **Find & Select** and then click **Find**.

**3**   In the Find what text box, type: united and click **Find Next**.

**4**   Click **Find Next** several more times and observe which cells are selected.

Now try different find options.

**5**   In the Find and Replace dialog box, click **Options** to display all find options.

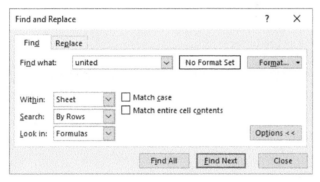

**6**   Click **Match case** to turn it on and then click **Find Next**.

A message box displays with the message "We couldn't find what you were looking for." Even though Excel did not have any difficulty earlier looking for the word *united*, none of the cells contains the word *united* in all lower case characters.

**7**   Click **OK** to close the message box.

**8**   Click **Find what**, and change the value to search for to: United (be sure to use upper case for the first letter).

**9**   Click **Find Next** several times.

**10**  In the **Find what** text box, delete United and replace it with spain.

**11**  Click **Match case** to turn it off, and then click **Find Next** several times.

**12**  Click **Match entire cell contents** to turn it on and then click **Find Next** several times.

Now only one row is found with the word Spain as the full name.

**13**  Click **Match entire cell contents** to turn it off.

Now try the Replace feature.

**14**  In **Find what**, type: x and click **Find Next** several times to find all words containing the letter *x*.

**15**  Click the **Replace** tab.

**16** In **Replace with** type: zh and click **Find Next**.

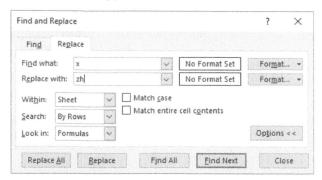

Excel has now found the first word with an *x* in it.

**17** Click **Replace**.

Instead of using Replace, you could click Replace All to replace all occurrences in the worksheet at one time.

**18** Click **Replace All** to replace every instance of the letter *x*.

Excel has completed replacing all specific text occurrences when a message box appears with "All done. We made 3 replacements."

**19** Click **OK** to close the message box.

**20** Click **Close**.

**21** Close the workbook and discard all changes.

# Using Hyperlinks

A hyperlink is a clickable element in an electronic document that you can use to jump to or open another document. Hyperlinks were introduced with the Internet to allow users to navigate from one web page to another whether the next web page was in the same website or another. Web pages are simply documents containing text, images, videos, and hyperlinks to other web pages.

By clicking a hyperlink, you can display the referenced document. Each hyperlink contains a code in the form of a Uniform Resource Locator (URL) which is the unique address for this document or page at this particular location on the Internet or intranet.

Over time, hyperlinks have evolved to link to any type of document in any location, not just on the Internet. A hyperlink in an Excel workbook can be used to:

- launch web pages from the Internet or the internal corporate intranet, or
- open a workbook or document located on a computer (including your own) within your home or corporate network, or
- jump to another cell in the same workbook, or
- create a new workbook, or
- create an email with a specific set of recipients and a subject line.

# Inserting Hyperlinks

**Objective 1.2.3**

To insert a hyperlink, use one of the following methods:

- on the Insert tab, in the Links group, click the **Link** button, or
- right-click on a cell and click **Link**, or
- press CTRL+K.

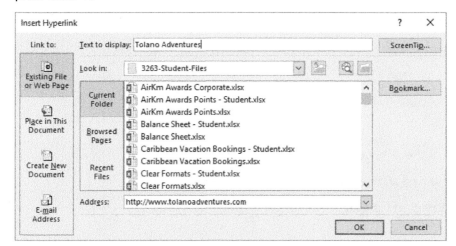

The displayed Insert Hyperlink dialog box allows you to insert one of four types of hyperlinks:

**Existing File or Web Page** — Used to link to workbooks, files or documents stored on a local or networked hard drive, or websites on the intranet or the Internet.

**Place in This Document** – Used to link to a cell or named range of cells in the current workbook either in the current worksheet or another worksheet.

**Create New Document** – Used to create a new workbook using the name that you specify in the Name of new document text box and located in the folder specified under Full path.

**E-mail Address** – Used to launch the e-mail program (for example, Outlook) installed on the local computer and create a new e-mail message using the e-mail address and subject line specified in this dialog box.

A mailto URL is a special type of URL used by e-mail systems.

# Modifying and Deleting Hyperlinks

**Objective 1.2.3**

Hyperlink addresses are unique, specific locations to a document whether it is stored on the Internet, the local intranet, or a local computer. If you move or rename the referenced document, you must change the hyperlink.

You may also want to change the text displayed in the worksheet for the hyperlink or add a custom ScreenTip.

To modify a hyperlink in the worksheet, use one of the following methods:

- right-click the hyperlink and then click **Edit Hyperlink**, or
- move the cell pointer to the cell containing the link and then, on the Insert tab, in the Links group, click **Link** to display the Edit Hyperlink dialog box. Make the necessary changes and close the dialog box.

When you no longer need the hyperlink, you can remove the reference. The text displayed for the hyperlink remains in the cell.

To delete a hyperlink in the worksheet, use one of the following methods:

- right-click the link and then click **Remove Hyperlink**, or
- move the cell pointer to the cell containing the link and then, on the Insert tab, in the Links group, click **Link** to display the Edit Hyperlink dialog box. Click **Remove Link**.

# Learn to insert hyperlinks

This exercise demonstrates how to create and modify hyperlinks in an Excel workbook.

**1**  Open the *Financial Statement Links* workbook and save it as: Financial Statement Links - Student.

Insert a hyperlink to a website in cell B3.

**2**  Select cell **B3**.

**3**  On the **Insert** tab, in the Links group, click the **Link** button to open the Insert Hyperlink dialog box.

**4**  Click in the **Address** field and type: www.tolanoadventures.com.

**5**  Click in **Text to display** and change the contents to: Tolano Adventures.

**6**  Click **OK**.

Now insert a hyperlink to an Excel workbook.

**7**  Select cell **B5**.

**8**  On the Insert tab, in the Links group, click **Link**.

**9**  Scroll down and select the *Income Statement* workbook. If necessary, select the student data files folder in the **Look in** list.

**10**  Click in **Text to display** and change the contents to: Income Statement, then click **OK**.

Insert another hyperlink to an Excel workbook, using a fast method.

**11**  Right-click in cell **B7**, then click **Link**.

**12**  Scroll down and select the *Balance Sheet* workbook and click **OK**.

Test one of the hyperlinks by clicking on it.

**13**  Position the mouse cursor over the hyperlink in cell B5. The cursor changes to a white pointing hand.

Notice that a screen tip will appear with the URL for the *Income Statement.xlsx* workbook.

**14**  Click the **Income Statement** hyperlink.

The Income Statement workbook is now open on top of the Financial Statement Links workbook.

**15**  Close the Income Statement workbook.

The color of the hyperlink has changed to indicate that it has been used.

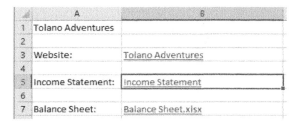

Now manually change one of the hyperlinks to point to a different workbook.

**16** Right-click the **Income Statement** hyperlink in cell B5 and then click **Edit Hyperlink**.

**17** In the Edit Hyperlink dialog box, scroll down and select the *Quarterly Income Statement* workbook.

**18** Click **OK** to save the updated hyperlink.

You can change the hyperlink text directly on the worksheet without having to launch the Edit Hyperlink dialog box. However, if you click on the cell containing the hyperlink, the workbook will open. The next two steps will show you how to work around the problem.

**19** Click in cell **A7** and then press the RIGHT ARROW key to make cell **B7** into the active cell without activating the hyperlink.

**Hint:** You can select any nearby cell and then use the cursor keys on the keyboard to select the cell.

**20** Press **F2** to switch to edit mode, change the link text to `Balance Sheet` workbook and press ENTER.

There are two other ways of selecting a cell without activating the hyperlink, by holding down the CTRL key while clicking on the cell, or by clicking and holding down the left mouse button on the cell for a few seconds until the mouse pointer changes from a hand to a white cross. Release the left mouse button and press the F2 key to go into edit mode.

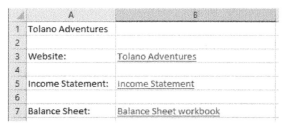

Now enter a custom ScreenTip for one of the hyperlinks.

**21** Right-click the *Balance Sheet* hyperlink in cell **B7** and then click **Edit Hyperlink**.

**22** In the Edit Hyperlink dialog box, click **ScreenTip**.

**23** In the Set Hyperlink ScreenTip dialog box, type: `This is the link to the Balance Sheet workbook` and click **OK**.

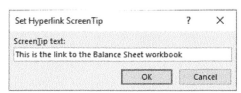

**24** In the Edit Hyperlink dialog box, click **OK** to close it.

**25** Position the cursor over the hyperlink in cell **B7** to view the ScreenTip.

Test the change to the Balance Sheet workbook hyperlink to make sure that it is working properly.

**26** Click the hyperlink in cell **B7**.

**27** Close the *Balance Sheet* workbook.

Now delete one of the hyperlinks.

**28** Right-click the hyperlink in cell **B7** and click **Remove Hyperlink**.

The hyperlink in cell B7 has now changed to plain text.

**29** Save and close the workbook.

# Importing and Exporting Data
## Importing Data Files from External Text Files

**Objective 1.1.2**

Most businesses use various specialized computer applications for their operations. Typically these systems reside on servers, other PCs within the same corporate network, or with remote servers (such as cloud providers). The challenge has always been to move data from one application to another without having to manually re-enter the data. Almost all of these applications have the ability to export data into files, and the text data file format is the most commonly used.

Excel uses the Office Open XML to store its own workbook data. However, most other applications do not support that format at this time. Fortunately, Excel has built-in tools to import external data easily.

On the Data tab, there are six icons in the Get & Transform Data group used for importing external data:

- **Get Data** – Displays a drop-down menu of options you can select to import data:
  - **From File** – Imports data from a selected Workbook, Text/CSV, XML, or JSON file. You can also navigate to a folder or SharePoint location to specify the file you want to import.
  - **From Database** – Imports data from a selected database file. You can select from among SQL Server, Microsoft Access, Analysis Services, SQL Server Analysis Services, Oracle, IBM DB2, MySQL, PostgreSQL, Sybase, Teradata, and SAP HANA database types.
  - **From Azure** – Imports data from a file stored in Microsoft Azure. Azure is a cloud-computing service created by Microsoft in which developers can build, test, install, and manage applications and services through Microsoft data centers. You can select files from SQL Database, SQL Data Warehouse, HDInsight, Blob Storage, Table Storage, and Data Lake Store services.
  - **From Online Services** – Imports data from files stored in various online services, such as SharePoint, Microsoft Exchange, Dynamics 365, Facebook, Salesforce Objects, and Salesforce Reports.

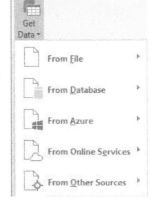

- **From Other Sources** – Imports data from files that come from various sources, some of which you can access directly using the options in the Get & Transform Data group. You can select data from sources such as a Table/Range, the Web, Microsoft Query, SharePoint List, OData Feed, Hadoop File, Active Directory, Microsoft Exchange, ODBC, OLEDB, and Blank Query.

- **From Text/CSV** – Imports data from a file containing numeric and alphabetic data in text format, in which the values are separated from each other by a tab, space, comma, or some other character.

- **From Web** – Imports data that is displayed in specific locations of a Web page.

- **From Table/Range** – Imports data from a selected Excel table or named range.

- **Recent Sources** – Imports data from a recently-opened source file.

- **Existing Connections** – Imports data using an existing data connection that was previously created for this workbook, this computer, or your network.

When you click the **From Text/CSV** option to import data from an external text file, the Import Data dialog box will display from which you select the name of the text or comma-separated value file whose contents you want to import.

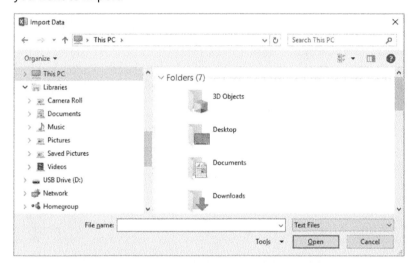

After you select a file and open it from the Import Data dialog box, the contents of the file will display in a preview window showing the overall structure of the data.

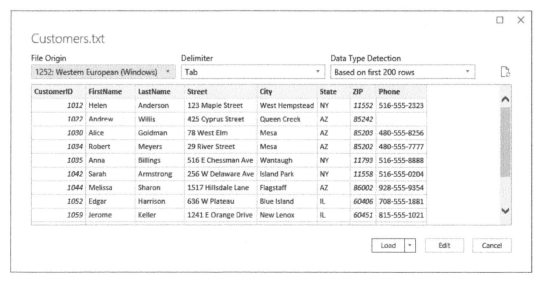

The preview window contains the following options:

| File Origin | Select an option to specify the character set used to create the data in the text file. In most cases, you can accept the default setting. |
|---|---|
| Delimiter | Select an option to specify the character used to separate each field of text in the text file. Excel attempts to detect each instance of the delimiter in the text file to determine the value that should appear in each column in the worksheet. |
|  | You can select from among the Colon, Comma, Equals sign, Semicolon, Space, Tab, Custom, and Fixed Width delimiters. Select Custom if you need to specify a delimiter that is not part of the default list, such as the quote or double-quote character. Select Fixed Width if the values are vertically aligned in columns (possibly with no gaps between the columns), and blank spaces are used where necessary to align the data. |
| Data Type Detection | Select an option to specify the number of rows in the text file that Excel uses to interpret the type of data contained in the text file. |
| (Preview) | Click this button to preview the imported data based on options you select in the File Origin, Delimiter, and Data Type Detection drop-down lists. You should always preview the data to ensure it will display correctly in Excel. |
| Load | Click this button to load the imported data. |
|  | You can click the arrow on the right side of the Load button and click the Load To command to specify how to view the imported data in your workbook, whether you want to place the data in the existing worksheet or a new worksheet, and the worksheet cell to use as the starting point for the imported data. Clicking the Load command in the drop-down menu is the same as clicking the Load button, which will import the data as a table into a new worksheet starting in Cell A1. |
| Edit | Click this button to display the Query Editor, in which you can determine how the data will appear in the worksheet. For example, you can transpose the columns and rows, filter the data, sort the data, and so on. |

# Learn to import text

In this exercise, you will import a text file into a worksheet.

1   In File Explorer, navigate to the *3263-Student-Files* folder, and then double-click the **Eco Cruises** text document file to open it in Notepad.

This is the data that you will import into an Excel workbook. It contains plain text data, and at first glance appears to be aligned into proper columns. However, a closer examination shows that the first row does not align with the rest of the rows. This indicates that a tab character, that is not easily visible in Notepad, is being used to separate the data into columns.

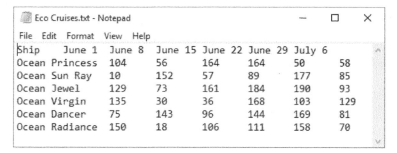

2    Close Notepad and discard any changes that may have been made to the file.

3    Create a new blank workbook and click the **Data** tab.

4    In the **Get & Transform Data** group, click **From Text/CSV**.

The Import Data dialog box is displayed.

5    Navigate to the student data files folder, select the **Eco Cruises** text document file, and click **Import** in the Import Data dialog box.

A preview window appears showing how the imported data will display in an Excel worksheet.

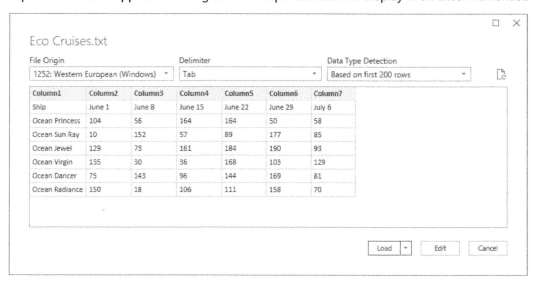

Notice that *Tab* appears in the Delimiter field. Based on the data in the text file, Excel determined that the TAB character was used to separate (or delimit) the values in each field, and placed each delimited value in a separate column.

Let's try different delimiters to see what effects they have on the data.

6    Click the **Delimiter** drop-down arrow to display the list of delimiters.

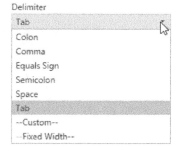

If you select a different delimiter, Excel will attempt to detect each instance of the delimiter in the text file and place each value separated by the delimiter in its own column in the worksheet.

**7** In the **Delimiter** drop-down list, click **Comma**.

The preview window displays how the imported data will appear in the Excel workbook.

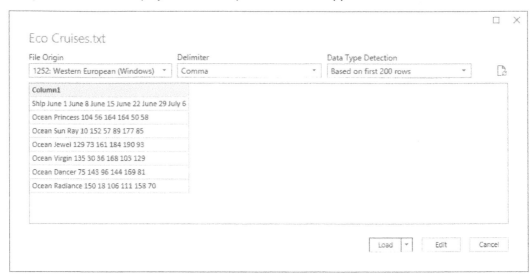

Because Excel was unable to detect comma delimiters in the text file, it had no way to determine where to split the data into separate columns. Therefore, all data appears in the first column.

**8** Display the **Delimiter** drop-down list, and then click **Space**.

The preview window displays how the imported data will appear in the Excel workbook.

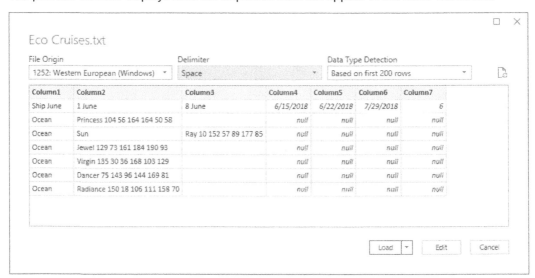

In this scenario, each time Excel detected a space in the text file data, it placed the value immediately after the space in a separate column. Notice that several date values were placed in their own columns, and null values appear in the rows under the dates for which no other data is present.

**9** Change the delimiter back to **Tab**. The preview window displays how the imported data will appear in the Excel workbook. In this scenario, Excel detected the TAB characters separating the values in the text file and placed each value in its own column.

10  Click the arrow on the **Load** button, then click **Load To**. The Import Data dialog box associated with the Load To command appears.

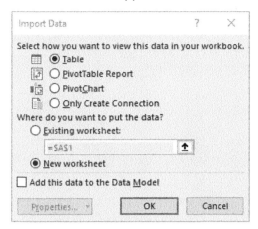

Notice that the default selections specify to import the data in a table format, and load the data into a new worksheet starting in Cell A1.

11  Ensure that **Table** is selected, select **Existing worksheet**, and then click **OK**.

Excel loads the imported data into the current worksheet as a table starting in Cell A1. You can edit and format the table as desired.

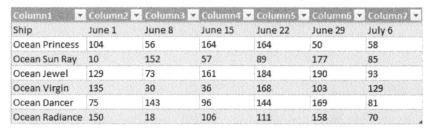

| Column1 | Column2 | Column3 | Column4 | Column5 | Column6 | Column7 |
|---|---|---|---|---|---|---|
| Ship | June 1 | June 8 | June 15 | June 22 | June 29 | July 6 |
| Ocean Princess | 104 | 56 | 164 | 164 | 50 | 58 |
| Ocean Sun Ray | 10 | 152 | 57 | 89 | 177 | 85 |
| Ocean Jewel | 129 | 73 | 161 | 184 | 190 | 93 |
| Ocean Virgin | 135 | 30 | 36 | 168 | 103 | 129 |
| Ocean Dancer | 75 | 143 | 96 | 144 | 169 | 81 |
| Ocean Radiance | 150 | 18 | 106 | 111 | 158 | 70 |

12  Save the workbook in the student files folder as: Eco Cruises - Student and close it.

# Importing Data from External CSV Files

**Objective 1.1.2**

A CSV (Comma Separated Values) file contains data in text form, just like a text file with the filename extension of .TXT. But because CSV files must follow a set of rules in how the data is laid out inside the file, Excel is able to open CSV files directly. It almost treats CSV files like an Excel workbook.

The example screen below demonstrates how Windows displays this type of file in File Explorer.

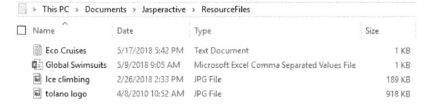

Notice that the icon to the left of the Global Swimsuits file name is similar to the icons of Excel workbooks, but it is not the same. Also, the file type is Microsoft Excel Comma Separated Values File.

If you open this file using Notepad, you will see the contents appear similar to the following:

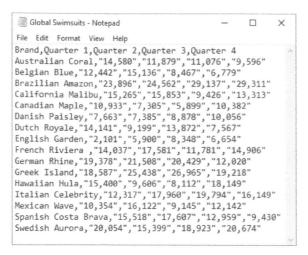

This example file demonstrates that a CSV file is simply a text file with commas used as a delimiter to separate the values between columns. The numbers have commas inside, so the double-quote character (") is used as the text qualifier around each number.

When you open a CSV file in Excel, Excel displays the values in columnar format using the comma delimiter to determine which values appear in which columns.

# Learn to open non-native files in Excel

In this exercise, you will open a comma delimited text file as a workbook.

1   In File Explorer, navigate to the *3263-Student-Files* folder.

2   Right-click the *Global Swimsuits* file, click **Open with**, then click **Notepad**. Alternatively, start Notepad first and open the file *Global Swimsuits.CSV*.

   Notice that this CSV file contains text data (including numbers) with commas used as a delimiter to separate the values between columns.

3   Close Notepad and discard any changes that may have been made to the file.

4   In File Explorer, double-click the *Global Swimsuits* file to open it in Excel.

   Alternatively, in Excel, you can click **File**, **Open**, then click **Browse** to display the Open dialog box, change the file type to **Text Files**, select the file, and click **Open**.

5   Increase the width of column A to display the full text in every row.

6   Click **File**, **Save As**, then click **Browse**.

7   Click the arrow for **Save as type**, and click **Excel Workbook**.

8   Click **Save**.

   The CSV file is now saved as an Excel workbook. If you go into File Explorer, you will see both a *Global Swimsuits* workbook using the workbook icon 📗, as well as a *Global Swimsuits* CSV text file using the CSV icon 📄. If both files are kept together in the same folder, you should closely examine the icon and the file type description.

9   Close the workbook.

## Exporting Excel Data as CSV

### Objective 1.5.2

Excel provides an easy-to-use method of exporting data to other file formats, including the CSV format. In the Save As tab in Backstage view, or in the Save As dialog box, the Save as type drop-down list includes an extensive list of different formats for saving the worksheet data:

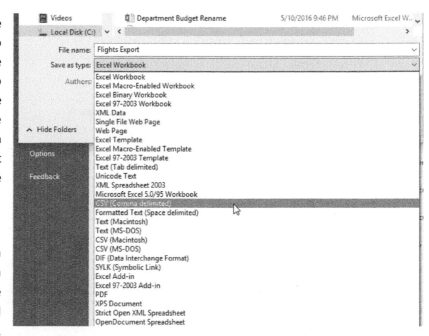

Note that CSV files only contain text data. This means that when saving a workbook using the CSV format, Excel will discard anything that is not pure data. Therefore, your CSV workbook should not use Excel features such as formulas, cell formatting, charts, and multiple worksheets. Excel will display the following question as a reminder:

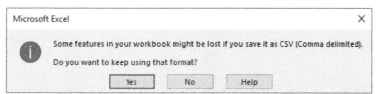

# Learn to export data

In this exercise, you will export worksheet data to a CSV file.

**1** Open the *Flights Export* workbook.

Export this worksheet to an external CSV text file.

**2** Click **File**, **Save As**, **Browse**.

**3** Click the **Save as type** arrow, select **CSV (Comma delimited)**, then click **Save**.

The warning message box appears.

**4** Click **Yes**.

Use Notepad to check the contents of the CSV file.

**5** Start Notepad, then click **File**, **Open** from the menu.

**6** Change the document type from Text Documents (*.txt) to **All Files**.

**7** Navigate to the student data files folder and select the *Flights Export* CSV file and click **Open**.

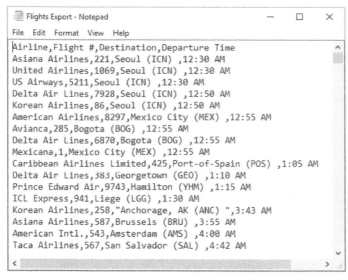

**8**   Close Notepad without saving any changes.

**9**   Go back to Excel. Close the *Flights Export* workbook and discard any changes.

**10**  Navigate to the student data files folder and double-click the *Flights Export* CSV file to open it using Excel.

Notice that all of the cell formatting that was in the original workbook has been removed, and only the text data remains.

**11**  Close the *Flights Export* workbook and discard any changes.

# Accessing Workbook Properties

### Objective 1.4.6

All files contain *metadata*; that is, information about the files such as date and time created and last modified, who created it, and the size of the file. Excel workbooks contain additional metadata such as your company name, the name of your computer, the number of times the workbook was modified, and comments.

This metadata – also known as document properties – is useful for sorting, organizing, and finding workbooks, especially when you have a large number of them.

File Explorer displays the file-related metadata in the Details tab of the Properties dialog box.

From within Excel, you can also access this same metadata, plus additional metadata that are specific to the Microsoft Office suite. This metadata can be displayed and set in the Advanced Properties window.

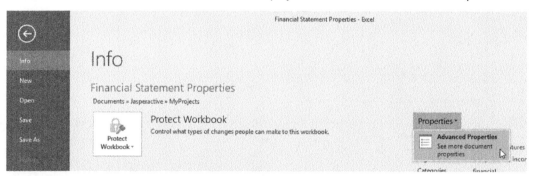

All files have four types of document properties:

**Standard properties** – These are properties that are created by all Microsoft Office software such as Excel and Word. These include author name, document title, and subject.

**Automatically updated properties** – These properties are the statistical information about the file, including the size, and dates when the file was created or modified. Users are not permitted to change these properties.

**Custom properties** – Excel allows users to create any number of customized properties of their own, or select from 27 pre-defined custom properties.

**Document library properties** – A document library can be created with rules set for all members. Therefore any file added to this document library will prompt users to enter valid property values to help identify it, and make it easy to search for by others.

# Learn to edit workbook properties

This exercise demonstrates how to view and modify Excel workbook metadata.

**1**   In File Explorer, navigate to the folder where your data files are stored.

**2** Right-click the *Financial Statement Properties* file, and click **Properties**.

**3** Click the **Details** tab, then scroll down the window to view its contents.

Notice that you can click the Remove Properties and Personal Information link at the bottom of the window.

**4** Click **Cancel** to close the Properties window.

**5** Open the *Financial Statement Properties* workbook and save it as: Financial Statement Properties - Student.

**6** Click the **File** button, click **Info**, and then click **Properties**, and click **Advanced Properties**.

**7** In the Summary tab, enter the following:

Title:      Tolano Adventures
Subject:    financial statement
Author:     <your own name>
Category:   financial
Keywords:   links, website, income statement, balance sheet

**8** Click each of the tabs to view their contents.

**9** Click **OK** to close the dialog box.

Notice that some of the property values that you entered now appear in the Info screen. They will also appear externally in File Explorer.

**10** Save the workbook.

**11** In File Explorer, navigate to the student data files folder, then right-click the *Financial Statement Properties - Student* file, and click **Properties**.

**12** Click the **Details** tab, then view its contents.

The window now displays the new property values you entered in the Excel workbook.

**13** Click **Cancel** to close the Properties window and close File Explorer.

# Using the Document Inspector

**Objective 1.5.6**

Although metadata is useful to the person who created the workbook, this collection may not be appropriate if shared with other users. For example, the Labor Relations department in a company may send a workbook containing personnel information to a union representative. That file may contain some metadata that may seem innocuous, such as the person who created it. However, the union may use that information to strengthen their position during upcoming negotiations.

The Document Inspector is designed to look for certain types of data stored in workbooks and report them to you. Some of these items include:

- Comments, revision marks, document versions, or annotations containing names of people who have made changes or made notations in the workbook.
- Workbook metadata that may include information about the originator.
- Information in any headers or footers, including watermarks.
- Hidden data rows, columns, and worksheets.
- Custom XML data that is not visible in the document.

The report is often useful to help users find hidden or private information in the workbook that they intend to share or publish for other people to use. By knowing that these types of data exist in a workbook, you can make a decision on whether it is appropriate to leave this data in or remove it.

## Learn to use the Document Inspector

This exercise demonstrates how to use the Document Inspector to find facts about the workbook that are "hidden" from view.

1   Ensure the *Financial Statement Properties – Student* workbook is open.

2   Click **File**, and in the Info screen, click **Check for Issues**, then click **Inspect Document**.

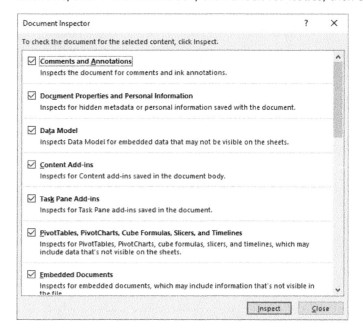

This graphic shows the items in your workbook that Document Inspector reports. You can then choose which items to keep or remove.

**3**  Leave all default options unchanged and click **Inspect**.

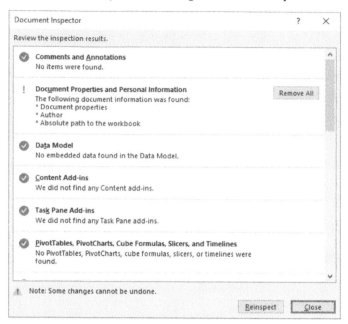

This dialog box shows items that the Document Inspector identified which you may choose not to share if you intend to distribute this document to others. Document Inspector provides the option to remove the items automatically, so that you do not have to remove them manually.

**4**  Scroll down the Document Inspector window to look for all sections that show the exclamation mark icon that need your attention.

**5**  Scroll back up to the top of the Document Inspector window and click **Remove All** in the Document Properties and Personal Information section.

The Document Properties and Personal Information section now shows a check mark to show that the issues have been resolved. You can do a re-inspection to check again.

**6**  Click **Reinspect** and then click **Inspect**.

**7**  Scroll down the Document Inspector window to look for any sections that show the exclamation mark icon.

**8**  Close the Document Inspector dialog box.

**9**  Click **Properties**, then click **Advanced Properties**.

Notice that in the Summary tab, the Title, Subject, Author, Category, and Keywords fields are now blank.

**10**  Click **OK** to close the Properties window.

**11**  Save and close the workbook.

# Using the Accessibility Checker Tool

**Objective 1.5.7, 5.3.4**

Computers have opened many new opportunities for persons with disabilities to enable them to become more self-sufficient and enhance their career opportunities. Windows and the Microsoft Office suite are designed with several features to assist persons overcome their physical limitations. However, workbooks should avoid certain attributes that can make it more difficult for users with disabilities.

By following these guidelines, your workbook can be used by more users of all abilities:

- Use descriptive text for images and objects. The text to speech tool in the computer can then read these descriptions for persons with sight disabilities. The descriptions are entered into workbooks using the Alt Text option.

- Worksheet tab names should clearly describe the purpose of their respective worksheets. For example, rename a worksheet to "Addresses" instead of using the default name of Sheet1.

- Use descriptive headings for data rows and columns.

- Use range names wherever possible to allow users to move quickly between significant parts of the worksheet.

- Create dense spreadsheets by minimizing the use of empty cells. Avoid using empty rows and columns wherever possible.

- Hyperlinks should display as descriptive text instead of the default URL. For example, "company intranet" instead of "https://corp.intnet.com".

- Use text fonts that are plain. A sans-serif font such as Arial, Helvetica, or Verdana is recommended. Sans serif fonts are more block-like and lack the little extensions on the end of the strokes.

- Use a high contrast color difference between the foreground and background.

To help with analyzing a workbook to improve its use by persons with disabilities, Excel includes an accessibility checker tool. To run this tool, go to the Excel Back Stage, click the **Info** category, click **Check for Issues**, then click **Check Accessibility**.

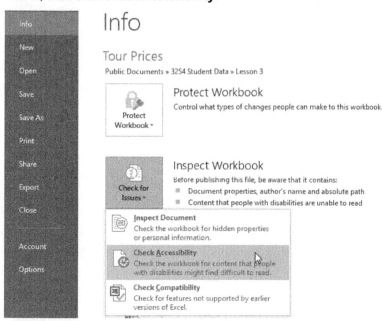

The Accessibility Checker pane will display a report suggesting improvements that can be made.

---

# Learn to check for accessibility issues

This exercise demonstrates how to check a workbook for its compliance with accessibility guidelines, and make corrections where necessary.

**1** Open the *Tour Prices Accessibility* workbook and save it as: `Tour Prices Accessibility - Student`.

**2** Click **File** in the Ribbon, then click **Info** if necessary.

**3** Click **Check for Issues**, then click **Check Accessibility**.

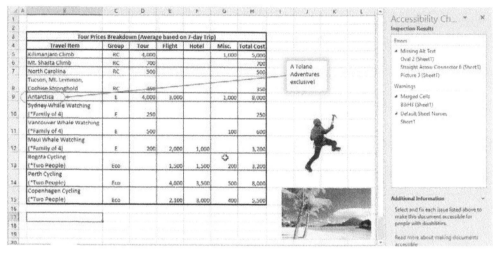

The Accessibility Checker pane lists a number of problems that need to be addressed, and some warnings that also should be corrected.

**4** Close the Accessibility Checker pane.

Correct the first error by adding a description for the image named Picture 3.

**5** Click the **ice climber** picture in the cell range J10:K14. The Name Box shows the object name Picture 3.

**6** Right-click on the **ice climber** picture, then click **Size and Properties**.

The Format Picture pane is displayed.

**7** If necessary, click the **ALT TEXT** arrow to open this section.

**8** In the Title text box, type: `Ice climber`.

Now correct the second error by adding a description for the oval and the arrow.

**9** Click on the **oval** shape in cell B9. The Name Box shows the object name Oval 2. Click in the **Title** text box in the Format Shape pane, and type: `Oval shape that highlights Antarctica travel item`.

**10** Click on the **arrow** line shape connected to the oval shape, then click in the **Title** text box in the Format Shape pane, and type: `Arrowed line to Antarctica travel item`.

Correct the first warning about the merged cells in B3:I3.

**11** Click in cell **B3**, the on the Home tab, in the Alignment group, click **Merge & Center** to turn it off.

Correct the second warning about the default sheet name.

**12** Double-click the **Sheet1** tab name for the worksheet, and replace it with: `Tour Prices`.

**13** Close the Format Shape pane.

Re-run the accessibility checker.

**14** Click **File** in the Ribbon, click **Check for Issues**, then click **Check Accessibility**.

**15** Save and close the workbook.

# Lesson Summary

Now that you have completed this lesson, you should be able to:

☑ customize the Quick Access Toolbar

☑ find data in the worksheet

☑ replace data in the worksheet with different data

☑ create, modify, and delete hyperlinks

☑ import and export data between other programs

☑ change workbook document properties

☑ use the document inspector tool

☑ use the accessibility checker tool

# Review Questions

1. You can add any Excel command to the Quick Access Toolbar including those that are not currently in the Ribbon.

   a. True                b. False

2. You can remove the Save, Undo, and Redo buttons from the Quick Access Toolbar.

   a. True                b. False

3. You can search a worksheet for every occurrence of a value (text label or number), function name, or cell reference.

   a. True                b. False

4. Lydia created a worksheet and wants to change the column title Cost to Expenses. Examine the following figure, then select the statement(s) that is/are true.

   a. Lydia can use either the Replace or Replace All commands, because in either case, only one replacement will be made.

   b. Lydia should use the Replace All command because it would be more efficient.

   c. Lydia should use the Replace command to ensure Excel does not make undesired replacements.

5.  A hyperlink in a workbook can be used to:

    a.  Open a different workbook that is stored on your computer, Jump to another cell in the same worksheet, Launch an Internet web page.

    b.  Run the Formula Annotator add-in, Create a new workbook.

    c.  Open Document format, Run the Formula Annotator add-in.

6.  Where will you find the options you need to import data from a text file into Excel?

    a.  The Data tab            c.  The Developer tab

    b.  The Formulas tab        d.  The Insert tab

7.  Which of the following is not permitted as a delimiter character?

    a.  ″ (double-quote)        f.  = (equal)

    b.  , (comma)               g.  (tab)

    c.  | (pipe)                h.  (blank space)

    d.  ~ (tilde)               i.  $ (dollar sign)

    e.  * (asterisk)            j.  All of the above characters are permitted to be used as
        delimiters

8.  Where will you find the options you need to export Excel data to a Comma Separated Values (CSV) file?

    a.  The Export & Transform group on the Data tab

    b.  The Export Forms group on the Developer tab

    c.  The Save As dialog box

    d.  The File Export group on the Formulas tab

9.  The workbook properties include the date and time when the workbook was last modified and saved.

    a.  True                    b.  False

10. The Document Inspector will not identify which of the following for corrective action:

    a.  Hidden rows, columns, or worksheets.

    b.  Custom XML data, even any that is hidden.

    c.  Misspelled names of people.

    d.  The name of the person who created the workbook.

    e.  Names of people who entered comments or other annotations anywhere in the workbook.

11. The Accessibility Checker Tool will not identify which of the following for corrective action:

    a.  Worksheets that still have their default names instead of customized ones.

    b.  Worksheet cells that do not have volume controls to assist people who are hearing impaired.

    c.  Picture images that do not have a description.

    d.  Shapes that do not have a description.

Microsoft®

# Excel 2016

Core Certification Guide

# Appendices

## Appendix A

Courseware Mapping

## Appendix B

Glossary of Terms

## Appendix C

Index

# Appendix A: Courseware Mapping

Skills Required for the Microsoft® Office Specialist Excel 2016 Core Exam 77-727:

| Objective Domain | | Lesson |
|---|---|---|
| **1** | **Create and Manage Worksheets and Workbooks** | |
| **1.1** | **Create Worksheets and Workbooks** | |
| 1.1.1 | create a workbook | 1 |
| 1.1.2 | import data from a delimited text file | 8 |
| 1.1.3 | add a worksheet to an existing workbook | 2 |
| 1.1.4 | copy and move a worksheet | 2 |
| **1.2** | **Navigate in Worksheets and Workbooks** | |
| 1.2.1 | search for data within a workbook | 8 |
| 1.2.2 | navigate to a named cell, range, or workbook element | 7 |
| 1.2.3 | insert and remove hyperlinks | 8 |
| **1.3** | **Format Worksheets and Workbooks** | |
| 1.3.1 | change worksheet tab color | 2 |
| 1.3.2 | rename a worksheet | 2 |
| 1.3.3 | change worksheet order | 2 |
| 1.3.4 | modify page setup | 5 |
| 1.3.5 | insert and delete columns or rows | 2 |
| 1.3.6 | change workbook themes | 4 |
| 1.3.7 | adjust row height and column width | 2 |
| 1.3.8 | insert headers and footers | 5 |
| **1.4** | **Customize Options and Views for Worksheets and Workbooks** | |
| 1.4.1 | hide or unhide worksheets | 2 |
| 1.4.2 | hide or unhide columns and rows | 2 |
| 1.4.3 | customize the Quick Access toolbar | 8 |
| 1.4.4 | change workbook views | 5 |
| 1.4.5 | change window views | 5 |
| 1.4.6 | modify document properties | 8 |
| 1.4.7 | change magnification by using zoom tools | 5 |
| 1.4.8 | display formulas | 3 |
| **1.5** | **Configure Worksheets and Workbooks for Distribution** | |
| 1.5.1 | set a print area | 5 |
| 1.5.2 | save workbooks in alternative file formats | 8 |
| 1.5.3 | print all or part of a workbook | 5 |
| 1.5.4 | set print scaling | 5 |
| 1.5.5 | display repeating row and column titles on multipage worksheets | 5 |
| 1.5.6 | inspect a workbook for hidden properties or personal information | 8 |
| 1.5.7 | inspect a workbook for accessibility issues | 8 |
| 1.5.8 | inspect a workbook for compatibility issues | 1 |

| Objective Domain | | Lesson |
|---|---|---|
| **2** | **Manage Data Cells and Ranges** | |
| **2.1** | **Insert Data in Cells and Ranges** | |
| 2.1.1 | replace data | 8 |
| 2.1.2 | cut, copy, or paste data | 2 |
| 2.1.3 | paste data by using special paste options | 2 |
| 2.1.4 | fill cells by using Auto Fill | 2 |
| 2.1.5 | insert and delete cells | 2 |
| **2.2** | **Format Cells and Ranges** | |
| 2.2.1 | merge cells | 4 |
| 2.2.2 | modify cell alignment and indentation | 4 |
| 2.2.3 | format cells by using Format Painter | 4 |
| 2.2.4 | wrap text within cells | 4 |
| 2.2.5 | apply number formats | 4 |
| 2.2.6 | apply cell formats | 4 |
| 2.2.7 | apply cell styles | 4 |
| **2.3** | **Summarize and Organize Data** | |
| 2.3.1 | insert sparklines | 6 |
| 2.3.2 | outline data | 7 |
| 2.3.3 | insert subtotals | 7 |
| 2.3.4 | apply conditional formatting | 4 |
| **3** | **Create Tables** | |
| **3.1** | **Create and Manage Tables** | |
| 3.1.1 | create an Excel table from a cell range | 7 |
| 3.1.2 | convert a table to a cell range | 7 |
| 3.1.3 | add or remove table rows and columns | 7 |
| **3.2** | **Manage Table Styles and Options** | |
| 3.2.1 | apply styles to tables | 7 |
| 3.2.2 | configure table style options | 7 |
| 3.2.3 | insert total rows | 7 |
| **3.3** | **Filter and Sort a Table** | |
| 3.3.1 | filter records | 7 |
| 3.3.2 | sort data by multiple columns | 7 |
| 3.3.3 | change sort order | 7 |
| 3.3.4 | remove duplicate records | 7 |
| **4** | **Perform Operations with Formulas and Functions** | |
| **4.1** | **Summarize Data by using Functions** | |
| 4.1.1 | insert references | 3 |
| 4.1.2 | perform calculations by using the SUM function | 3 |
| 4.1.3 | perform calculations by using MIN and MAX functions | 3 |
| 4.1.4 | perform calculations by using the COUNT function | 3 |
| 4.1.5 | perform calculations by using the AVERAGE function | 3 |

| Objective Domain | | Lesson |
|---|---|---|
| **4.2** | **Perform Conditional Operations by using Functions** | |
| 4.2.1 | perform logical operations by using the IF function | 3 |
| 4.2.2 | perform logical operations by using the SUMIF function | 3 |
| 4.2.3 | perform logical operations by using the AVERAGEIF function | 3 |
| 4.2.4 | perform statistical operations by using the COUNTIF function | 3 |
| **4.3** | **Format and Modify Text by using Functions** | |
| 4.3.1 | format text by using RIGHT, LEFT, and MID functions | 3 |
| 4.3.2 | format text by using UPPER, LOWER, and PROPER functions | 3 |
| 4.3.3 | format text by using the CONCATENATE function | 3 |
| **5** | **Create Charts and Objects** | |
| **5.1** | **Create Charts** | |
| 5.1.1 | create a new chart | 6 |
| 5.1.2 | add additional data series | 6 |
| 5.1.3 | switch between rows and columns in source data | 6 |
| 5.1.4 | analyze data by using Quick Analysis | 6 |
| **5.2** | **Format Charts** | |
| 5.2.1 | resize charts | 6 |
| 5.2.2 | add and modify chart elements | 6 |
| 5.2.3 | apply chart layouts and styles | 6 |
| 5.2.4 | move charts to a chart sheet | 6 |
| **5.3** | **Insert and Format Objects** | |
| 5.3.1 | insert text boxes and shapes | 6 |
| 5.3.2 | insert images | 6 |
| 5.3.3 | modify object properties | 6 |
| 5.3.4 | add alternative text to objects for accessibility | 8 |

# Appendix B: Glossary of Terms

**Accessibility Checker tool** – An Excel feature that inspects a workbook for data and objects that may have accessibility issues.

**Active cell** – The currently selected cell.

**Alignment** – The positioning of the contents of a cell; e.g. left, right, or centered.

**AutoFill** – A method of copying data and formulas or creating data series by dragging the lower right corner of a cell or range.

**AutoFit** – A feature that will automatically adjust the width of a column or the height of a row so that the cells are just wide or high enough to display the values in all of those cells.

**AutoFilter** – See Filter.

**AutoFormat** – A feature that enables you to apply many different formatting characteristics with a single command by choosing from a selection of format templates; see Cell Styles also.

**AutoSum** – A tool that will quickly insert a SUM function into the current cell, and determine the appropriate cell range to be used.

**Backstage** – Introduced in the Microsoft Office 2010 suite, replacing the Office button. The Office Backstage is a single view that allows you to manage the workbook, including printing, opening and saving in different formats, and changing the metadata.

**Bold** – Dark or highlighted text.

**Borders** – The feature that enables you to add lines or surrounding borders to the selected cells in the worksheet.

**Built-in Functions** – Pre-programmed formulas to do specific calculations. You can either type these functions in or use the Insert Function wizard to assist.

**Cell Styles** – A feature that enables you to apply many different formatting characteristics to one or more cells with a single command by choosing from a selection of format templates; see AutoFormat also.

**Center** – To place text in the center of a cell.

**Chart Wizard** – The automatic feature that Excel provides to help you create a chart in a step-by-step process.

**Chart** – A pictorial representation of the data you enter in a worksheet.

**Circular References** – A type of error that occurs when one or more cells refer to each other directly or indirectly.

**Clear** – Removes information (and/or formatting and comments) from selected cells and leaves the cells blank.

**Column** – A vertical arrangement for text or numbers, separated from other columns by a grid line and denoted with alpha letters per column. Excel has a maximum of 256 columns, denoted from A to IV.

**Comma Separated Values (CSV) file** – Also known as Comma Delimited text file. One of the formats available to create from an Excel workbook. All data in this file is of variable length. Each cell value is followed by a comma, except for the last value in each row. See also Fixed width text file.

**Comments** – Similar to a post-it note where you can enter information for yourself or others to review.

**Copy** – An editing function used to duplicate selected cells.

**Cut** – The editing process of transferring selected cells to the Clipboard so that you can move them from one location and place them into another.

**Data Table** – A table that displays one or two input variables and the result of a calculation using the input variables.

**Database** – Used for compiling and sorting (typically large) lists of data.

**Document Inspector** – A tool to assist in removing any personal or hidden information you don't want others to see when they open this file.

**Error Checking** – An auditing tool to assist in checking any errors that may exist in the formulas. Any errors are marked with a dark green triangle in the upper left corner of a cell.

**Excel Services** – A component of Microsoft SharePoint that is used to publish Excel data to others, whether they have Excel installed on their computer or not. It is used in business intelligence applications to help users analyze business data.

**Extensible Markup Language** – A set of rules developed by the World Wide Web Consortium to facilitate data to be transferred from one computer system to another over the Internet.

**Filter** – A feature that will suppress the display of data that do not meet the filter criteria.

**Fixed width text file** – The format of the data exported from a program such as Excel. All data in the same column have the same length, usually the defined width of the column. Cells that have less data than the defined width will have extra blank spaces added at the right side of the cell. See also Comma delimited text file.

**Font** – A specific typeface and point size.

**Footer** – Text that repeats at the bottom of every page and may include automatic page numbers.

**Format** – Instructions to Excel as to how it should display and number styles, fonts, colors, etc.

**Formula Bar** – A field on the screen that displays the formula in the active cell. It can also be used to make entries into the worksheet.

**Formula** – Used in a cell to calculate new result values to be displayed. Composed of values, cell references, arithmetic operators and special functions. These results may be used in other formulas located in other cells.

**Function** – A feature designed by Excel that enables you to perform quickly a calculation or formula using a specialized function.

**Graphics** – Illustrations that can be inserted into a worksheet such as pictures, clip art, charts, text boxes, shapes, etc.

**Header** – Text that repeats at the top of every page and may include automatic page numbers.

**HTML** – Acronym for Hyper Text Markup Language. It is the underlying language for the set of instructions used by web browsers to display information on a web page.

**Hyperlink** – A link to another document. It is usually stored in the form of a Uniform Resource Locator (URL), which is the unique address to find this document; e.g. on the Internet, the intranet, folder on local or network hard drive, location in current document or workbook.

**Insert Function** – The feature that Excel provides to help you select the desired function to perform calculations.

**Insert** – An editing function that enables you to add text between other text, including entire columns or rows.

**Insert Worksheet Tab** – The tab at the end of the worksheet tabs on the lower left corner of a workbook to assist in inserting/creating a new worksheet at the current location.

**Justification** – The formatting function that determines how Excel will align the data within a cell or cells.

**Legend** – A box on a chart that explains the meaning of each line in a line chart, or bar in a bar chart.

**Linking** – The process of referencing cells or worksheets in one file to another, so that changes made on one file will automatically change in the linked file.

**Macro** – A feature that "records" keystrokes for future use. Macros save time in operations where the same series of commands is repeated.

**Margin** – The white space or area from the edge of the paper to the text.

**Name Box** – This box displays the cell address of the active cell. It is located on the left below the toolbar.

**Named Range** – A range of cells that has been assigned a name.

**Office Open XML** – A set of rules developed by Microsoft that defines how spreadsheet, chart, presentation, and word processing data is stored in files.

**OneDrive** – A file storage and sharing service that can be accessed from a web browser or mobile device. All Windows users are given 5 GB of free personal storage.

**Page Break** – The division between two pages.

**Page Setup** – The feature that determines how Excel will display and/or print the worksheet — e.g., margins, headers/footers, gridlines, etc.

**Paste** – The editing function of placing cut or copied data into a new location.

**Quick Access Toolbar** – A toolbar that is displayed in the upper left part of the Excel window. It is customizable to give you ready access to commands that you want to use frequently without having to select a tab in the Ribbon.

**Range of cells** – A contiguous block of cells with one or more rows and one or more columns of cells.

**Ribbon** – The collection of commands grouped under different tabs across the top of the Excel screen. Each tab is aimed at a type of activity, such as page layout or inserting items into a worksheet. Some tabs are only shown when appropriate.

**Series** – Each set of data used in a graphical chart.

**Shared Workbook** – A feature in Excel which enables more than one user to update a workbook at the same time. If the same cell(s) are updated by different people, Excel will display the conflicts and allow one of the values to remain.

**SharePoint** – A Microsoft software product that allows multiple users (usually within an organization) to collaborate by sharing documents, files, and workbooks. This concept is that end products are better through team work.

**Solver** – A tool designed to reach a solution, by changing a number of variables.

**Style** – A combination of formatting features you can save and apply as a set.

**Table Styles** – A feature that enables you to apply many different formatting characteristics to a table with a single command by choosing from a selection of format templates; see AutoFormat also.

**Template** – A pre-designed workbook that may already contain data, formulas, and other objects, thereby saving you time and effort in entering these items.

**Tracing Errors** – An audit tool that draws arrows to help you find or trace formula errors in cells that are precedents or dependents of the current cell.

**Tracking Changes** – A process that displays all changes made to the worksheet, including editing actions and formatting changes.

**Trendline** – A common method of analyzing data using charts or graphs based on the data in a worksheet.

**What-if analysis** – The ability to pursue an almost endless cycle of trial-and-error use of base numbers in formulas and therefore be able to make important decisions quickly.

**Workbook properties** – A group of data that is used to help users sort, organize and find workbooks. This data is stored internally and can be displayed in Windows using the File Explorer.

**X-axis** – The horizontal edge of a chart, marking the scale used there.

**XML** – See Extensible Markup Language.

**Y-axis** – The vertical edge of a chart, marking the scale used there.

# Appendix C: Index